Benedetto Cotrugli – The Book of the Art of Trade

Carlo Carraro • Giovanni Favero
Editors

Benedetto Cotrugli – The Book of the Art of Trade

With Scholarly Essays from Niall Ferguson, Giovanni Favero, Mario Infelise, Tiziano Zanato and Vera Ribaudo

palgrave
macmillan

Editors
Carlo Carraro
Ca' Foscari University of Venice
Venice, Italy

Giovanni Favero
Ca' Foscari University of Venice
Venice, Italy

Translated by John Francis Phillimore

ISBN 978-3-319-82004-0 ISBN 978-3-319-39969-0 (eBook)
DOI 10.1007/978-3-319-39969-0

Printed on acid-free paper

This Palgrave Macmillan imprint is published by Springer Nature
The registered company is Springer International Publishing AG
The registered company address is: Gewerbestrasse 11, 6330 Cham, Switzerland

Preface
A Brief History of An Extraordinary Project

A gondola slowly skimmed the dark waters of the Grand Canal on a winter's evening of 2010. Niall Ferguson and Fabio Sattin, dressed as Venetian merchants from the fifteenth century, spoke quietly, listening to the sound of the oars in the water, as the gondola brought them towards a large, brightly-lit, noble palace, where a beautiful and mysterious Carnival party was under way. Normally dressed as an awkward professor of the twentieth century, and overwhelmed by the beauty of the masks and costumes, I was waiting for them in the main hall of the palace, at the party to which I had also been invited. I didn't know Niall personally at that point, so I was interested in talking with him. Fabio had organized the meeting in order to discuss a project that he has already talked to Niall about, a project regarding a little-known but extraordinary book to make known to a broad international public. I was truly intrigued.

They slowly climbed the grand staircase, scheming just like real Venetian merchants—just like Benedetto Cotrugli must have done, as he was always dissatisfied with the way that business matters were managed. Amidst the Venetian masks, Fabio and Niall, simultaneously elegant and surprising, approached me in order to discuss translating a book by Benedetto Cotrugli into English, a little jewel then available only in its original language, difficult even for an Italian to understand, yet so full of outstanding, innovative ideas for the year it was written, and still so modern today.

The book that they presented to me is *The Book of the Art of Trade*, which you will read for the first time in English in the pages that follow. It is a fascinating book for the way in which, for the first time in history, modern accounting concepts were presented, as well as for the basic concepts of corporate social responsibility and many other economic issues. I was immediately enthusiastic about Fabio and Niall's proposal. At the time, neither Niall nor I was familiar with the book and, thus, we listened to Fabio's fascinating stories about Cotrugli's life and the contents of his book, of which he owned a copy from the last, no longer available, printing. The ambience of the grand hall resembled that of Renaissance-era Venice, which Fabio's tales made even more real.

Benedetto Cotrugli was neither an author nor a professor—he was a merchant, but one that possessed a great cultural depth and an awareness that allowed him to look behind his occupation in order to understand organizational ineffeciencies, accounting approximations, and moral weaknesses that characterized the merchant class of his era. He didn't just present criticisms of the system but, most importantly, proposed solutions. And, thus, *The Book of the Art of the Trade* is a book filled with ingenious proposals and practical ideas.

Translating a rich, concise and very meaningful book is never a simple task, and it is even more complex in a case like Cotrugli's. First of all, due to the language in which it was written, which, for a translator, is difficult to decipher. Secondly, due to the explicative and exegetical work that was very necessary in this case. I decided then to construct a team that would work along with the translator in order to correctly adapt the original text into English. I thank my colleagues Giovanni Favero, Tiziano Zanato, Mario Infelise and Vera Ribaudo from Ca' Foscari University of Venice for their tireless work, which is insufficiently evident in the essays published in this book.

We decided together that a new critical edition, transcribed from the earliest and most recently found manuscript version of the book, was necessary. The outstanding edition by Vera Ribaudo is contained in the volume entitled *Benedetto Cotrugli, Libro del'arte dela mercatura*, published by Ca' Foscari University Press in 2016. The book is available on line at http://edizionicafoscari.unive.it/en/edizioni/libri/978-88-6969-088-4. Vera Ribaudo was als asked to provide a paraphrase in modern

Italian of Cotrugli's critical text to make translation easier and more precise. Using that version, John Phillimore would then create the English version, which is published in this book. John Phillimore's translation is also extraordinary, as it was able to confer to the reader all of the subtleties and the sophistication of Cotrugli's original text.

The work of the Ca' Foscari team was both intense and difficult. It was a feat of rediscovery, that wholly renders Benedetto Cotrugli's intellectual greatness in a time when Venice was a capital of the world, a major business center, similar to modern day New York or London. The book, in its English version, slowly came to light, becoming more and more modern and interesting as it was being translated.

The difficulties that occasionally emerged during the course of the project were overcome by the enthusiasm and encouragement of Fabio Sattin, the diplomacy and friendly smile of Veronica Gusso, the support of Dante Roscini, the home cooking of Elena, Fabio's wife. I am truly grateful to them all.

This book was an extraordinary and massive project that required a considerable level of investment. Without the financial support of Ca' Foscari University of Venice and the steadfast support of its rectors, this project would not have been made possible. I am, thus, extremely grateful to Ca' Foscari for the enormous contribution it gave to this project. I thank my colleagues Giovanni, Tiziano, Mario and Vera for what they have done on the scientific and cultural end and my staff for having shared with me as much the best moments as the more difficult ones.

Benedetto Cotrugli probably did not enjoy being a merchant. He would have perhaps preferred to be a university professor. In the end, his book, due to his ability to look at the business world from different perspectives, is that mixture of theory and practice that modern business schools teach as the most effective way to train today's good managers, the modern-day merchants.

That day in which Niall, Fabio and I met in that majestic palace, we probably didn't expect the hardships that we would endure in completing such a large-scale project. In the pages that follow, reading the introduction by Niall Ferguson and the essays by Giovanni Favero, Tiziano Zanato, Mario Infelise and Vera Ribaudo, the reader will become immediately aware of the significance of Benedetto Cotrugli, the originality and the relevance of his book and, thus, the inherent difficulty of the project. I can't help but to thank everyone, especially Niall and Fabio, for the success of this extraordinary book, which surely, even in its English translation, will not fail to intrigue many other readers.

Cotrugli's book is a little jewel that has remained hidden for centuries. Let's enjoy its splendour.

Carlo Carraro
Ca' Foscari University of Venice
Venice
June 8, 2016

Contents

Part I Introduction 1

Benedetto Cotrugli, *The Book of the Art of Trade* (*Libro del'arte dela mercatura*) 3
Niall Ferguson

A New Edition of Benedetto Cotrugli's *The Book of the Art of Trade* 9
Giovanni Favero

Part II The Book of the Art of Trade 21

Preface 23

Part 1: On the Origins and Principles of Trade 27

Part 2: On the Religion Incumbent on the Merchant 85

Part 3: On the Civic Life of the Merchant 111

Part 4: On the Economic Virtues of the Merchant 141

Part III Essays 173

Benedetto Cotrugli, Merchant Writer 175
Tiziano Zanato

The Printed Editions of Benedetto Cotrugli's Treaty 213
Mario Infelise

A Note on the Text 219
Vera Ribaudo

References 223

Index 233

Part I

Introduction

Benedetto Cotrugli, *Book of the Art of Trade* (*Libro del'arte dela mercatura*)

Niall Ferguson

Foreword

In any airport bookshop from Boston to Beijing you will find entire shelves of books on how to succeed in business, the more credible of them written by authors who have themselves done so. It is a sign of just how long capitalism has been around that one of the earliest such books was written over half a millennium ago. It is a sign of how little business has changed that Benedetto Cotrugli's *Book of the Art of Trade* should still repay reading.

That is not to say that Cotrugli's *Art of Trade* is the fifteenth-century equivalent of Donald Trump's *Art of the Deal*. For Cotrugli was no Trump. Amongst many pieces of wise advice, Cotrugli warns merchants against involving themselves in politics. "It is not expedient," he writes,

N. Ferguson (✉)
Laurence A. Tisch Professor of History at Harvard University, Harvard University, Cambridge, MA, USA
e-mail: nfergus@fas.harvard.edu

C. Carraro, G. Favero (eds.), *Benedetto Cotrugli – The Book of the Art of Trade*, DOI 10.1007/978-3-319-39969-0_1

"for a merchant to have to do with the courts, nor above all to involve himself in politics or the civil administration, because these are perilous areas." Far from glorying in verbal vulgarity and ostentatious displays of wealth, Cotrugli was a highly educated humanist whose ideal merchant combined the classical virtues of the commoner-citizen as they had been conceived by the ancient Greeks and Romans and rediscovered by Italian scholars in the Renaissance.

As a young man, Cotrugli had in fact attended the University of Bologna, but (as he ruefully observes): "Destiny and ill-luck contrived it that right in the midst of the most pleasurable of philosophical studies, I was seized from studying and made to become a merchant, a trade I was obliged to follow, abandoning the sweet delights of study, to which I had been utterly dedicated…" Returning to run the family business in Ragusa (present day Dubrovnik), Cotrugli was disgusted by the low intellectual level of his new milieu. In the absence of any kind of formal business education, there was nothing more than an "inadequate, ill-organised, arbitrary and threadbare" system of learning on the job, "to the extent that my compassion was aroused and it pained me that this useful and necessary activity had fallen into the hands of such undisciplined and uncouth people, who carry on without moderation or orderliness, ignoring and perverting the law." In many ways, *The Art of Trade* was Cotrugli's attempt not just to raise the standard of business education but also to elevate the standing of business itself. Though it is best known to scholars as the earliest work to describe the system of double-entry bookkeeping—more than thirty years before Luca Pacioli's better known treatise *De computis et scripturis* (1494)—*The Art of Trade* is most remarkable for the breadth of its subject matter. Cotrugli offers much more than just practical advice on accounting. He offers an entire way of life. This is not a dry textbook but an exhortation to his fellow merchants to aspire to be Renaissance businessmen, in the manner of Cosimo di Medici.

Cotrugli's book also gives the modern reader a fascinating glimpse of a vanished world. Born in Ragusa (present-day Dubrovnik), Cotrugli and his brother Michele were importers of Catalan wool as well as dyes, paying in Balkan silver or, more commonly, bills of exchange. In the course of his business life he spent time in Barcelona, Florence, Venice and, finally, Naples, where he lived from 1451 to 1469. This was truly a Mediterranean life; indeed, Cotrugli knew the sea well enough to write another book in the subject, *De navigatione*, which he dedicated to the Venetian Senate He also served Ferdinand, king of Aragon, as ambassador to Ragusa and master of the Naples Mint. Life in the fifteenth century was precarious even for a successful merchant. In 1460 Cotrugli was accused of, and tried for, allegedly exporting bullion illegally. *The Art of Trade* was written in rural Sorbo Serpico while he was escaping an outbreak of plague in Naples. Life was shorter in those days. Cotrugli was in his early fifties when he died in 1469.

Yet the reader gets a keen sense from this book of a life well lived. Cotrugli might have missed the libraries of Bologna, but he took considerable pride in his commercial calling. Indeed, parts of *The Art of Trade* read as a defense of merchants against the frequent charges—of usury, of greed, of avarice—leveled at them by religious zealots at the time. Cotrugli declared himself "astonished that exchange, being so useful, easy and entirely necessary to the conduct of human affairs, should be condemned by so many theologians." He was careful to show his respect for members of the nobility, who were prohibited from sullying their hands with filthy lucre, but not to the extent of disparaging the upright bourgeoisie to which he clearly belonged. We find here an early and eloquent celebration of what would later be thought of by Max Weber (wrongly) as a Protestant work ethic. "To turn a profit, or to accomplish the aims of the art of trade," writes Cotrugli,

> it is essential to set aside every other concern, and to dedicate oneself as diligently as possible to all the things that may prove useful to or advance that occupation. This means sometimes putting up with privations day and night, travelling on foot or on horseback, and by land and sea, working one's hardest at buying and selling and in making attractive the goods bought and sold, and applying as much diligence as possible to these and similar matters. And every other consideration, as I have said, must take second place, and not only superfluous things but even those necessary to the maintenance of human life. It may well be required sometimes that eating and drinking and sleeping be postponed to another occasion, indeed that one endure hunger and thirst and white nights and other similar inconveniences deleterious to the normal equilibrium of the body, which

> were it not an instrument prepared for these eventualities and trained for such hardships, could not sustain them, and undergoing them could cause such suffering as to lead to sickness and even death.

In short, a career in commerce was not for the weak.

The first book of *The Art of Trade* is the one most concerned with business itself. Chapter V, for example, deals with barter, while chapter IV discusses cash payment. ("Make sure that the other side declares the price first," advises Cotrugli. "Get used to always asking what he expects for his goods: it is all too easy to be outwitted here.") A key issue discussed in the next chapters is credit. At a time when religious prohibitions on usury (lending at interest) still remained on most European statute books, Cotrugli was careful to spell out his view that, as a general principle, "selling on credit is itself legitimate, indeed reasonable and necessary." Credit contracts were "legal, useful and indeed necessary to the sustenance of individuals and their families and cities." But not all lending was good. "You must consider the expiry date of the credit," warns Cotrugli, "which we should always try to make after as short an interval as possible. … you need to be very prudent about this and not do as many foolish men do and agree a timescale of eighteen months and more, time for four popes to perish and who knows what unforeseen events to occur." Moreover, you should beware of bad debtors. "A debt has this characteristic that it deteriorates with time," he notes, "and after a year has passed from its settlement date it has lost 50 % of its value, and continues to do so proportionately, because for the merchant losing time and losing money are the same thing." In Book Two, however, Cotrugli defines usurers as "those who, on the maturation of a debt, will not extend it without interest to borrowers unable to pay immediately." As is clear from the accounts of banks like the Medicis', debt finance remained a grey area so long as usury was formally illegal. Italian lenders at this time did not explicitly charge interest, but instead collected commissions or even charged insurance premia to compensate themselves.

Cotrugli was an early believer in diversification as a way of managing and reducing risk. He imagines a Florentine merchant entering into various partnerships with merchants in Venice, Rome and Avignon, investing some of his capital in wool, some in silk. "Having in a safe and orderly way put my hand so many transactions," he observes, "I will gain nothing but advantage from them, because the left hand will help the right." And again: "You must never risk too much on a single throw, by land or by sea: however rich you may be, at the most five hundred ducats a shipload, or a thousand for a large galley." But here, too, there are caveats: "Be careful not to take on too many or too large transactions: do not try to net every bird that passes, because many have failed for taking on too much, but no one for exposing himself too little."

It is in Book One, chapter XII, that Cotrugli explains the importance of double-entry bookkeeping, perhaps unintentionally switching the conventional location of credits and debits:

> Thus, every item that you write in the book must be written down twice, once as a debt from who must pay out, and in the other case a credit to the receiver. … In the same way, every item must be written on both sides of the sheet, that is, on the right-hand side of the book under "sums owed" and on the left "sums owing."

Elsewhere he strongly condemns "those that keep only one column of accounts, that is how much is owing to themselves and not how much others are expecting from them," urging his readers "to repudiate them and condemn them publicly, and eventually take them to court. For these are the worst type of merchant, the basest and most iniquitous." Yet this is only one of the relatively novel business skills of the era that Cotrugli emphasizes. He explains the importance of bills of exchange in long-distance trade. He explains the essential role of insurance for ship-borne commerce.

Nevertheless, *The Art of Trade* would be a rather full book if these were its sole contents. Its most engaging passages are in fact to be found in Books Three and Four, where Cotrugli turns from business tips to what we would now call questions of lifestyle. He dismisses businessmen "who are proficient at chess, board games, cards, dice, and at fencing, wrestling, playing instruments, dancing, hunting, fishing, etc." as "indiscreet and uncivilised." Nor should a man of affairs be over-dressed. "Do not get yourself up in silk," he advises his reader, "or you will look like a monkey in fancy dress or a king bee. Make it your choice to dress cleanly, simply and elegantly." Cotrugli's ideal merchant has his mind on higher things, and with good reason: "A merchant should be the most universal of men and one that has the most to do, more than his fellows, with different types of men and social classes." Consequently, "everything a man might know may be helpful to a merchant," including cosmography, geography, philosophy, astrology, theology, and law. Cotrugli's ideal Renaissance businessman was truly a polymath.

Finally, Cotrugli turns to the private sphere, offering all kinds of intriguing suggestions about marriage, sex, the siring and raising of children and the management of servants. Each page reveals how profoundly Western social attitudes to the family, and especially to women, have changed over five hundred years. And yet still the questions are the perennial ones. How can one raise a child to appreciate the hard work that is necessary to run a business? When should a businessman retire from the counting house to cultivate his garden? How much time and money should one devote to philanthropy? To religion? The notion of "work-life balance" was not an invention of our modern age. In many ways, it is Cotrugli's central theme.

The Book of the Art of Trade survived by sheer good luck. Only the discovery of the original text in two Florentine manuscripts revealed that the printed edition of 1573 had been badly abridged. Cotrugli's third book, *De Uxore Ducenda*, was not so fortunate. That is a matter for regret. Cotrugli tells us that it "discoursed at some length, in the Latin tongue, of all the matters in which a wife should obey, of her duties, of the education of her children, and of all the instructions that ought to be followed by each member of the household." Still, these are probably the subjects on which we and the men of *quattrocento* Naples are least likely to see eye to eye. What has survived is a marvelously illuminating self-improvement manual that reminds us not only that the world has changed very much since the 1400s, but also that the ethos of capitalism has changed very little. The ascent of money began longer ago than most of us think.

A New Edition of Benedetto Cotrugli's The Book of the Art of Trade

Giovanni Favero

A Changing Book

Benedetto Cotrugli's *The Book of the Art of Trade* (as we may translate the title of the manuscript, *libro del'arte dela mercatura*) is a particularly clear case of relevant changes in the historical interpretation of a text following new archival discoveries.

Cotrugli's humanistic treaty on commerce was written in 1458 yet published in print only in 1573. As a consequence, it was for centuries neglected as a handbook dealing with the mercantile practices of a previous age. The historians of accounting rediscovered it in the nineteenth century as the first book citing the practice of double-entry bookkeeping, pre-dating in composition Luca Pacioli's famous treatise *De computis et scripturis*, included in the 1494 Venetian printed edition of his *Summa de Arithmetica*. It is true to say, however, that the thirteenth chapter of the first volume of Cotrugli's 1573 book dealt with bookkeeping very

G. Favero (✉)
Department of Management, Università Ca' Foscari Venezia, Venice, Italy
e-mail: gfavero@unive.it

C. Carraro, G. Favero (eds.), *Benedetto Cotrugli – The Book of the Art of Trade*, DOI 10.1007/978-3-319-39969-0_2

summarily, stating in the end that it was almost impossible to explain it, as it was difficult to learn without practical experience.

In 1990 Ugo Tucci published a new edition of Cotrugli's book based on two Florentine manuscripts of the late fifteenth century (the earlier dated 1484), demonstrating that the 1573 Venetian editor had heavily altered the original version both in its language and contents, transforming it from a book for merchants' education into a humanistic treaty. In particular, he abridged the thirteenth chapter eliminating all practical examples, extracting the procedure of bookkeeping and adding the above mentioned conclusion.[1] Reading Tucci's edition, it is clear that Cotrugli had described in detail the practice of double-entry bookkeeping some decades before Pacioli. Despite of his priority, as Tucci (1990, 12–13) highlighted, Cotrugli was neither the inventor nor a theorist of double-entry accounting, and Pacioli's merit for spreading this method is not in question. Cotrugli's book is rather of interest as a pivotal link between the medieval handbooks of mercantile technique and early modern accounting treaties following Pacioli's (Doni 2007, 70–74).

Yet the question was not finally closed. Paul Oskar Kristeller (1989) in his *Iter Italicum* mentioned a 1475 copy of Cotrugli's book, made in Naples but preserved in the National Library of Malta. This manuscript was briefly described in a biographical sketch of Cotrugli in Tafuri (1760; Sangster 2014a). Tiziano Zanato (1993) was then able to reconstruct by way of linguistic analysis a *stemma codicum* of the three known manuscripts. Žarko Muliačić (1995a) studied in detail the differences between the Venetian edition, the Florentine manuscripts and the new Maltese version. Miroslav Buzadzic, Mladen Habek and Vladimir Stipetic (1998) used the latter to build a stronger argument in favour of the priority of Cotrugli over Pacioli in the description of double-entry bookkeeping. In the same year, indeed, Joanna Postma (Postma and van der Helm 2000, 148) discovered that the eleventh chapter of the first volume of Cotrugli's book on letters of exchange "is identical" with the first part of Pacioli's chapter on the *tariffa mercantesca* of his *Tractatus*

[1] According to Muliačić (1995a), Patrizi abridged chapter 13 of Cotrugli's book because at the time better instructions on double-entry bookkeeping were available. The interest aroused by publishing the book in the late sixteenth century would not be in its priority in describing this accounting technique, but in its more general value as an humanistic treaty on the virtues of commerce.

mathematicus ad discipulos perusinos (1478). It is likely then that Pacioli may have been in possession or well acquainted with Cotrugli's book long before the publication of the *Summa* in 1494, as Vladimir Stipetić (2002, 128) concludes. Postma and van der Helm (2000, 148) suggest also that both may have drawn on an earlier common model. In any case, they also discovered that the Maltese manuscript contained, bound together with the copy of Cotrugli's book, the transcription of a set of earlier bookkeeping instructions (not by Cotrugli) including a short theoretical part. This would make these instructions more than merely a set of examples, but themselves the oldest known bookkeeping textbook that was used outside the workplace, probably together with Cotrugli's book (Sangster 2014b). The contents and structure of the instructions are different from Pacioli's but can be found in quite similar form in subsequent treatises (Tagliente 1533[1525]), suggesting that a parallel tradition of bookkeeping textbooks accompanied the diffusion of Pacioli's. Yet such instructions are not the subject of the present edition, which focuses on Cotrugli.

Following the latter discoveries, we can say that the issue of authorial priority in describing double-entry bookkeeping, if not to be discarded altogether as unrealistic, is no longer crucial in justifying the historical interest of Cotrugli's book. Its importance lies rather in the description of the late medieval mercantile techniques and practices, widespread in the Mediterranean world, in his defence of their legitimacy and in the enunciation of principles reflecting the prevailing ethics of the time.

This Edition

This introduction aims at offering the English-speaking reader an overview of the current state of historical knowledge on Cotrugli and his book on the art of commerce. A more detailed study of the author's biography, of the origin of the book and of its content is provided in the essay by Tiziano Zanato, which follows Cotrugli's text. A further essay by Mario Infelise focuses on the early modern printed editions of Cotrugli's book, analysing the characteristics of the 1573 Venetian *editio princeps* (then reprinted in 1602 in Brescia and translated into French in Lyon in 1582) and on the life and business activities of its first publisher, Francesco Patrizi. A final note by Vera Ribaudo summarizes the tradition of the manuscript text of the book and the criteria followed to elaborate its critical edition.

The reader will find here the first available translation in English of Cotrugli's book made by John Phillimore, complete with indexes. This translation is based on the critical edition of the original text, curated by Vera Ribaudo on the basis of the 1475 Maltese manuscript and its comparison with other existing versions. The critical edition is published by Edizioni Ca' Foscari—Digital Publishing, and is available at the following link: http://edizionicafoscari.unive.it/it/edizioni/libri/978-88-6969-088-4/

The Author: Benedetto Cotrugli (Benedikt Kotrulj/Benedictus de Cotrullis)[2]

The author of the book, Benedetto Cotrugli (ca 1416–1469), was a merchant from Ragusa (Dubrovnik) who spent part of his life in the Kingdom of Naples then under Aragonese rule.

The Cotrugli family originated from Kotor, but around 1350 the merchant Zivo (Johannes) Kotrulj moved to Ragusa, where one of his three sons, Rusko, became a member of the St. Antun confraternity of merchants and traders, named after St. Anthony the Great. Benedetto was born around 1416 from Nicoletta Ilic (from a family of the same confraternity) and Giacomo (Jakov) Cotrugli, one of Rusko's sons, together with Giovanni (Ivan) and Nicola (Runjić 1989, 515; Luzzati 1984, 446).

Giacomo was active as a merchant and contractor in Angevin Naples (the Kingdom of Naples was contested by the Aragonese and the Angevins for much of this century), where the queen Joanna II put him in charge of the mint. Meanwhile the whole Cotrugli family was deeply involved in the import trade of wheat and other cereals, salt and saltpeter from the Kingdom of Naples to Ragusa (Luzzati 1984, 446). Around 1430 Benedetto moved to Italy, probably to Bologna (Tucci 1990, 31), to study law and philosophy. Yet after Giacomo's death in 1436 he was forced to go

[2] These short biographical notes on Benedetto Cotrugli are mostly based on Luzzati (1984), Spremić (1986), Tucci (1990) and Janeković-Römer (2009).

back to Ragusa to take charge of the family trading business. He became in his turn a member of the St. Antun confraternity, from 1436, and got married in 1444 to Nikoleta Dobric-Bozic (Nicoletta Natale Bondenalio: Kheil 1906b, 240), from another merchant family of the confraternity. It is possible to presume that from the death of his father to when he got married, Benedetto was learning trading techniques and travelling, while most of his father's business was managed by other members of the family, in particular by his uncle Giovanni.

Benedetto Cotrugli's activity as a merchant has been reconstructed from archival evidence by Zdenka Janeković-Römer (2009). It spans the central decades of the fifteenth century, when the Aragonese Kingdom extended from Catalonia to the South of Italy and Athens, and maintained a privileged relationship with the Republic of Ragusa as the gateway to the Balkan route to the Levant and as its main ally against the Venetian hegemony in the Eastern Mediterranean (Del Treppo 1973; Spremić 1986).

Cotrugli is the first Ragusan whose name appears in archival records in Barcelona, where he was officially sent from 1444 to 1446 to follow a legal dispute concerning the right of the "Italian customs" to impose duties on Ragusan merchants' activities (Janeković-Römer 2009). Together with his brother Michele (Mihoc), Benedetto traded Catalan wool to Ragusa and Florence, from where he also imported dyes, paying for the goods with Balkan silver which he had sent from Ragusa to Florence and Southern Italy. Most of the business consisted in small and rapid trading operations using credit financing (Tucci 1990, 27–28). The trading network of the young Cotrugli brothers involved the Ragusan patricians Nikola and Sigsmund de Giorgi and the Florentine merchant company of Francesco Neroni, whose main business relation in Ragusa was still Benedetto's uncle, Giovanni. From Benedetto's letters to Neroni kept in Florentine archives, it is clear that the Cotrugli brothers were trying to make their company independent from Giovanni's protection (Boschetto 2005).

In 1450 Benedetto and Michele split their company and possessions: Benedetto made Michele his proxy to manage his business in Ragusa and moved to Naples in the early months of 1451. Despite the lack of official appointments, Cotrugli was probably able to exploit his family connections to gain access to the court of the King of Naples Alfonso of Aragon. In 1452 he was back in Ragusa to negotiate with the Republic the purchase of a credit to be claimed from King Alfonso in compensation for the damages caused by the assaults of pirates on Ragusan merchants. He rapidly sold the bulk of the credit to two Ragusan patricians and to his brother, and took on another credit that he was able to get reimbursed from the King but never paid back to the Republic. In 1454 he was then officially sought after by the Ragusan authorities, who were however unable to prosecute him in Naples, where he enjoyed the protection of the King, who according to some sources appointed him as auditor of the Royal tribunal[3] and urged the Republic to make him its consul in Naples, as it perhaps finally did in 1458, only to immediately annul the appointment.

When Alfonso of Aragon died in the summer of 1458, the succession to the throne of Naples of his illegitimate son Ferrante (Ferdinand) was opposed by the Pope, Calixtus III, who however died some months later, in August: his successor Pius II recognised Ferrante's rights. Although appointed by Ferrante as his ambassador to Ragusa, Cotrugli was forced to settle temporarily in the castle of Serpico to escape a plague epidemic in Naples,[4] and there, as stated in the closing section of the *Book on the Art of Trade*, he wrote his treatise.

In the meanwhile, the Ragusan Republic, following the complaints of other Ragusan merchants in the Kingdom of Naples, and perhaps taking advantage of the occasion of King Alfonso's death, ordered him to appear in court in Ragusa. The banishment following his non-appearance was however repeatedly suspended on Ferrante's request (Luzzati 1984, 447). Cotrugli was even able to pass through Ragusa without consequences at least twice, as an ambassador of Ferrante to Bosnia in 1462[5] (Spremić 1986, 100) and in 1466 to establish official

[3] Cotrugli is cited as auditor of the Royal tribunal in the dedication by Giovanni Giuseppi to the Ragusan merchant Francesco Radagli (Frano Radaljevic) that appears in a limited number of copies of the 1573 Venetian edition (see below the essay by Mario Infelise on the printed tradition).

[4] Privitera (2010) argues that no plagues are recorded in Naples in that period. However, Corradi (1972, I, 296) records an epidemic lasting six months in 1458 (Tucci 1990, 37).

[5] The interpretation of this appointment as 'prime minister' of the Kingdom by Appendini (1803, II, 98–100) is due to the equivocation of the term used by the Ragusan Senate granting Cotrugli a safe-conduct as "plenipotentiary minister", actually meaning ambassador.

relations between the Kingdom of Naples and the King of Hungary Matthias Corvinus (Matyas Hunyadi), who had just retaken Bosnia from the Ottomans who had occupied it in 1463.

Ferrante in 1460 appointed Cotrugli as chief of the Mint in Naples, the same position his father had held before him, although he was in court the same year following an accusation of illegal exportation of bullion. However he kept the position until 1468, when he was moved to the Mint of L'Aquila, where he died in 1469. His son Iacopo (Jakov) succeded him until 1474, and continued the family's merchant activities. A daughter, Caterina, got married in L'Aquila, and another, Eleonora, in 1483 became a nun in the San Girolamo monastery in Naples. A younger son, Girolamo (Jeronimo), remained in Ragusa.

The Book: il Libro del'arte dela mercatura

Of the four works attributed to Cotrugli, only two are known to have survived up to the present. A bio-bibliographical repertory (Farlatus and Coletus 1800, 17) cites a book in the Italian vernacular on the nature of flowers (*Della natura dei fiori*) that Cotrugli may have written in 1460, but its existence and attribution are very dubious. Another book written before 1458 is cited in the opening of the sixth chapter of the fourth volume of the Art of Trade, "*Dela muliere*" (to be interpreted not as "on the woman" as in Latin, but as "on the wife" from the Venetian): the title was *De uxore ducenda*, and its possible content is discussed in Tiziano Zanato's essay, included in the present edition.

However, the *Book of the Art of Trade* (*Libro del'arte dela mercatura*) is no longer the only surviving literary work of Cotrugli. Two editions were in fact recently published of a treatise on navigation (*De navigatione*), written in the Italian vernacular in 1464–65 and dedicated to the Venetian Senate: the first edition is based on a manuscript from the Yale University Library[6] and includes a Croatian translation by Damir Salopek

[6] The first manuscript of Cotrugli's book on navigation was found by an antique dealer in Naples and offered in vain to the Marciana library in 1913–14, to be then purchased by the American collector Henry C. Taylor, who finally donated it to the Yale University Library, where it is now catalogued as Ms. 557 (Trovato 2009). Another manuscript is kept in the private collection of

(Kotruljević 2005a); the second includes a commentary in Italian and compares the Yale manuscript with another manuscript from the private collection of Lawrence J. Schoenberg with a commentary by Piero Falchetta (2009). Interestingly, Falchetta (2012, 59) has shown that in this work Cotrugli aims at establishing a proper "science" of navigation, by mixing or alternating practical notions deriving from the actual experience of sailors with philosophical and moral considerations drawn from other texts or from personal reflections. In his essay, Tiziano Zanato discusses here this interpretation in relationship with the *libro del'arte de la mercatura*, where the same approach to the foundation of a proper "art of commerce" can be detected.

The book on trade was then Cotrugli's second literary work. It is dedicated to the Ragusan merchant Francesco di Stefano ("di Rizzato" is added in one of the Florentine manuscripts), who, following Janeković-Römer (2009), was Cotrugli's brother in law, having married the sister of Nikoleta Dobric-Bozic. As stated above, it was written, according to the author's own statement, in the castle of Serpico (today Sorbo Serpico, not far from Avellino) during the summer of 1458 when a plague epidemic hit the city of Naples. The choice of the Italian language ("volgare et materna"—vernacular and mother tongue) instead of the Latin is justified by Cotrugli in the introduction as more commonly used and understandable by merchants, for whose benefit the work was written. The explicit aim of the book was indeed to explain to merchants how it was possible to earn money honorably and without offense to God and to their fellow men. On the relationship between the definition of morally legitimate trading behaviour and the idea that commerce should be practiced following its own principles see again the essay by Tiziano Zanato below.

The book is divided into four volumes (called "books") and an introduction (*prefatio*). The first volume is the closest in content to a technical handbook, dealing not only with the origin (ch. 1) and the definition of commerce (ch. 2), and with the qualities required in a

Lawrence J. Schoenberg as Ms. 473: it was described as anonymous by de Polo Saibanti (1985) but is clearly a copy of Cotrugli's *De navigatione*. Falchetta (2012, 54) cites also a third manuscript Ma. 334 at the "Angelo Mai" Library in Bergamo.

merchant (ch. 3), but also with the local conditions that may favour the settlement of merchants (ch. 4), such as a healthy position, the presence of other merchants, conditions of peace and the possibility of accessing the faster and more informal mercantile justice system rather than Roman Law procedures ("leggie Iustiniana"). This was a clear statement in favour of the jurisdictional autonomy of merchant communities and of the mercantile justice procedure called "*sommaria*". The volume deals also with specific mercantile instruments, such as barter or mixed selling (ch. 5), or selling against cash (ch. 6), and forward selling (ch. 7), to be avoided but sometimes necessary for some specific merchandise. Here is an exhortation not to repose one's confidence in nobles, priests and friars, student, scholars, soldiers, as they are not used to dealing with money and will not reimburse the payment. Other chapters deal with the collection (ch. 8) and repayment of debts (ch. 9), with choosing the the goods and instruments of trade (ch. 10), with letters of exchange (ch. 11). As said above, the latter chapter was replicated by Pacioli in a part of his treatise for Perugian students (1478). Interestingly, as highlighted in Tucci (1990, 32), despite being the chief of a royal mint, Cotrugli dedicates only a few words here to the exchange of different coinages and to the possibility of speculating on their scarcity or abundance: it was perhaps a matter of maintaining trade secrets, that in his case had been transmitted from his father Giacomo to him and from him to his son Giacomo. A chapter (ch. 12) on deposits and pawns is followed then by the renowned section (ch. 13) on bookkeeping. He explicitly describes double-entry accounting, even if debits are placed on the right and credits on the left, an inversion probably due to a scribal error (Sangster 2014b, 5). Cotrugli invites in particular the merchant to keep three distinct books, i.e. a scrap book for direct records, a journal that orders them chronologically, and a ledger with an alphabetical index making it possible to search the records by subject or date. He insists on the need to close the accounts at the end of each year. A chapter on (maritime) insurance (ch. 14) follows, and then a series of specifications concerning the particular characteristics of the trade of jewellers (ch. 15), drapers and haberdashers (ch. 16), who can be considered lower-grade merchants as their art is mechanical, wool traders and other guilded merchants (ch. 17). Finally, a section focuses on the things that are prohibited to merchants (ch. 18), among them gambling, drunkenness, alchemy and smuggling, and another (ch. 19) deals with the need for the merchant to periodically settle and pay off all his outstanding liabilities (he says each seven years following the Genesis model).

The following volumes shift the focus from the specific, if not always technical, qualities of the merchant to his religious, moral and family behaviour. Tucci (1990, 63–64) suggests that Cotrugli's book should be set against the background of the Italian early Renaissance and of the writing genre of the treatise on the family: a comparison of the 1573 Venetian edition of Cotrugli's book with Leon Battista Alberti's books on the family (*Libri della famiglia*) was indeed proposed by Tenenti (1978).

The second volume deals then with the religion incumbent on the merchant, focusing on the obligation to attend mass (ch. 1), to pray (ch. 2), on how and to whom the merchant should give alms (ch. 3), and on matters of conscience (ch. 4). In the last chapter, Cotrugli explains what is and what is not permissible, dealing at length with the prohibition of usury and how the merchant should interpret it in practical cases, a crucial issue for the legitimation of trade in a Christian society.

The third volume focuses on the public life of the merchant, dealing with his need to be honourable and trustworthy (ch. 1), prudent (ch. 2), to have an extensive scientific and also literary culture (ch. 3), to be confident in his own reason, while knowing its limits (ch. 4) and acknowledging the role of luck (ch. 5). The volume includes a series of short chapters listing the main virtues of the merchant: his honesty (ch. 6), diligence and care (ch. 7), easiness and fluency (ch. 8), but also the ability to detect guile (ch. 9). Good manners (ch. 10) should go together with equity (ch. 11), steadfastness (ch. 12), an authoritative presence (ch. 13), liberality (ch. 14), peace of mind (ch. 15) and modesty (ch. 16). Such virtues should affect not only his public life, but become his nature (ch. 17), the main features of which should be moderation and restraint (ch. 18).

Finally, the fourth volume concerns family matters. It starts by dealing with the best location and disposition of the main house (ch. 1), and with the usefulness of also having a farm for income and a country residence (ch. 2). For Cotrugli the merchant should be the master of the house ad exert his authority (ch. 3), and avoid oddness in apparel (ch. 4) and furnishings (ch. 5). The following chapters focus on how to choose a wife and deal with her (ch. 6), how to raise children (ch. 7), how to deal with servants and menials (ch. 8). Yet the merchant should not have too large a property to take care of, as it would divert his attention from trade (ch. 9). The final chapter focuses on the necessity for the merchant to retire before his last years, in order to settle his material and spiritual business (ch. 10). The attitude that Cotrugli displays on family matters is utterly conservative. It seems somehow that in his effort to legitimise trading practices Cotrugli was making his best to explicitly conform to traditional norms in all other sensitive issues.

Part II

The Book of the Art of Trade

Preface

Men of a certain education generally derive pleasure less from physical beauty or good fortune, than from strength of mind and from virtue, which consists not only in having gained experience in many fields but also in committing what they have lived and learned to the eternal memory of the written word, so as to spread their knowledge among future generations. I can think of nothing that is more congenial, more necessary, more praiseworthy or more remarkable than the lessons enshrined in writing. And credit must be given therefore for their expertise to all those who have lived a long time or read many things, because it is difficult or almost impossible to acquire a wide knowledge in a short time, still less by reading little or nothing. Having mastered the teachings of wise and educated men, I maintain therefore that young people who are essentially uncultivated and inexpert in the ways of men do not deserve to be praised for their wisdom. For which reason I often find myself wondering in no small measure at the idleness or rather inertia of those who, setting aside and belittling matters of the spirit, |f. 1'| have consigned and invested all their felicity and wellbeing to changeable Fortune, that purveyor of disappointments. And were these persons to consider all aspects of the matter carefully, above all, were to look within themselves

C. Carraro, G. Favero (eds.), *Benedetto Cotrugli – The Book of the Art of Trade*, DOI 10.1007/978-3-319-39969-0_3

rather than without, and if they are favoured by God with some degree of talent, they would understand clearly that extraneous things do not bring happiness, and would not seek them if they lack them, and if they have them, would make the most liberal use of them and benefit thereby. For we human beings are composed of both body and soul, in the former being kin to the beasts, in the latter to God. And the bodies of all of us shall die, and our souls live in eternity.

If we want to make our way using our reasoning and the powers of our minds, we must see to it that we recognise these earthly things for what they are and that the higher and eternal things are not unknown to us; and consequently we must study attentively how we must behave in order not to follow in the tracks of the beasts but rather to walk in the footsteps of the immortals. And anyone who looks for these things not in the soul's riches, but instead in the fragility, in the weakness and irrationality of Fortune, will be misplacing his hopes and will strive uselessly and in vain.

And since we have examined all these things thoroughly and wish to share the benefit of our studies with those that will come after us, we will set out, on the subject of the practice of trade, what we know from our daily exercise of the art, and what we have discovered by the application of our intelligence, |f. 2| since destiny and ill-luck contrived it that right in the midst of the most pleasurable of philosophical studies, I was seized from studying and made to become a merchant, a trade I was obliged to follow, abandoning the sweet delights of study, to which I had been utterly dedicated. And in this profession I found the state of general education inadequate, ill-organised, arbitrary and useless, to the extent that my compassion was aroused and it pained me that this useful and necessary activity had fallen into the hands of such undisciplined and uncouth people, who carry on without moderation or orderliness, ignoring and perverting the law, and that this profession should be considered of so little importance and be so neglected by the wise, and so mangled and given over to those who know nothing, a forum for empty chatter where anything goes.

For this reason I have many times and again promised myself to take up my pen and offer some instruction and lay down some salutary axioms concerning this profession, eliminating the errors and abuses that have reduced it to a joke, a profanity surrounded by lies, faithlessness, perjury and licentiousness, neither venerated nor cultivated, lacking modesty and commitment, completely without any sense of our duty towards humanity, and marred by acts of great incivility. And having omitted for a long time to set these things down, due to various pressing claims and responsibilities, and particularly from having lived away from my lovely homeland, which is so dear to me, as you will read, it was you that came to my aid, dearest Francesco, my prompter and petitioner, and it is to satisfy your entreaties |f. 2'| that I am resolved to write what I think of the art of trade, not least because I do not doubt that in writing to you I will do a service to many, and especially those that desire and are prepared to trade in things with honour and without offence to God or their neighbour.

Now, trade, whether we call it a science, an art, or an unclassifiable discipline, owing its necessarily multiform diversity, given the variety each day brings to it, is governed none the less by specific rules, both general and particular, which must be understood by those who genuinely aspire to attaining an honourable return from it, in particular the young, because, as the prince of philosophers states in the second book of *De Anima*: "An active principle can only exist if what receives is adapted to it". Thus those who are callused and rooted in their ways, grown old in malpractice, are immoveable, undisciplined and incorrigible. But trade, if properly cultivated and conducted, is not only useful but, more than that, quite vital to human operations, and therefore it is the noblest activity. On this subject, Cicero said: "merchant(s) are the resources of the state," speaking of the better sort, expert and well-educated. For the same reason, Aristotle maintains that one of the principal and most necessary ornaments of the city is commerce, on which all other activities proliferate, as from a pure spring, until it deteriorates or fails. And it is |f. 3| a difficult occupation, being, as we have said, so various, and for this reason one hears often the common saying: "More goes into the making of a merchant than a High Court judge", because every science has its rules and regulations, by following which a man becomes expert therein. Only trade demands such a probing of one's natural intellectual ability, which is daily and hourly put to the test.

And so, having decided to write, I was uncertain which language I should adopt for my treatise, the Latin language or my maternal vernacular, and from this side and that came into my mind reasons pushing me in different directions now one way, now another. As far as Latin was concerned, I thought that it was a much worthier medium than the vernacular and would enable me to explain more elegantly what I needed to say in my treatise and give it a far greater polish. But then, considering the vernacular, I thought that, as I was writing my work for the benefit of merchants many of whom, for lack of education rather than any innate deficiency, would be inexpert in, or ignorant of, Latin, it was beholden on me to write in the language that was most commonly used and comprehensible to those merchants at whom the work was aimed. For this single reason therefore, I abandoned my original intention of writing in Latin and set out finally to write |f. 3'| in the vernacular, for which I ask your indulgence, but I do it, as I have said, for the benefit of my merchant readers, for all that the work will be judged less worthy of consideration than if it had been written in the Latin tongue. And being desirous that our book be useful not only to merchants in our present century, but also to those coming after, into whose hands it may happily fall, we have decided to proceed with our treatise according a particular scheme. And so it seemed to me to be necessary to divide the work into four books: and in the first we will deal with the origins, types and essence of trading; in the second, the manner in which the merchant should make his religious observances; in the third the attitudes proper to the merchant relative to the moral virtues and politics; in the fourth and last of the individual merchant and how he should administer his house, his family and his budget. And this will bring us to the end of our work, if it so please God.

Part 1: On the Origins and Principles of Trade

Chapter I

It is entirely natural, and indeed confirmed by the authority of the philosophers, that every thing that depends on the stewardship of men, if it is to be well and properly administered, should be first conceived and organised in the mind so that, when it is put into practice it is will be evident that, before proceeding to the exterior action, an interior synthesising was necessary, which we call theoretical speculation (f. 4), and it is from this, as from a mother, that the practical deed derives. Practical actions are the daughters of theoretical speculation in the same way that theoretical speculation is itself a daughter of nature, when properly exercised.

And thus, he who wishes to dwell on the true nature of things, as must any writer, should consider that Almighty God, when he created the world, put all things in their natural order. And since that divine order was corrupted by the sin of our forebears, it became necessary for the good government of the world and the salvation of the human race to promulgate additionally a written law that clarified which are the paths we should follow, and which avoid, by the express will of the Lord our Saviour. And this was the law given to the people of Israel by the hand of

C. Carraro, G. Favero (eds.), *Benedetto Cotrugli – The Book of the Art of Trade*, DOI 10.1007/978-3-319-39969-0_4

Moses, the first of all the prophets. And since after many centuries this law failed, due to the delinquency of the people, to produce the desired fruit, it was necessary in consequence for the salvation of men, to introduce another, new law to correct the old one and to assure the faithful, for their own good, that the prize promised them would be neither brittle nor ephemeral, but rather, solid and eternal: and this was the law of the Gospels.

And since it was the case that the natural things in creation were intended to be understood by natural instinct it was first necessary to understand individually from the outside what should be done and then (f. 4') to proceed with such actions as were indicated by the interior intelligence. And this latter intelligence was in the natural order of things given us before proceeding with exterior actions, and it is called theoretical, which means nothing less, according to the original Greek etymology, than 'intrinsic speculation and contemplation of things'. And having been given this intelligence as a natural instinct and means for considering any number of things, it behoves us to proceed to exterior actions, that is, to display openly for the general good of mankind what we have understood by means of that interior intelligence. And indeed this has been the procedure since the earliest philosophers, who, though pagans, were illuminated by the flame of natural philosophy. They investigated the natural order with diligence and having grasped it, proceeded to exterior action in such a manner that we can confidently state that these first philosophers were indeed theoreticians of that natural order, and that those coming after them were the doers, who put into practice what their predecessors had contemplated and understood with such great assiduity and wonderful intelligence. We can therefore conclude that practical activity is the child of theoretical intelligence, theoretical intelligence the child of nature, and nature that of God. Reasoning thus, we can see that it is quite impossible to bring any action to a profitable conclusion without an inner intelligence and without taking into consideration the natural state of things.

In virtue of the above, it must seem evident that the arts, particularly those expressed in practical activity, derive from nature, not without a due consideration (f. 5) of the natural order of things. And although this is indeed the proper sequence, none the less it appears that we sometimes work in the opposite direction, in that in some arts, thanks to experience and induction from particular incidences, we can arrive at universals which are the moving forces behind both the arts and the sciences. This we know from shared experience and from two cases in particular, one being the use of simples, experimented in different ways and in different places, on different persons and at different times; by way of example we can take rhubarb, which is by nature always and everywhere a purger of choler: from many instances we can therefore arrive by induction at the universal axiom that all rhubarb expels choler. And I would say that the same holds true for the art of oratory, because before it was revealed as such, some men were by natural instinct so well versed in that art that they applied the rules pertaining to the constituent parts of an oration no less well than was the case after the art of oratory had been theorized, which arose out of natural practice, as can be seen in the well known instance of the Bosnians: these people by their very nature, without knowing the art of oratory and without any form of training in the discipline, exercise most wonderfully the art of speaking, which they possess by natural instinct.

It is though in the sequence we first outlined, and not in the reverse fashion, that I dare to place our own art of trade, which, if we consider it properly, had its origin in nature after the human race had multiplied over the face of the earth: it being then necessary to produce a great quantity of goods for the sustenance of the (f. 5') individual citizen and his family, a man after having conjoined himself with a woman, and eventually becoming let us say a public figure or governor of a state, could not maintain any of those three roles, of private citizen, of a man dedicated to his family, or of public figure, without exchanging for goods he had need of such others as he had incidentally a superfluity of, because up until that time, there had yet to be invented, out of man's ceaseless industry, the need for money, a usage which quickly became universal, substituting barter, which had formerly been the original and only means of exchange, before the use of money, as we have said, supervened. As men grew in numbers and became more expert in their day-to-day activities, as it is in their nature to do, they began to understand that some universal measure of exchange would better answer to their needs present and future, and that this universal measure should be one that everywhere and in every age would ensure that such things as are necessary for human sustenance would be guaranteed by the exchanges effected whenever necessity arose. And consequently they fixed on money as the means in question and from this, as from a gushing spring, sprang forth commerce.

And therefore, with reference to the matter of our treatise, while we can say that every branch of knowledge, every discipline and every occupation have their origin in natural instinct, there are some which, notwithstanding what we have deduced previously, are expanded and enriched by the actual practice thereof, as demonstrated by the arts we spoke of (f. 6) above.

And to return to our theme, we can say that the art of trade, with which the present work is concerned, for all that it has its origin in nature, as we have said, none the less, propelled by man's need of life's necessities, has become so widespread in practice and has come across many centuries to our own time that we can truly say that its first and true origin is nature and that subsequently through the ingenuity of men, it was so expanded and propagated that it and its application have immeasurably eased the daily administration not only of private persons but also their households and families, republics and principalities, kingdoms and empires.

And although the exercise of this art, as conducted down to the present time, has never been made the object of study, none the less through its continual practice, its employment, exercise and customs can be understood, and their intrinsic nature is such that, while respecting the rules of the art of trade, this familiarity is, in my view, more instructive than any training that could be given in the subject. And this I believe to be the reason and the motive why no written precepts have been set down for a profession that is at once so natural, so necessary and so useful. And I myself would also remain silent on the matter were it not that, in the course of my long practice of this calling, I have understood, indeed seen and had closely to do with, the confusion and abuse of proper procedures perpetrated daily by the merchants of our times. And this has been my main motive for setting down, in the manner proper to a treatise on the art of trade, what has never perhaps been written before from the creation (f. 6') of the world down to our own times.

Chapter II On the Essence and Definition of Trade

To keep things in their proper order, we will describe what trading is, because, as Cicero says, if we want to understand things properly, we must begin by defining them. And as we are going to be dealing with trade, before proceeding we must first of all resolve a question that might create difficulty among uneducated merchants, that is, clarify the difference between two similar words *mercatantia* (merchandise) and *mercatura* (trade). By the term *mercatantia* in fact we mean all those things which are bought, sold or bartered, or concerning which contracts may be in any other way entered into, while the term *mercatura* refers to the art or discipline of trade, or all that is covered by the precepts and guidelines according to which everything that belongs to trading, of which we have already spoken, should be practised and negotiated.

And therefore, having made it clear that the term *mercatantia* embraces all those things that a merchant might contract a sale for, we must proceed to an initial definition of *mercatura*, which we will define as follows: *mercatura*, or trade, is "an art, or rather a discipline, practised between qualified persons, governed by the law and concerned with all things marketable, for the maintenance of the human race, but also in the hope of financial gain". And as this matter is the basis of our entire work, it seems opportune to clarify a little better the various constituents (f. 7) of our definition of trade. And thus we will be able to claim that our definition is, as it seems to us, perfect, in that embraces both its intrinsic nature through universals and its variations through particulars. Its essential, universal nature is what is meant by calling it an "art or rather a discipline", a term signifying no more than that it is governed by a set of precepts directed to a particular end. The variations are made up of everything remaining that is covered by the above definition, which we may clarify as follows.

The persons who are not qualified to engage in trade are of two types. The first includes all those who cannot exercise the art without bringing discredit to themselves or without coming up against a prohibition to their so doing, which is to say, kings, princes, barons, knights, gentlemen and any others of noble birth to whom the practice of trade is forbidden according to the provisions of civil law, lex *Nobiliores,* to be found in the commercial section of the Code of Justinian, *de commerciis*, where it says: "We hereby forbid those of nobler birth, those who have achieved distinction for the splendour of their honours and those who have obtained great riches, to engage in harmful trade, so that the common citizen and the broker can the more easily effect their transactions".

Other prohibited persons are those in holy orders, for this is the teaching of the apostle Paul, in his Second Letter to Timothy, chapter 2, "No man that warreth for God entangleth himself with the affairs of this life"; and St John,[1] *distinctio* LXXXVIII: "Avoid like the plague the cleric turned merchant, become rich having been poor, proud having been humble". And these two categories of men, belonging to our first type, are disqualified by the dignity of their station.

The second type comprises unfit persons, who are that is to say themselves deficient in (f. 7') their ability to practice the profession, or in the type of merchandise they wish to sell. Those that are deficient in themselves and therefore unfit, are young persons yet to reach majority, women of all ages, peasants, children under guardianship, servants, the insane, wastrels, and other uneducated persons incapable of exercising the art. Others are unfit to engage in trade on account of the things they would offer for sale, which is to say, thieves, footpads, counterfeiters, alchemists and others of similar stripe.

"Governed by the law": refers to the price at which an item is be bought or sold, which should be a fair one, at least approximately; in the contrary case, according to the common law, the contract is invalid, most particularly when the fair price is exceeded by more than half; and the subject of legal safeguards is treated at greater length in the tenth chapter, second *quaestio*.[2]

"Concerned with all things marketable" is intended to exclude those things which ought not be the burden of a contract, which are sacred objects, pawned goods, items deposited as collateral or stolen, or things that have always been forbidden, in every age and to all, such as poisons

[1] Cotrugli's error for St Jerome.

[2] Of the *Rosarium ad Decretum*.

or gaming dice and suchlike, or things bought for personal use only or for one's family, or as gifts for others.

Nor have we added without reason to our definition of trade that it should serve "for the maintenance of the human race": for it is a fact that, right from the beginning, as soon as the human race had spread itself over the earth, this art of trade was adopted out of a general need for things that were lacking to one and superfluous to another, having its origin in exchange and barter, before money was introduced. None the less, following on the invention of this facility, (f. 8) once what nature had ordained to be done, out of necessity and for the maintenance of the human race, as we have said, had been achieved, merchants then began to exercise their art in the hope of gain. And the same thing happened with clothes, which to begin with were created rough and ready, because their only function was to cover and protect the human body from excessive heat and cold, and likewise from rain and snow and ice and other phenomena harmful to human nature.

And after their initial invention, which answered to man's basic needs, men turned to making ornate and beautiful what had first been rough and ready and without ornament, and have continued to adorn them with ever greater embellishments down to our own day, when they amaze all that cast eyes on them. And the same seems to have happened with trade, which first took shape, as we have said, from the promptings of nature and human necessity; then, over the centuries, it showed itself to be very useful to merchants, who, thanks to this utility, were able to embellish it with so many admirable innovations that only a most expert merchant could credit them, as will become clear as our treatise proceeds.

We have explored all this purely in order to clarify that part of our definition of trade from the point where we have called it "an art, or rather a discipline primarily instituted for the needs of the human race", moving on to speak of the invention of money, which proved so useful for those merchants who engaged in the profession to answer to the needs of humankind (f. 8') and in the hope of financial gain. We might add "as distinct from those who sell out of necessity", or those who buy for the use of their own families or for some other reason than with a view to reselling, these being the principal actions involved in trade; and these last therefore cannot be defined as merchants, even if they are apparently acting as such, in so far as they are not intent on the proper goal of this art which is the profit of anyone that exercises it, as Aristotle has it in his *Economics*, according to which the end of trade is profit and enrichment.

Chapter III On the Personal Qualities of the Merchant

It is well known that the ancient authors who were expert in such matters have handed us down their verdict that earthly things are governed by the influence of celestial bodies. These, by virtue of the order ordained by God, have such power over all inferior things as to impose on them their natural qualities. Only men are able to defend themselves against such influences, having received this exemption from God, for they, although swayed by the power of the constellations more towards one course of action than another, none the less because of the dignity of free will vested in them together with the gift of an individual soul, are possessed of a freedom which allows them to resist any predisposition or inclination which might induce them one way or another in accordance with the different influences of the various constellations. And this fact is enshrined in a proverb, much, indeed almost too often, cited, derived from Ptolemy: "The wise man will be the master of the stars".

For all that it is difficult to fight (f. 9) the influence of the stars, which can so largely determine the behaviour of individuals, none the less such resistance is not impossible, particularly for those men endowed with a superior intelligence, above the common run, in that their good judgement will stand firm against that influence and they will be neither guided nor directed by it. But if such resistance proves too intransigent and pushes them towards some occupation other than that which they ought to follow under the celestial influences that determine their natural bent, as often as not they will fail to keep faith with their natural calling.

For this reason we need to take particular care, when we are beginning to channel the dispositions of a son, or of some one else for whom we are responsible parentally or through some other blood relationship, when directing them towards the practice of trade, because if that son has a leaning elsewhere, or towards some activity under an opposing sign, he might well not prosper in that life, or would only get on with difficulty and remain stuck half way with small profit to himself and without reaching his objective, which should be to enrich himself honourably. In this sense, during the formative years of a young person whom we wish to direct towards such an employment, it is essential to ascertain in what direction he is inclined by nature.

And discovering this inclination means, during his boyhood, which is free of moral corruption, understanding what occupation the child enjoys and how he usually spends his time. And he if he is lively by nature, well turned-out and of noble character, and not too fickle nor an idler, but rather aspires to acquire both honour and profit or victory in war, then we can say that he is suitable material for a career in trade (f. 9'), the goal of which is honourable enrichment. And when we identify such inclinations in our children or in others closely related to us, we must direct them towards the activities they are predisposed to, and not set ourselves to fight against nature thinking to get the better of her, because she can defeat any man however strong he be.

For proof of this fact we have the example of the Titans who, so the poets tell us, trusting in their immense strength, sought to usurp the kingdom of the heavens from Jupiter, who struck them down and killed them, which myth Marcus Tullius Cicero interprets in his treatise *On Old Age* in which he says, among other things: "To take on the gods, as did the Titans, is nothing less than to set oneself against Nature".

We have too the example of the Greeks and Romans, both of whom, during the epochs when they were at their respective zeniths, applied the rule of encouraging their sons and relatives in the careers to which nature inclined them, with the result that in those times, in the case of both peoples, we find in every worthwhile field of endeavour the best men there had ever been, or that there have ever been since.

And examples that this was the case can be found in all of the liberal and mechanical arts, as in philosophy for example, among the Greeks we find the very greatest philosophers, almost beyond numbering: chief among them were Pythagoras, Socrates, Plato and Aristotle; and in the mathematical sciences, Euclid, Archimedes (f. 10), Ptolemy and many others; and in poetry Homer, Hesiod and Pachivio[3] and closer to ourselves Virgil, Ovid and Horace; and in oratory Demosthenes, Aeschines, Hortensius and Cicero; and in history Thucydides, Herodotus, Polybius, Livy, Cornelius Nepos, Tacitus and Justin; and in painting Apelles and Zeuxis and many others like them; and in sculpture Phidias and Praxiteles; and in the arts of war Alexander, Lysimachus, Caesar, Scipio, not to mention Hamilcar, Hasdrubal and Hannibal if we were to include the barbarians. And therefore it seems to me that the judgement of Apollonius of Alabanda is particularly praiseworthy, of whom it is said that after he had been invited to Athens to teach rhetoric, when brought a pupil predisposed to that discipline he would receive him willingly but when he was unsuitable or incapable he would exhort him to follow some other profession and decline to teach him so as not to waste time.

Assuming he is endowed with a natural aptitude, as we have said, the boy electing to be educated in the art of trade should possess one further qualification, which is surely well enough known from experience and sanctioned besides by natural law, that is that he be the son of a merchant, because, as we can readily observe, there are many similarities of feature between a father and his son, passed on naturally in his seed, and the same thing holds for interior resemblance, which is why the bard Cecco d'Ascoli, appropriating the philosopher's saying, wrote: "The eyes reveal the qualities of the heart". And if the external appearance reveals the interior and is derived (f. 10') from the father's seed which has imprinted the family resemblance, there is no reason to doubt that the intrinsic virtues of the son will be similar to those of the father.

And leaving aside any number of demonstrations of this fact, I will limit myself to saying that I have certainly myself verified it, recognising in myself my father's imprint; in fact he has left his particular stamp on me to such a degree as to cause general amazement, and not only with regard to practical matters but also in our common manner of dealing with providence. As soon as he is born a child should be helped and tempered betimes, and instructed from the cradle in the precepts and principles of discipline, as Quintilian enjoins us to do at the beginning of his work on 'How an orator should be moulded': he would have it that even

[3] Wrong reading, maybe instead of Pindaro.

his wet nurse and all those with whom the infant will converse should be chosen for their fine articulation, so that a good and pure elocution be imbibed by the child along with his nurse's milk; and that there should always from his earliest years be teachers in the house from whom he can learn eloquence.

And we would say exactly the same of the merchant: that from his earliest years he should absorb the gestures, manners, habits and speeches of merchants and display fluency and sober dignity in every action. And we read further that Cornelia, the mother of the Gracchi, much helped her sons in developing their eloquence. And when these two requirements are combined, so that one reinforces the other, and if a third is then added, that is, the teaching of the essential rules of discipline and their putting into practice as a constant reflex, the outcome will be the ideal merchant who will achieve his potential, above all if he is assisted in some degree by good fortune. Fortune, as often as not, will smile (f. 11) on those who manage their lives wisely and by the light of reason, and conversely will abandon those who conduct themselves without rule or irrationally. From which derives the common saying which has it that good fortune does not frequent the house of the fool and if it find itself there will not lodge long. And if it should sometimes happen that one who handles himself poorly none the less succeeds in some enterprise, it is a rare occurrence and happens by chance and seldom in day-to-day affairs: certainly it should not be taken as a rule or example, in fact the opposite course should be followed.

And since everything explained thus far about the character of a merchant has been concerning only the inclination of his mind, it remains to add briefly something about his body's workings. In this regard we can say that although the proper set of his mind and his soul, which must underpin the intentions of anyone wishing to follow the merchant's calling, are most crucial and conducive to achieving his aims, none the less a degree of physical ability is also necessary.

And this is why I have called this chapter "On the personal qualities of the merchant" because the word "person" embraces both the mind and the body. And if it seems to the reader that this section where we deal with physical aptitudes is useless or superfluous, let him but think how and to what extent the practice of trade is physically demanding and he will perhaps no longer be sceptical but will admit that this part far from being useless and superfluous, is actually useful and necessary. In fact, to turn a profit, or to accomplish the aims of the art of trade, it is essential to set aside (f. 11') every other concern, and to dedicate oneself as diligently as possible to all the things that may prove useful to or advance that occupation. This means sometimes putting up with privations day and night, travelling on foot or on horseback, and by land and sea, working one's hardest at buying and selling and in making attractive the goods bought and sold, and applying as much diligence as possible to these and similar matters. And every other consideration, as I have said, must take second place, and not only superfluous things but even those necessary to the maintenance of human life. It may well be required sometimes that eating and drinking and sleeping be postponed to another occasion, indeed that one endure hunger and thirst and white nights and other similar inconveniences deleterious to the normal equilibrium of the body, which were it not an instrument prepared for these eventualities and trained for such hardships, could not sustain them, and undergoing them could cause such suffering as to lead to sickness and even death.

The consequence then must be one of these two following: either, by not exercising his profession as he should, the merchant will not achieve the necessary yield from his art and not obtain his proper aim, that being profit with honour, or alternatively, even if he does succeed in earning, will do so at the cost of being unable to carry on his vocation due to the weakness of his body, or, if continuing to do so with a body inadequate to the task, will sicken and die. And although these two outcomes, being extreme cases, are sufficiently obvious to avoid, we still maintain and will demonstrate that it is exceedingly useful and even necessary to maintain the body in good condition (f. 12) so that it will be suitable to an activity that requires a proper instrument to achieve its ends, just as a hammer, being the tool adapted to the purpose, best suits the workman for driving home a nail; and the same thing applies to other activities. And the mind and the soul guide the body like an artist imposing due proportion on his works. And while I maintain that the body should be used to sustaining hard work I also say, as Aristotle reminds us in the second book of his *Ethics*, that all excess is dangerous: I am referring here to the excesses of those who have a powerful physique, who can sustain hard labour and have indeed what goes beyond what is required of the merchant, who while he must certainly be able to work hard, none the less should not be a common porter, because generally those who are strongest and most robust are not those most gifted with intelligence. Nature in fact compensates for deficiencies in one person with gifts in another, according to Aristotle's teaching, where he says that tender flesh is easier to grasp, whereas firm things are resistant.

The merchant should therefore be capable of supporting his calling's challenges but at the same time have a tender and delicate body, which goes with a nobility of intellect; I am not talking of bodies too weak to be suitable to the exercise of trade, nor those of great strength and sturdiness like those of load-carriers, which tend to belong to those lacking a lively intelligence, uncultivated people with little substance to them, whom a merchant will normally shun, whence the celebrated proverb "A strong man is the ruin of a household".

(f. 12') Chapter IV On the Proper Location for the Merchant

Notwithstanding Seneca the moral philosopher's verdict that "The place does not make the man", none the less, while the place does not form the man, the volume of mercantile activity does depend on a suitable location, and consequently the merchant should choose a place favourable to trade and shun unsuitable addresses. In fact a merchant's choice of residence can contribute a great deal, from its natural advantages, to his enrichment or ruin. This truth is very little understood, its opposite in fact widely believed by those inexpert in trade, in so far as these people, ignorant and untutored in the art, are prone to choosing unfrequented places where they can live at small expense and there are few other merchants.

What I say is that the best place for a merchant to practice his profession and one that will improve his state should above all boast good clean air, which is the element most essential to human existence: wholesome air is very good for healthy human life, while foul air can cause great harm, bringing illness, frequently of a serious nature, resulting in loss of income and the wreckage of all one's gains.

Secondly the place should be populous and frequented by merchants and gentlemen. Just as the soldier is best able to demonstrate his proficiency with the sword if he frequents places where arms are employed, so the merchant, by living (f. 13) in places frequented by other merchants, will become day by day ever more expert and experienced, and as a result richer. And what is more, in a place where many merchants live, he is in a position to observe well and continuously improve his mercantile practices; and in such a place although a merchant may not become inordinately wealthy, it is all but impossible that he will be poor, because here there will always be many sources of sustenance and refuge, thanks to which he can find aid and assistance and thus be kept from ruin.

Thirdly, he should live in a place where peace and not fear reigns, because as Cicero says in his *On Choosing a General*,[4] war renders men unhappy in many ways but for trade the fear or rumour of war is sufficient, and the merchant needs to live freely and with a quiet mind untroubled by disturbances.

Fourthly, he should live in a place where mercantile law is applied rather than the Code of Justinian, because the disputatiousness of lawyers, who are hostile to his profits, is no small problem for the merchant. Besides, mercantile affairs require rapid preparation and speed in execution, while in legal disputes the exact opposite is the general rule. Furthermore the practice among merchants is to honour simple private deeds, a procedure quite alien to jurists. And there are many other matters in which many now seriously question the applicability of the ancient laws, not that the laws are not in their essence just and divinely inspired, but due to the greed of many of their modern interpreters they have become corrupted (f. 13') and reduced to fallacious disputes. And where it is necessary to see straight to the heart of a question and unravel the knots it has wound itself into, these men would instead convert the whole matter into fallacious disputes, or rather an occasion for corruption. Mercantile norm is that their judgements should not be *de rigore iusticie*, nor directed towards punishments, but governed by the principles of equity and moderation.

---

[4] That is *Pro Lege Manilia*.

Fifthly, the merchant should avoid living in those places where the volume of business and general wealth is excessive, for such places are overrun with dealers, which is a dangerous state of affairs for the merchant who frequently fails as a consequence. And this one learns by experience, because there are certain places where the foreign merchant rarely manages to conduct his business over any length of time without failing. One of these is the kingdom of Valencia, which is possessed of great natural wealth, but in my times, and as far as I have been able to establish, in times past likewise, rarely has anyone been able to establish a business that does not eventually go to the bad and fail. And the same is true of Calabria, and even more so in Sicily. Here the merchants typically overextend themselves investing in tax farms on food more than they are able to collect. It is essential therefore to be alert, as these are places that are evil by nature. And one may well encounter many places that in proportion to their character and size abound in all kinds of merchandise: and yet in some of these the wealth of men does not seem as a general rule to exceed five hundred ducats and it appears that however hard they try they cannot better this sum, or as soon as they get above it they become enmeshed in the clutches of usurers (f.14) and end up as bricklayers or peasants. There are some places where the wealth of men never rises above a thousand ducats, in others four thousand, in others again ten thousand, and so on, place by place, and this derives from the intrinsic character of the place.

For which reason, if you wish to achieve the goal of the merchant, which is, as Aristotle says, to get rich, endeavour to live in some place where those who reside there and follow the merchant's calling have succeeded in accumulating the greatest wealth. For it from this that the saying arises "The biggest fish are netted in the biggest lakes"; and therefore you must live where you can engage in large enterprises and obtain honour and riches therefrom.

Chapter V On Exchange Selling

To continue with our treatise in due order, we will now speak of the actual actions and procedures involved in the practice of trade. And we will speak first of barter, the first and principal part of trading, which was formerly called 'commutation': barter in fact consists in the simple exchange of goods for goods, with no added money element, while commutation now involves the exchange of one thing for another with a cash addition from one of the contracting parties.

With regard to the first type of exchange we should remember that it was introduced for the benefit of the two parties, in so far as both, wishing to dispose of merchandise they were holding, and being unable to do so for money payment, had necessarily, to bring this about, to have recourse to this first type (f. 14') of barter, which is to say exchanging the goods they had previously held for others which they believed or were certain that they could dispose of more easily, more quickly and more advantageously. Which is why I say that this first type of barter was invented for the convenience of both the contracting parties as we can confirm every day with obvious examples.

And as a readily understandable demonstration of our discipline is best achieved by examples, we will take a case that demonstrates the usefulness, indeed the necessity of barter. Florentine merchants frequently take their cloth and fine fabrics down to the Kingdom of Sicily to sell for cash, and it often happens that they cannot find ready payment for their goods, particularly those that can only be sold on over a long period; these merchants, finding themselves in Sicily with their goods, and desiring to dispose of them but not managing to do so for cash, in order not to lose time or render the journey fruitless, have to decide on some local product that they can take in exchange which will have a better chance of being sold advantageously in their native city than their own cloths and fabrics, were they to take them back. By choosing thus to barter, they manage to exchange the said merchandise for wheat, either through a broker or otherwise, which the Florentine will be able to dispose of at home more easily than the cloth and fabrics, other things being equal. The broker in fact, applying his expertise, manages to barter the goods for wheat with a Sicilian (f. 15) who has a large quantity of grain to dispose of. This Sicilian, not managing to dispose of his wheat for cash, willingly accepts in exchange the cloth and fabrics which he expects to be able to sell more easily than his corn. From this we can see the usefulness of the first type of barter.

And since it can sometimes be difficult to exchange one kind of merchandise for another, without a rounding up of cash, also in this case, to meet the requirements of the contracting parties, the second kind of barter was invented, which is the exchange of goods with a cash addition: this addition aims at successfully completing the transaction which could not otherwise be concluded. One needs however to be alert when bartering merchandise as swindles are rife in this field and one can suffer serious losses. Not for nothing do merchants have a proverb "He who risks barter, risks himself". And among other precautions, you need to be quite sure that the goods you acquire by exchange are really more convenient and easy to dispose of than those you part with.

Secondly, you must do your best to obtain a higher price than the other side. And in order to work this out, you must calculate the worth of your grain in money, the premium you are adding to the exchange and the percentage which the other side is adding, and the same holds for the cloths. Having made this calculation (f. 15'), you must deduce from the comparison who is getting the better of the exchange, and to what degree; and in this context you must consider carefully the potential sale value of the merchandise you are taking in exchange, notwithstanding its lower value in the forum where the contract is made. The valuation should refer to the place where you will resell the goods, where the more favourable market conditions will give you greater opportunities for their disposal. And having weighed these three elements, you must adjust the respective totals (drawing up a balance sheet) before concluding the barter.

Furthermore, make sure that the other side declares the price first. Get used of always asking what he expects for his goods: it is all too easy to be outwitted here, because if we are asked to make an offer for the merchandise, which we calculate according to the suitability of our goods to high or low market conditions, we are likely to be caught out, because the other side becomes more confident of selling when he sees that the merchandise sells on well, and will raise the price considerably by increasing his premium, rather than basing himself on what he can expect to get from selling the other party's goods, if necessary transporting them by land or sea to other markets. That the other side thinks the arrangement will be a success is no bad thing, so you should always offer the other party a fair price if you aim to barter well.

Fourthly, you should always manage to have some cash with you, if possible, or, when you don't, try not to disburse cash to the other party yourself. And if you must pay over money on top (f. 16), you should make your calculations carefully and work out exactly how much extra corn you will get by paying over that cash which the other has added to the exchange, as the other side will always try to increase his take. You must therefore work out how much is being added on top and convert that sum into goods value: in short you must try to discern and calculate his cash mark-up. By these means, taking proper consideration of all the elements listed above, you will succeed in your project and barter to your advantage.

And now that we have dealt sufficiently with barter and commutation in this introduction, it seems the right point to move on to selling merchandise for cash.

Chapter VI On Selling for Cash

Since we must now, following our subject order, deal with selling, we should begin with the necessary distinctions. We will specify that one can sell in two ways, other than by barter, which we have dealt with in our preceding chapter, firstly for cash, and secondly on credit. We will deal first with the one and then with the other. And since a sale entails a purchase, because these are reciprocal actions, we intend in this chapter to deal with both buying and selling for cash. First of all in this regard we will say that one cannot buy or sell goods that are not the property of the seller, or that one cannot buy from a seller not authorised to sell on his behalf by the owner of the merchandise or from one he has not commissioned to do so. And selling for cash was invented as soon as money came to be used by men (f. 16') and only in the absence of this, due to unavoidable time lapse or distance, was it necessary to introduce selling on credit. And therefore, whenever it is possible to sell for cash, we would exhort every merchant to do so, rather than on credit.

And we would say the same thing of buying, not least because cash sales are transparent transactions, without risk or anxiety, bringing with them the certainty of achieving that gain which had induced you to make the sale in the first place; furthermore you will always buy with advantage, because the seller, as soon as he sees ready money, will be more amenable in his dealings if he is to collect immediately.

Besides, this is a type of transaction which is always lawful, provided that one is not selling at a higher than reasonable price, which is the second matter of Chapter X, 'Hoc ius', and of our treatise, where we deal with issues of conscience.

It is lawful also as long as one is not selling prohibited articles such as gaming dice, playing cards, poisons and suchlike; or defective goods, as in St. Thomas II[a], II[e], q. LXXVII; or where no commitments on oath or perjuries or other improper or untoward circumstances are involved. And thus far we can agree that any article can be sold for cash without prejudice to one's conscience, provided that the necessary conditions as outlined above are observed.

But it is not the case that every article, though legal in itself, can legally be sold on credit, as we will discuss in the chapter on contracts: in fact, although selling on credit is itself legitimate, indeed reasonable and necessary, under certain circumstances it may become illegal.

Chapter VII Selling on Credit

(f. 17) Having dealt with selling for cash quite summarily because it seems to us a straightforward matter, we will now consider selling on credit. And since the matter is more complex, we will approach it more systematically and thoroughly, above all bearing in mind that this form of selling has provoked a considerable difference of opinion among our theologians, both ancient and modern.

And we will add, about what we said in the preceding chapter, that selling on credit came about from the lack of immediately available cash, is certainly true; none the less, this kind of transaction has turned out to be so useful, necessary even, to merchants that little would be concluded, or is concluded, without it. In addition, all dealings between merchants would close down and the art of trade come to an end, to the destruction of private property and the public weal; indeed the ruin of all the families in the city would surely follow, in so far as without this facility there would be no commercial voyaging among the Turks or the Tartars, or the Moors, nor among the more distant barbarians, peoples who supply us with merchandise not otherwise available to Christian folk, with consequent loss of profit.

And thus all the principal occupations, especially those practised most widely and bringing the most income to many peoples, such as the wool, the silk, the spice and similar trades, would be no more, bringing insolvency to whole cities and the families in them. And if it were to be objected that all this could be done instead with ready money, (f. 17') the answer that this would be utterly impossible for the shortage of cash in these times among the Christian nations, which is insufficient for even day-to-day transactions; nor is the amount in circulation increased by the addition of the foreign goods we obtain from the above-mentioned barbarian peoples. From all of which it is evident that credit selling, for all its origin, as we have said, being the simple lack of ready money, has none the less proved so useful to merchants that without it the art of trade could hardly be carried out, nor households nor cities remain solvent. One may therefore, indeed must, logically allow that, on the grounds outlined, this type of sale is not only useful but necessary. The reason for this can also be clearly demonstrated in another fashion with a fresh example: those who travel for commercial reasons cannot carry large amounts of cash around with them, but carry merchandise, which they buy in places where it abounds and sell where it is in short supply. And in so far as travel and portage expenses, together with the length of time spent travelling, could easily eat away their profit, and their capital too, merchants cannot waste the further time required to sell their goods retail, but must dispose of them wholesale; and since in wholesale transactions it is rare to find buyers or entrepreneurs ready to pay in cash, the merchant, if he does not want to lose his profit and his investment, must opt for selling on credit, and on the basis of the credit notes thus received buy (f. 18) the goods that will serve him in his country of destination, where they will for the most part be sold on credit in their turn. In this manner he will succeed in paying off the debt incurred in buying the original goods and emerge with honour and profit. And from this many advantages derive, both particular and general, to the benefit of many persons, craftsmen and unskilled workers, porters, shipowners, sailors, watermen, customs officers and others in a similar line, each bringing work to the next.

And apart from this spread of general benefits, there are the greater and more specific ones earned by those who have had the enterprise to buy on credit and provide a living for the above-mentioned categories and take home themselves an honourable profit. And all this only comes about because rich men who have ready money at their disposal are not given to travelling far from home or exposing themselves and their wealth to the uncertainties of the sea, and furthermore, in line with their social standing, are happy to avoid physical effort.

And since this matter of selling on credit is particularly hard to get a good grasp on, even for those familiar with the art of trade, on account of the numerous difficulties the daily exercise of this kind of selling can come about, it is also the case that many men of wide culture, but without practical knowhow or any expertise in mercantile affairs, condemn as a matter of course credit selling as an entirely improper procedure without drawing any distinctions. And since this form of contract is in fact in itself legal, useful (f. 18') and indeed necessary to the sustenance of individuals and their families and cities, we are greatly surprised to find it expressly condemned by those who have compiled *Summae* on moral questions. And since we are desirous of clarifying this matter, which is of no little importance to us, we will explain anon, drawing clear distinctions between different cases, how and when a contract for sale on credit can on occasion become an illicit one. This form of contract, which is not of its nature in any way corrupt, is always itself lawful, useful and necessary. None the less, credit selling does involve a number of rules which must be observed in order that its practice can be useful and beneficial. We must therefore review with the greatest attention six elements in particular involved in selling for credit: the objects being sold, the person to whom they are being sold, the agreed expiry date of the credit, the amounts involved, your margin of profit and the modalities of final payment.

The first point to be considered then is the merchandise itself, which should be well chosen and suitable for sale, free of defect or damage, unlike what is offered by many sellers who put up for sale on credit the worst and basest goods they have in their warehouse which they have not managed to shift otherwise. In these cases "the glutton makes one calculation, the innkeeper another". You may think to ruin some poor sap with old and shoddy merchandise, and he may be thinking to avoid payment, and is buying only as a last resort: but if he goes bankrupt, so will you. The wise merchant therefore will always be wary of extending credit to men in a great hurry to buy even on disadvantageous terms, without regard for the true value of the merchandise. And as soon as one such arrives on your doorstep, even if his credit seems to be good (f. 19), steer well clear of him, and look on him as already a failed bankrupt, or sure soon to become so.

Thus, secondly, look carefully at the person to whom you are selling your goods, who should be a man with good credit and reputation, a good payer. You should try to find out about him and know him intimately. And in the case of those of whom you have no direct acquaintance, you should pay attention to many elements: first, you should look to the physiognomy, beginning with his eye, since as Pliny says in his Natural History: "The soul dwells in the eyes"; and Cecco d'Ascoli: "The eyes reveal the qualities of the heart". And as Solomon says: "Beware of the man marked by some physical defect", like the lame, the cross-eyed, the crooked-mouthed, the red-haired and suchlike, and above all those who when talking to you will not meet your eye. And observe how when a man asks for deferred payment and seems overcome by hesitation, is cautious about answering or committing himself to any position, this is because lack of money and weakness make a man timid, as Seneca said[5]: "Miserable poverty has this further curse, that every question makes its victims blush." While bashfulness can be admirable in the very young, as Aristotle argues in the Ethics, it is to be condemned in later life.

Beware too of men whose names suggest iniquity, since, as the proverb has it "the name suits its wearer" or "Adam named each creature according to its nature", and St Augustine and other sages are of the

[5] Sentence not attested in the corpus of Seneca.

same opinion: so you may well come across men called Pietro Zacchera [Peter Mudball] (f. 19') Giovanni Imbrattamondo [John Worldfouler], Antonio Gabbadio[6] [Anthony Godswindler] and suchlike. None the less I should make clear that in my own experience I have met and had to do with many common and attractive names behind which a man of worth was in no way to be found, and the opposite too, names I will not cite to avoid rancour from any side. And if therefore good and attractive names can turn out to be hateful, how much more so are names that within and without testify to villainy! And the lesson we can draw from this is that one gift a father can bestow on a son, at no cost to himself, is a good name; another is to rear him in a good area or in a good country; and a third to give him a good grounding in a profession, since, as they say: "Where there's a craft, there's a raft".

Do your business then with men whom nature has created with pleasing proportions: I am sure that Nature, just as she troubles to form well and in due proportion the principal organs, that is, according to the physicians, the heart and the brain, so she will see to it that the other members which depend on the above will be in proper proportion, unless they be damaged or distorted by some misfortune; in the same way, the opposite is true, that in those whose hearts are perverted by nature, cheating and sly, the other members will grow awry, crooked and out of true. And it cannot be doubted that you will rarely find a well-proportioned man with well balanced limbs whose inner self does not correspond to his outer aspect. And this explains and helps us to understand why, as Aulus Gellius recounts in the first book of his *Attic Nights*, the philosopher Pythagoras (f. 20) would have his disciples be good-looking and well-made fellows. And thus we should take care that those with whom we have to do, and to whom we entrust our merchandise, be of a pleasing aspect and cheerful and easy in their speech. And if one should sometimes become passionate when talking with friends or sigh on occasion and let fall a tear from his eye, then he is a man of fine qualities, and lovable too. Be sure that he looks you straight in the eye with a sincere gaze, civilised and not predatory, truthful and open, not deceitful, and not concealing many secrets: such a man is worth cultivating and having as a friend.

---

[6] Of course, these are three feigned names.

Thirdly, you must consider the expiry date of the credit, which we should always try to make after as short an interval as possible. You should also try to see to it that the payment deadline of others to yourself comes at a favourable moment or coincides with some obligation of your own, such as attendance at a fair, or a sea voyage, or the maturation of some debt to be liquidated on your part, or investments in goods to be made or avoided if you suspect a plague season may be in the offing. Anyone anticipating the arrival of such an event should prepare his defences in advance; if you have any suspicion, from any straw in the wind, of the imminence of a plague epidemic in the summer for example, you should see to it that repayments come in before the end of March, because as the atmosphere gets warmer the disease will increase in vigour; and similarly if you think a war might break out or some other calamity, for a month can be vital in such circumstances. And you need to be very prudent about this and not do as many foolish men do and agree a timescale of eighteen months and more, time for four popes to perish and who knows what unforeseen events to occur that would impossible to predict, unless from (f. 20') a reliable written forecast. But it is impossible to be found, and subject to mutation into its opposite at the drop of a hat, and even were that not so, long-term maturations are never without risk.

Fourthly, you must give consideration to the amounts involved: be sure not to extend too much credit, neither in a retail nor a wholesale contract, that is to say neither in a small nor a large transaction. Consider the nature of what you are dealing in and the financial capacity of the man to whom you are offering credit: under no circumstances allow the concession of large credits.

Fifthly you must take into account your profit from the transaction, that is, your premium on the merchandise. Make sure that your price is a fair and honest one, because if you push your poor buyer too far, you will risk losing both your gain and your investment: the sale price should be equable, as we will argue when we come to deal with matters of conscience.

Sixthly, you should look to the modalities of payment. When you consign your merchandise, have a clear contract drawn up, in the form of a public document, that is, one protected by the legal safeguards in force in the place where you are signing. Because contracts are drawn up in different ways in different places, in accordance with local usage. And for every transaction be in the habit of involving a broker, because this is a worthwhile precaution; and even if he needs to play no active role, give him something to countersign the contract, for this will be money well spent, ensuring that there are no errors or improprieties in the document. And the more the other party is a friend of yours, the more you should take care, because. as the common proverb goes: "with an enemy one covenant, four with a friend". For there is nothing wrong, nor would any true friend think the worse of you for it, in asking for a legal guarantee at the point when you hand over your merchandise (f. 21): a merchant should in fact always be provident and cautious in his actions.

One last piece of advice regarding credit selling: if you see that your debtor's affairs are not going smoothly and you are worried about a favourable outcome, avoid denouncing him or imposing a payment injunction on him, because talking publicly about his difficulties or pursuing him with injunctions will drive him to bankruptcy. Be wise, wait before extracting yourself from dealing with him. And if you are in a condition of being able to help him, extend his credit and get him back on his feet, this will be a thing well done; and do not despise him or be angry with him, make an agreement and a covenant with him, be welcoming to him and put him at his ease, and help him in any way you can, because his good standing is your salvation.

Beware of offering credit to patricians or priests, friars, students, professors or soldiers, as these are not men used to managing money, and by extension, honouring their debts. Money is a tasty dish and when a man unaccustomed to spending comes into possession of it, he is overcome by such a pleasurable sensation that he is unable to administer it wisely, or consequently pay what he owes. Merchants would in fact, I am sure you will agree, behave in much the same way themselves, were they not continually paying and receiving money so that disbursing becomes a habit for them because they look on giving and receiving without emotion. "Since habit does not excite the passions" as the Philosopher has it; while those unused to handling money will find the opposite.

And be careful when you come across one seeking credit for goods that he has no experience of selling and is not a merchant operating in many sectors, expert in buying all kinds of merchandise, particularly if you know he is buying to sell on: do not sell to such a man, (f. 21') because he is buying to incur a loss in that commodity, which is dishonest. Secondly, if he goes bankrupt, how will he pay you, and so on? And it may be that you can get something back from others, but when the time for reckoning comes, the amount recovered will not cover a good part of his debt, and bankruptcy will likely follow.

But to conclude this chapter, my advice is not to extend credit if it can be avoided, because credit is frequently sought by those who are unfamiliar with the merchandise and cannot or do not know how to manage their money day to day, like usurers, bailiffs, gentlemen, the uneducated, widows, peasants and men generally who are inexpert in the mercantile profession. Only, then, extend credit when you have no choice, because there are some commodities that frequently cannot be sold in any other way.

Chapter VIII On Receiving Payment

Since, keeping to our schedule, receiving payment comes next after selling on credit, we must now deal with the correct manner of obtaining settlement.

A merchant should be prompt in obtaining payment on the expiry of a credit and not let it grow old. A debt has this characteristic that it deteriorates with time, and after a year has passed from its settlement date it has lost 50 % of its value, and continues to do so proportionately, because for the merchant losing time and losing money are the same thing. Anyone is capable of placing merchandise on credit but by no means all know how to get paid, yet this is a task which ought to take precedence over all others for the merchant (f. 22), and should be accomplished professionally.

Every month he should seek out maturing credits in his ledger, make a note of them and go and collect. Rescrutinise your accounts constantly and do not let debts languish; either pass them on to others or collect them, or group them and renew them to make a new arrangement, which even if it is old to you will be new to the party you are extending it to. See to it that you are not book-rich and cash-poor. And a few days before the debt falls due, go to your debtor, as it can do no harm to give him a reminder, and say "X number of days from now, you are due to pay me such and such a sum: you would do me a real favour, as I have need of it right now, if you could advance me the money a little before the due date". For all that he will probably demur, as debtors are inclined to, you will have discreetly and honestly reminded him of the deadline and explained in advance that for the valid reasons given you cannot wait beyond the agreed date. Then the day after the latter, with prompt courtesy but firmly, you should go and ask for what is due to you, for "he who asks fearfully invites refusal" as our great moral philosopher Seneca observed in one of his tragedies. And to this end I strongly suggest that all merchants employ young men, who are well suited to debt collection, because you will collect more effectively through the young who do not blush at being importunate and insistent. Whereas the opposite can be the case with more seasoned dependants, who must greet friends as the merchant himself does and display a human face; while the younger ones are more persistent and will not let go until the debtor has paid up, and are happy to cause red faces over and over again. The Genoese and the Florentines in particular favour (f. 22') this practice, as I have seen and experienced in their territories.

Chapter IX On Paying Your Debts

To be a good collector, as well as a correct merchant, you must necessarily be also a good payer, and there is certainly a deal of truth in the proverb "he who is honest with money is honest in all things". I thoroughly subscribe to and admire this saying and I have seen it much honoured among the Catalans especially in the noble city of Barcelona: the first thing they say in praise of someone they are thinking of electing to a political office is "He's a good payer". And generally speaking they all try to appear so, to be good payers, and for the most part they are; and in this they imitate our Saviour who instructed us not to let our workmen's wages remain the night under our roof. And he meant that anyone owed money should be paid punctually and given his recompense; and St Augustine meant likewise when he defined justice: "Justice is giving each man his due". And know that paying punctually you will acquire credit and reputation among your friends. From this derives the proverb "the good payer is lord of others' purses". And it is the merchant, more than any other category of person, who should desire this accolade, as in the case where, when the settling day arrives, the credit-giving party omits to send a request for payment: you should then seek him out and pay him. And every item of debt that you concede (f. 23) or receive, write it in your ledger with the name of the creditor.

And if you are ever called on to adjudicate and you have to deal with those that keep only one column of accounts, that is how much is owing to themselves and not how much others are expecting from them, you should repudiate them and condemn them publicly, and eventually take them to court. For these are the worst type of merchant, the basest and most iniquitous. And similarly those who, when collecting goods or money from you, do not give you a receipt, or if they do, have it written by another hand, these are the most iniquitous, sly, false, lying and villainous of men, from whom you should flee as from the plague, they are either utterly treacherous types or men who arouse suspicion as moral renegades or transgressors of the norms of the associations of good, honest and fair merchants, among whom there should be no cheating, nor any suspicion of fraudulence.

If you receive a payment on someone else's behalf, let him know immediately how much you have received and from whom, so that you cannot say later that you have not received it, and the devil does not find your door open. And see to it that even if you should die unexpectedly your heirs cannot pretend the money was not received. Always write down what you have received and copy out the transactions you are a party to so that no mistakes are made, for those who do not do this, act in this way for no other purpose than to make a negative entry at the opportune moment, should the need arise. And whenever you see someone not writing things down, keeping back the possibility of committing some wickedness in the future, do not trust him at all, as you would avoid any other ruffian.

Pay promptly, and acknowledge your indebtedness to those to whom you are obliged, and if you do not have the wherewithal to pay, pray humbly, for debts are not paid (f. 23') by those who have nothing, but by those under obligation to do so.

Chapter X On the Manner and Universal System of Trading

In so far as all things in this world have been fashioned in a certain order, and we must so manage them, particularly those of greatest importance, such as the dealings of merchants, that are directed towards the preservation of the human race, as we have said, it follows that a merchant must manage himself, his stock and his money systematically, with a view to the proper end of all mercantile activity, which is wealth. But this system must be adapted to the merchandise and capital at his disposal: thus a very rich man will organise himself in one way, a man neither rich nor poor in another, and a poor man in yet another. It follows that some men are suited to the handling of large sums of money, others to small sums, others again to being servants, and so on. For those that are rich and administer large and various assets must direct their minds upwards and and pursue higher goals, and rightly so, because, as they say, "great ship, great effort". And they should not make large investments on the word of common sailors or other persons of limited intelligence or layabouts, because your sailor when he drinks in the tavern and buys bread in the market square will always find them expensive, and tell you that you would make a pile by selling wine or bread in that place.

The sober merchant, and above all one who has to do with large enterprises, should not invest (f. 24) casually in wheat or wine, but display a merchant's knowhow; thus he will independently address his mind to meticulous enquiries, not forgetting that excellent saying of Lactantius in the second book of his treatise *On Religion*[7]: "Above all when it comes to the conduct of one's life, it is essential to have faith in oneself, and when seeking out and assessing truths, trust in one's own judgement and intelligence rather than relying on the errors of others and being led astray, as if without the power of reasoning. God has given wisdom to all men, according to their ability, so they can enquire into things they do not know and evaluate what others say". It follows that, since we are all given as a gift of nature a capacity for rational enquiry, those who turn

[7] That is *Divinarum institutionum libri.*

their backs on wisdom and rationality and go along with the opinions of others without an independent rational assessment, are steered by others like sheep.

And to narrow the matter still further remember how many have said "trade seeks no advice", and I have subscribed to this maxim myself, because while in almost every field, civil, political or economic, the opinion of others can be useful, in trade seeking the opinion of others is inadvisable. I mean this with regard to analysing and formulating one's decisions, primarily because, if you need to ask for advice, you will have to ask another merchant, to whom you will explain either all or a part of your affairs. If you tell him everything, you are afraid this could hamper you, if only a part, he will not be able to advise you. If you ask a man who is not a merchant, and does not understand the basics of your profession, your projects and forecasts, or your ability, he will undermine your capacity for planning, raising some query or other, putting doubts in your mind, which will seem to have some substance; thus he will end up by undermining your enterprise.

(f. 24') There can be no doubt that a merchant, above all one dealing with large transactions, must acquire an expertise that becomes almost a habit of mind, so that he not only knows how to evaluate and plan, but foresee future outcomes, which comes with experience. In fact, as a valiant military commander, viewing the field of battle, knows how to deploy his troops, where he risks being overrun, where an attack will not succeed, and so on, so a merchant, once a transaction has been outlined to him, can tell you the probable outcome, the potential snags, the margin of risk and suchlike.

The merchant dealing with large contracts must above all consider carefully and manage his transactions in an orderly manner, and not simply accumulate money but spread his investments in reliable enterprises. And in this, in my opinion, the Florentines are more conscientious than other peoples. I mention the Florentines as exemplary, though others too diversify. I might hypothesise: "I am a rich and substantial merchant from Florence; I will make a partnership with others trading with Venice; I will invest two thousand ducats in exchange for 25 % of the profit and a division of the capital agreeable to all the partners. I will also enter into another partnership in Rome, investing a thousand ducats, and another in Avignon, again with a thousand ducats, and into a wool workshop a thousand ducats, and a thousand into silk, and so on, according to my means and the investment required. And I will keep back six thousand ducats for individual ventures under my own name and such commodities as I may decide to invest in in the short term".

And having in a safe and orderly way put my hand (f. 25) to many transactions, I will gain nothing but advantage from them , because the left hand will help the right; whilst had I restricted myself to accumulating money, I would have reason to be worried, because there is no end to it and I would want to net every bird that passes, or would surely run up against bad debtors, that is I would ruin myself and go bankrupt if I wanted to expand into other activities. But instead, in this fashion, dividing up my capital, in each partnership the directors will have set limits and precise criteria; with their limited capital they will not seek constant expansion, both because there are no orders to justify it and because they will not be holding excess cash. This is the proper, safe and profitable method of management for the wealthiest merchants.

Those that dispose of only average wealth, say four thousand ducats, must operate in a different way: they should not divide their capital, but keep it intact, with few exceptions, and place sparingly orders between four and five hundred ducats. They should also refer back to and frequently re-examine their accounts and realise their profits, so that every penny spent comes back into their pocket. And in my opinion our own Ragusans are particularly skilful in this type of business and at operating within these limits: so that I would not hesitate to sing their praises at this point in my treatise were it not that my readers might think me biased towards my homeland. The Ragusans deal in merchandise that is easy to sell such as silver, gold, lead, copper, wax, crimson, leather and suchlike, and are naturally shrewd, at least until they have accumulated capital over the limit indicated above and start to build, clear the ground of rocks and make gardens (f. 25'), vineyards, and other projects outside their cities, rather than within them. And they adorn their buildings so that they are wondrous to behold. And I would say to them, along with Saint Paul: "I commend you in all things, but not in this"; and above all I will not commend those who need to maintain a family in prosperity, and warn them that luxury in the countryside is the ruin of cities: often indeed a nation, failing to confront the ruin threatened them by the countryside, will allow itself to be overrun and destroyed by its enemies. To be sure all would be well with us if man were able to live always in times of peace like those of Octavian! But I say that many countries would be the more blessed if it were laid down by law that only thatched cottages could be built outside the city.

Returning to our theme, so as not to give the impression we have abandoned our initial premise, we will speak next of those who have little money, up to two hundred ducats. With such a sum they will have to commit themselves personally and not enter into partnerships nor invest in numerous enterprises. They should make the greatest individual effort to ensure a flow of money, for otherwise they will end up by consuming what little they have: as a rule the profits of those who cannot invest are few and modest, and they cannot insure themselves against ruin with little capital.

Those with nothing must strive to dedicate themselves to any activity they can, without any shame in adapting to circumstances, as indeed the Tragedian recommends loud and clear: "it behoves us to adapt".

They must not be ashamed to work for others, for as Seneca, again, says: "Do not think ignominious anything misfortune imposes on the unlucky", and to engage in any activity, however lowly, as long as it is honest and allows them to start accumulating. (f. 26) And we would emphasise that we do not consider working for others in any way unworthy, indeed we think it necessary to a future merchant, because, as they say in Italy, "He who has not been a cadet cannot be a good man at arms, and he who has never crewed cannot be a good ship's captain", or as Boethius has it in his *Scolastica*[8]: "Let there be no masters who have not learned to be pupils: for such men blush to be instructed and are unashamed to know nothing. We have seen many servants become rich men, but very few, and then rarely, become good masters without first having been good disciples. Hercules, who was wise and strong, was not

[8] The sentence is not by the Latin philosopher Boethius, as rather being in a spurious pedagogical treaty of the thirteenth century wrongly attributed to Boethius in the late Middle Ages, *De disciplina scholarium*, chapter 2, first paragraph. The attribution was demonstrated false by humanists in the late fifteenth century. See A. Steiner, The authorship of *De disciplina scholarium*, *Speculum*, 12 (1937), 1, pp. 81–84.

ashamed to serve Eurystheus, as Seneca says in the character of Megara addressing Lycus "Do away with harsh commands and where would valour be?" The Genoese, the Florentines and the Venetians, who are well versed in the mercantile arts will even today do this, and not so long ago, in the years of my youth, it was the custom in our own city. I have seen many gentlemen place their children in the service of their own servants, so that they can absorb from a tender age those skills which we used to be keener to learn than we are now, since our incomes have risen and our pride fattened.

I have seen how their children accustom themselves to the meanest occupations, even minding the horses and sweeping out the shop. To this day the Florentines continue this usage of placing their children in the service of others, so that, if they should ever find themselves in difficulty, they will not scorn any kind of honest work, however mean.

I have seen great men, fallen on hard times, who do not disdain to hire out horses, act as middlemen or keep an inn, or similar kinds of work, and among these I have seen how some have acquired riches in a short time, reaching even ten thousand ducats. I will not name them out of scruple, lest they blush from my eulogising. And generally speaking, if (f. 26') you look, you will see that when the Genoese or the Catalans have the bad luck to become poor they will take to piracy, the Venetians and the Ragusans will become beggars, but the Florentines middlemen or artisans who pull themselves up by their own industry. Nature directs the magnanimous to their proper ends, the pusillanimous to theirs, artisans and labourers to theirs, and so the poor man must help himself in any way he can, be it legal and honest.

The merchant must further be clever in seeking business, weigh up opportunities and find new ones, for the proof of an active intelligence is finding new things, as Boethius says in his *De Consolatione*[9]: "It is a sign of the feeblest intelligence to be always going back to what is already known and not to what has yet to be discovered"; and Aristotle: "It is easy to stick to what we already know". And your enquiries should be directed towards opportunities proper to the forum, to those involved and to your own financial situation, and towards enterprises that can be realised with

[9] Actually, *De disciplina scholarium* (see note 8 above).

a degree of skill. And such men exercise their professions in an admirable manner, unlike those whose brains and intellects flit everywhere without any sort of constancy, and against whom Seneca, in one of his letters *ad Lucilium*, declared: "The first thing is to be at ease in one place and with oneself". And elsewhere: "It is the sign of a spoilt stomach to be dipping into many dishes".

So, one's enquiries should not be prolonged infinitely, because ill will come of it: first because infinite speculations rarely, if ever, bear fruit; secondly, even if successful they are so far outside the normal practice of the merchant pursuing them that a great number turn sour. And they are so far from his practice, because, as I have said, he continues to speculate endlessly. Let me take as example a merchant who ships wool from Catalonia to Venice: he is expert in this sector (f. 27), understands it, enjoys a certain eminence in the field and has good contacts and credit. But arriving in Venice he observes how the buyers of his wool sell it on to wool workers either retail, or even on extended terms, and this seems to him a more profitable mode of selling than wholesale. And so he too decides to sell directly to the wool workers whom he sees making a good profit selling woollen cloth, and resolves therefore to produce cloth himself. But, still not satisfied, he spies out the destination of the cloth, and hears that good profits are made in the Levant and decides to export there himself, and so on to infinity he continues to study transactions and their large and various margins, his mind devising endless projects. Such men are mad and their brains fly everywhere. I say to you, concentrate your mind and your dealings to a single profession and do not try to gain all the way down the line, leave room for others to profit: and in fact our ancestors used to say "he who wants all, dies of gall" and "he who wants everything, loses everything". Know when to stop; let everyone make his profit, stick to your business and practice it: "Dripping water penetrates the stone – not by falling twice, but repeatedly." Those who want to get rich quickly are dangerous, and I tell you, if you want to be rich, live a long life, and accumulate a little at a time, otherwise these are wasted words.

A merchant must also experiment astutely and assess what kind of product he is suited to, for some are lucky in dealing in metals, some foodstuffs of various kinds, some slaves, others commodities such as wool, cotton, pepper, etc.; others have a bent for trafficking in different goods, clothes and hand-woven cloths, or livestock, some for trading in the Levant, others in the West, others in the North, some to shipping goods, some to accompanying them, some to mastering a skill, others to supervising others in one, (f. 27') and so on, as Ptolemy's calculations in his *Astrology* have taught us, celestial influences affect all things that we have put our hand to since childhood.

A merchant should also know the right moment to switch merchandise, when he sees that profits are diminishing because a sector is becoming crowded. You must know how to extract yourself dexterously.

A merchant should never refuse to listen to a deal offered him; but do not be hasty, keep your cards close to your chest and delay your answer, limiting yourself to yes and no. And when you have given your word, you must keep it, because were the keeping of promises between men, and especially merchants, to disappear, nothing would remain to them: for they could no longer call themselves merchants, or men of decency.

Be careful not to take on too many or too large transactions: do not try to net every bird that passes, because many have failed for taking on too much, but no one for exposing himself too little. You must never risk too much on a single throw, by land or by sea: however rich you may be, at the most five hundred ducats a shipload, or a thousand for a large galley.

It is not expedient for a merchant to have to do with the courts, nor above all to involve himself in politics or the civil administration, because these are perilous areas: and magistrates and administrators, for good reason, are not numbered among the merchants but the judges.

The merchant must have ample credit at his disposal, but concede little.

Every time you make a purchase, seek immediate possession of the goods, because until then, you have bought but the other has not yet sold. When signing a contract, speak clearly and conclude the business punctiliously.

Do not chase useless friendships. Take a lively interest (f. 28) in the affairs of others and in the business being transacted around you, or you may find yourself in difficulty; similarly you should know what is going on everywhere. Do not be cast down by the setbacks you suffer, and do not tell everyone your business, particularly those that are not able to help you.

Combat ill fortune bravely, do not give in to it or let yourself be overcome, because a dispirited man makes his own bad luck. Remember Virgil's words: "Fortune favours the bold and rejects the timid".

Buy cheap and sell dear, but when you have a sufficient profit, sell, do not wait until the last moment, as the proverb has it "It is better to sell with regret than to keep with regret".

Do not burden yourself with interest hoping to make a profit, unless necessity forces your hand.

Do not move around too much: concentrate if you can on one kind of merchandise, because generally, as the Slavs say, "A rolling stone gathers no moss".[10]

Devote yourself to goods that can be stored and beware of perishables, such as wine, meat, cheese, cereals, horses and suchlike, I am not saying in view of the rapid conclusion of the business, but to buy up with a good chance of profit.

If you have a partner, you must respect him, honour him and live alongside him with loyalty and good faith.

A merchant must be diligent in all that he does, but dispassionate, without making a spectacle of his actions: there are in fact calm and balanced intellects who operate easily and unostentatiously, doing things at the appropriate time, who direct others steadily and in an orderly manner, and work readily and without strain, and do everything well and resolutely. But others are superficial types, weak-brained and lacking intellect, who have no backbone and cannot make up for these deficiencies without the support of (f. 28') tossing their hands, head and feet about, because as the doctors and natural philosophers say, "what is lacking in one place nature makes up in another". From which it follows that those traders who throw their heads and hands and feet about when

[10] Even if Cotrugli interprets it as a Slav proverb, in its Latin version ("Saxum volutum non opbdicitur musco") the sentence was credited in the Middle Ages to Publilius Syrus, even if it does not appear literally in his *Sentiatiae*. The desirable meaning attributed to the growth of moss by Cotrugli was in the original intent of the proverb. In the Renaissance its meaning was inverted, and Erasmus in his *Adagia* (published in Paris in 1500) cited it as "musco lapis volutus haud abducitur", metaphorically relating moss to stagnation and rolling stones to active people in motion.

talking do this from weakness of mind and no other reason. So things accomplished readily indicate a sound brain, such as instructing, talking, trading, playing, writing, dancing and suchlike, but those performed with difficulty reveal brains furred with moss, drowned in water, idiotic, feeble or obtuse.

A merchant therefore must be adept at writing, conducting his business and everything else. And this will be the case if he diligently puts into practice the precepts and procedures recommended in this work of ours.

A merchant should not refuse the commissions of others, because they can do him no harm: every letter contains some proposal or other and "one thing leads to another". For this is a profession that must be practised with a long view, because the guidelines covering merchandise are infinite, in that they have no fixed term, but are shifting rules that need to be adapted from day to day and hour by hour; what they do not amount to is saying "last year so and so dealt in certain goods from forum x to forum y and did well from it; so this year I will do the same". This will rarely prove to be the case in reality, because projects on their own will not bring success but must be supplemented by the merchant's own experience, which he should have acquired from the cradle upwards, as we have said. And so we must talk about specifics, if briefly, to leave room for other matters and not seem prolix to our readers.

Chapter XI On Exchanges

Bills of exchange are a perfect invention for the merchant, and are, one might say, an essential and necessary element in commercial transactions: just as the human organism cannot subsist without (f. 29) sustenance, equally trade cannot subsist without exchange. I am talking here of exchanges one makes through letters or bills of exchange between one place and another, because we will speak of less essential forms at the end of the chapter. And to demonstrate that exchange is a highly important element and entirely necessary to trade, and that without it trade would hardly be feasible, I offer the following argument.

As a merchant who understands his profession (and in truth to judge a merchant one needs to be oneself a merchant and to have studied the principles of our trade), you know well what advice to give to one such as yourself wishing to import cloth from Catalonia into the Kingdom of Naples? You will say: "I have need of a thousand ducats in Barcelona: but since I cannot take them out of the realm, owing to export restrictions, nor, even were that possible, could I convey such a sum so far safely and easily, I must find someone in Barcelona who needs money in Naples". And you will say to him: "I will give you a thousand ducats here and you will give me so much a ducat in Barcelona in Spanish money, say fifteen or sixteen shillings, etc.". Once you have the transaction details in hand, and after the other side has made their offer, you must make your calculations. Cloths in Barcelona are worth so many lire the piece, which corresponds to so many shillings a piece and therefore so many ducats: how much will a piece cost me in ducats?

And each of your calculations must be referred to this rate of exchange, that is how many shillings a ducat is worth. And likewise in the reverse case: say I am in Barcelona and want to send cloths to Naples and I must draw up an account of how many ducats a length of cloth will fetch in Naples. I will get (f. 29') fifteen ducats, and fifteen ducats at fifteen shillings the ducat are so many lire in Barcelona. Deduct my expenses, such as freight and insurance, and I will know what price my cloth will fetch in Naples and how much I will receive in exchange in Barcelona in Spanish money. So you see how the principal foundation of your transaction is exchange, for the corresponding amount in Neapolitan money.

Equally, exchange is a procedure hard to analyse and hard to copy, and one needs therefore a sound head to handle it, and everything depends on properly understanding its workings.

You know that when you want to make a remittance in another forum, you must be sure that the currency is trustworthy there, otherwise you will only achieve losses where you expected gain. You might say: "In Barcelona the currency is strong in October and November due to the large quantities of saffron being bought, and likewise in May because of the wool; in Venice in July and August for all the galleys that set out in that season, and again in December and January when the ships depart for Soria, and so on for other destinations, because every province and every country has its high season. And with this in mind, you will have need of constant correspondence and information on the variation in exchange values from place to place, and the beauty of this is that you will draw up your accounts knowing in advance the efficacy of your bills of exchange. You will collect money in one place and remit in another, where you will be able to pay in good time without dipping into your own money, as you might say: "You who are there in Barcelona with a bill of exchange from Valencia, check on the corresponding value in Venice", and again: "A Venetian ducat is worth eighteen shillings in Valencian money". You will give a commission to your correspondents in Valencia, being able to recoup from Barcelona the four percent deduction that the Valencians will take from the Venetians, and reapplying in Venice the rate of eighteen shillings the ducat as usual: you should do his and then write to your Venetian that, if someone from Valencia makes him a cash remittance, he should act according to your written instructions. The Valencian remits at eighteen shillings which costs me four percent in Barcelona. When the time comes for the Valencian exchange to be effective, (f. 30) I make my own exchange and in Venice get seventeen shillings and six pence, that is seventeen and a half shillings the ducat, and gain from the higher rate plus the fortnight it takes for the journeyman to arrive from Valencia, according to the usage of Barcelona. And so on for many similar situations, as often as you like, without ever having to touch your own funds but profiting all the while; and therefore it is essential that the exchanger enjoys good credit in the places where he needs to operate, and knows all the conventions, so you might say: "A bill from Rome to Naples honoured in eight days, from Naples to Rome in ten, Naples to Venice honoured in fifteen, Naples to Barcelona bills honoured in thirty days, Barcelona to Venice business concluded in sixty days", and so on. And knowing these periods you will know what to expect from each place.

There is also another type of necessary exchange, in addition to that outlined above, which is as we have seen at the base of every bill accompanying merchandise: I mean large-scale merchandise, because I am excluding those merchants or even merchandise that belong to faraway places, beyond the horizons of regular commerce; I am talking about those places most adapted to buying and selling and of merchants par excellence, because just as one does not number among the poets the two-bit verse-cobblers, and the same goes for philosophers and others, when we speak of merchants we do not mean the strugglers, hawkers of eelskins, as the saying goes; and likewise for places, because exchanges are necessary and without them one could not survive in the merchant's world.

I say again that exchange is a useful and necessary tool for men moving from one place to another and who (f. 30') need money in their country of destination which they must buy with that of the country of departure; such might be priests and knights, students, professional soldiers and suchlike, that cannot readily transfer money from the Kingdom of Sicily to Flanders, Bruges, etc.; and these need therefore a letter of credit, depositing their cash here in exchange for a letter of corresponding import, because more often than not it would be impossible to transfer money any other way.

Exchange being therefore so convenient and useful, necessary even, not only for merchants and their goods but also for gentlemen, priests and knights and travellers of all kinds, we can say that it is a mechanism of the greatest importance in human life and a most ingenious invention on the part of he who first thought of it. And for their deeply rooted tradition, and for the fluency, method and discipline that the Florentines, more than any others, display in the practice of exchange, we need not doubt that they were the first innovators to experiment with it.

And I am certainly astonished that exchange, being so useful, easy and entirely necessary to the conduct of human affairs is condemned by so many theologians, ancient and modern, as impermissible, embracing as it does uncertain gain, the circulation of goods, simple exchange, lending, the paying of interest, particularly hard work, realism, the risk of having credits pending on many occasions and being in a situation of potential profit or loss. I have little doubt that the matter has not been understood by those who have returned this negative verdict. I am a merchant myself and understand this art of exchange, but I was practising it for two years before grasping (f. 31) it fully, and my intelligence is above the mean and I was determined and desirous of grasping it. So that churchmen should not marvel that I so audaciously declare that it is more or less impossible for a man of the cloth to understand this art from simply having heard about it, and consequently he cannot make a judgement, 'like a blind man with colours'. Furthermore, they go further and posit the implausible, that is, say Pietro has a hundred ducats in Paris and is himself in Venice and cannot repatriate them, and he finds Giovanni who has a hundred ducats in Venice and says to him "Give me your hundred ducats here and I will see you have mine in Paris. "If you want", says Giovanni, "I will give you them and make this exchange, but I want ten profit on top": and they say, that for the favour to Pietro and Giovanni's risk such a mark up is lawful. And I say that genuine exchanges, being generally respected and taking place in the real world, are much more lawful.

And since we must deal with this material in its proper place and in a specific chapter, I will pass straight on to actual practice, and say that other exchanges are those which are made from currency to currency and paid out in a third, as they do in Avignon, where francs can be exchanged for payment in escudos, the account being drawn up in florins. That is to say, 132 1/3 Avignon florins are one hundred francs; and 1 florin, 7 shillings and 9 3/5 pence make one franc; one current Avignon florin is worth 30 shillings and 10 escudos of the Kingdom are worth 34 shillings. Every grosch is worth two shillings; one gives 5 florins for 4 francs.

Other exchanges may be between the same currencies, but with a certain percentage more or less according to its worth in different forums. Thus Barcelona and Valencia exchange lira for lira with x percent more or less for that of Barcelona or Valencia depending on the season, and likewise Perpignan and Barcelona exchange lira for lira with a so much percent discount for the Perpignan money; Naples and Palermo exchange their currencies, with a discount on Palermo's; and Venice also, Venetian ducats against Venetian ducats with whatever percentage (f. 31') more or less. Geneva changes in a different manner with Venice and Barcelona etc., that is for a gold mark they accept so many lire, and for a Genevan gold mark the Venetians give so many Venetian ducats, that is 62, 62 1/2 and 63, and thus one exchanges at a different rate in different countries, and in accordance with different customs. Oh Lord, when you think of it, how much hard work and ingenuity the first inventors of exchange must have applied to the matter!

The usage is to apply sanctions to non-payers, the exchange in these cases returning with a percentage more or less which the party that has had the money and not paid out must make good, because the other would otherwise have gained a certain profit. It is because of this that many think to condemn these contracts, a matter on which I cannot stay silent although our purpose here is another, and I will repeat what Aquinas (IIª, 2ᵉ, q. LXXVIII) has to say: "Anyone conceding a loan can, without sin, include in his agreement with the borrower a clause insuring himself against any loss depriving him of what he should have gained: for this is not selling the use of his money, but avoidance of loss. And it may well be that he who borrows avoids thereby a greater loss to himself than that incurred by the lender, because the borrower makes good the other's loss to his own advantage".

And the cited Aquinas adds (IIª, IIᵉ, LXII) that one who holds back another's money and does not pay him "apparently does him injury by impeding him from obtaining what he was on the point of buying, and is therefore obliged to recompense him, according to the situation of those involved and the transaction in question". And Hostiensis[11] agrees on this, and Vilielmo,[12] who explains the matter more clearly: that the sanction I have been obliged to apply (f. 32) is on account of my being prevented from realising a profit and you must make this good with expenses.

There are further types of exchange between other currencies, and these are made on the basis of your valuation of those currencies depending on the amount of that money in circulation and its usefulness, or otherwise. And the procedure is the same with the banks: give me such and such a currency in exchange for so much, and I will give you x percent. And that is enough said about exchanges.

Chapter XII Of Deposits and Pledges

A pawnbroker or custodian must be more trustworthy than other men because as often as not the usage is to pawn without any formal contract. The custodian must faithfully keep the pledge, and return it immediately when requested, without delay or giving room for suspicion.

---

[11] Henry of Segusio.

[12] William of Ockham.

And when choosing a pawnbroker one must carefully ascertain he is of proven honesty because the cupidity of the world weighs heavily on a man's resolve, corrupting it and bending it with ease. For many are honest with a hundred or five hundred ducats, whom I could not vouch for at a thousand or two thousand. And when you return a deposit after concluding some other piece of business with the depositor before he lodged the deposit with you, do not reimburse yourself out of the latter: repay the deposit in full and then ask for what is owing you. The honesty and trustworthiness of a merchant requires as much, that one who has trusted you at the time of depositing sees the restitution of what is his, without any further obligation or reduction. One must not in fact make detractions, in whole or in part, even if such a detraction would be allowed in the case of cash money to cash money, and we give examples of this in the chapter *Bona Fides*.

And be aware that the custodian is legally liable to the depositor if the item deposited is damaged by his fault: for example, if I entrust my indentured servant to you and you free him out of compassion or he escapes, you are liable; and particularly if your own goods are untouched and you have lost those deposited with you, you will be suspected of fraud; again (f. 32') we have an example in the chapter *Bona Fides*. In the same way, if something is deposited with you with a stipulation that it not be used, if you use it you will commit theft, *Digestis*, chapter *De conditione furti, Qui furtum*; if on the other hand one has reason to believe the owner of the asset would have no objection, one is not so constrained.

In conclusion, it is a most dishonest procedure for a merchant to touch a deposit or make use of it. And we can say the same regarding pledges given as guarantees against a loan, as is clarified in the *Theft* chapter of the *Instituta*.

Chapter XIII On Keeping One's Books in a Mercantile Manner

The pen is so noble and excellent an instrument that it is extremely necessary not only to merchants but to all of the arts, liberal and mechanical. And you can readily see how a merchant whose pen weighs heavily, one, that is, indisposed to put it to paper, can hardly be said to be a merchant.

And he must not only have skill in writing, but must know how to organise his writings, of which we will speak in the present chapter. A merchant should not in fact conduct his business by memory alone, unless he be Cyrus the Great who (f. 33) knew by name each one of the soldiers who made up his immense army; and likewise the Roman Lucius Scipio, and Cineas, Pyrrhus's ambassador, who on his second visit to Rome greeted every senator by name. And given the impossibility of this, we must move on to the practicalities of mercantile writing, which serves not only to preserve and have accessible to the memory all the matters negotiated and brought to a conclusion, but to avoid problems, quarrels and disputes; for records prolong the lives of men of letters for thousands and thousands of years, retaining in the memory so many glorious names and illustrious careers, which could not be the case without the marvellous instrument that is the pen. How much the human race owes to Carmenta, mother of Evander, who, the ancients tell us, was the first inventor of the use of the pen! And we see continuously the usefulness of writing, even at the simplest level of communicating between one place and another, keeping abreast of large things and small in other cities.

But to return to our theme, let us come to the point, that is, the practicalities of ordering our records in a proper mercantile manner. These records enable us to remember everything we have done, who owes us and to whom we owe, the costs of goods, profits, losses and every transaction on which a merchant's activity depends. And we emphasise that knowing how to keep records in proper order in itself teaches us to negotiate, to trade, and to earn. And the merchant should not trust blindly to his memory, relying on which has led many into error. Of such a reliance the scholar Averroes has written (f. 33') criticising Avicenna, who had great faith in his own intellect, saying: "Two things lead man into error in his study of nature, overestimation of one's intellect and ignorance of logic".

The merchant then must keep at least three sets of books, that is, his Scrap Book Records, his Day Book and his Ledger. And to take these in order, we will begin with the ledger, which must be organised alphabetically so as to be able to locate what you are looking for quickly. Your ledger must be kept as follows: first you must label it and give it a name; and the first book is usually marked 'A'. Then when book 'A' is full, you move on to the next, marking it 'B', and so on through the whole alphabet. And your records in the Scrap Book and your Day Book should be labelled with the same letter as the ledger volume to which they correspond.

Having done this, you should write the title at the top of the first page, and make clear (not failing to invoke the name of the Lord) to whom the book belongs, who are his business partners, how the book is arranged, number of pages, etc.

That done, you must calculate your total capital and how it is made up, and you should enter it as follows: post the merchandise you are holding in the debtor column and the capital in the credit column. For example if you have a hundred lengths of cloth valued at a thousand ducats, make an entry as follows: my capital must be credited on such and such a day of the month with a thousand ducats for the hundred lengths of cloth in my possession, having posted that the cloths must be debited the same amount in the relevant page of the ledger. And this same item must be recorded and entered in another place: on a certain day of the month the cloths must render a thousand ducats (f. 34) for the hundred lengths that I have in hand, having posted that my capital receive the same on such and such a page of the ledger.

Thus, every item that you write in the book must be written down twice, once as a debt from who must pay out, and in the other case a credit to the receiver, so I can say: "Here I am selling a length of this cloth at ten ducats which I have in cash and put into the till": how shall I enter this item? And you will say: "The cash column must give ten ducats for a length of cloth, we sell the cloth to someone on such and such a day, having posted that the merchandise column be credited", and relating the transaction to the cloths you will say: "The merchandise must receive on such and such a day ten ducats a length, we sell them and collect the cash, having posted that the cash column must disburse": the cash column must appear as debtor, because it receives the money, and the merchandise column credited because it disburses the money.

In the same way, every item must be written on both sides of the sheet, that is, on the right-hand side of the book under 'sums owed' and on the left 'sums owing'. And for every item you must say when, how much, to or from whom, and why: when, that is to say; on which day, how much, that is, the amount of money; to or from whom, identifying by name the debtor or creditor; why, that is, the justification.

And furthermore, you should enter first and then disburse, receive payment first and then cancel. As you have entered the cloths, so must you enter the other merchandise: if you have a thousand ducats at the beginning of the ledger, you should enter the merchandise as a minus and the capital as a plus; and when the cash-in-hand capital has been noted in this manner, your debtors and goods should be entered in the 'must pay/owing' column and the capital in the 'must be paid/owed' column.

You should then continue, transaction by transaction, to enter under 'owing' and 'owed', in such a way as to record each item of merchandise: in the case of cloth outlay makes the cloths debtors (f. 34'), while receipts makes them creditors; and once they are all sold, in that they are 'owing' you lose the sum for which they were in debit, while if they are 'owed', you are left with the amount they are in credit; and if they are, say, fifty ducats in credit, you need to settle the account and make them debtors. And you will say: "And on such and such a day fifty ducats, from the cloths remaining in stock, having entered that they are held over, must be credited on such and such a page". And you will create in the ledger a section headed 'surplus': and having written here what remains in the 'sums owed' column, and what you spend and lose in the 'sums owing' column, everything that remains at the end of the year you return to capital, which must be credited with what the surplus is debited, so the transactions will balance and your capital be updated; and you will do the same at each year-end.

Every transaction should be written down first in the Day Book, and then transferred from the Day Book to the ledger. And what you enter in the Day Book you record as a single entry, while in the ledger you enter twice, because the Day Book is not organised by page numbers, but by dates. And you will say: "This lot of cloth that you have sold for ten ducats owes the till ten ducats, for the length of cloth sold to Pietro", this transaction must be recorded in the cash column of the ledger, therefore, as an 'owing' item and as an 'owed' in the cloths column, while in the Day Book it is a single item, and likewise for other items.

In your Records in the Scrap Book you must write all contracts and obligations taken on and your exchange transactions, and everything you do as soon as you have engaged to do it, before actual transactions derive therefrom that need entering in the Day Book: there are in fact many things you agree to, that do not become entries in your account books, but which none the less it is necessary (f. 35) to remember and have noted down in your records.

And remember that any one making use of the exchanges must record in his double entries when he disburses the cash: that is, one line for the calculation of the equivalent value in the currency of the city you are trading in, and another, with appropriate symbols, accounting for monies corresponding to the currency in which you are accustomed to keep your Day Book, according to the usage of your city. You do this in order to be always be in control of situations you are involved in. And in these lines you will record the profit and loss on that account. And if you follow this practice, you will fully understand what I say; and if you administer your trade books according to this system you can, indeed must, call yourself a merchant, and if you do not, you are not worthy of the name.

Finally, you must keep your desk in good order, and for every letter that comes in you must note down from where and whom it comes, the year, month and day; you must record this in one place, answer each one and mark it 'replied'. File the letters in separate packs for each month and keep them. And similarly file in order all the bills of exchange you pay on; and the important letters, dealing with private signed bonds or registered deeds, must be conserved with particular care. And keep your head in your records constantly, because they bear witness to every movement of a merchant's assets.

To keep things brief, that will be enough on the subject of mercantile records and the system by which they should be kept, both to avoid prolixity and because it would be impossible to explain every procedure in detail.

Chapter XIV Of Insurance and Insurers

Insurance is a common contract, convenient and useful not only to the merchants that insure and take out insurance, but also most beneficial (f. 35') to cities and republics for two very important reasons: first, because insurance allows a merchant to embark on many more ventures. In fact, if I were unable to take out insurance, I would not be able to risk the large sums needed to rent a ship, I could not run so great a risk, lest I suffer a great loss, and I would necessarily have to renounce substantial enterprises. For this reason, only because I am able to insure myself can I rent a ship, even a large one, risk as much as I want to, and insure the rest. Significant advantage will derive from this, both to the city treasury and to the benefit of particular groups of people, for the ships, for the customs and for all kinds of private citizens. And as to the second reason, when some disaster overtakes a ship, if it were to the charge of a single merchant, he would be impoverished or be bankrupted and a generator of profits would be lost, while if the loss is spread among many, no serious damage results: and generally each merchant will take on a hundred or two hundred or three hundred ducats of the insurance, so that while all are affected by the misfortune, no one is ruined by it, and so this is a highly praiseworthy procedure and essential to any well-organised city where commerce is engaged in.

Having spoken of the usefulness and necessity of insurance, it remains to talk of the parties involved, first of those who take out insurance, then of those who insure. Those who take out insurance must take care about three things, first the detail of the insurance contract, that it be well thought out and contain a clear definition of obligations, so that no disputes will arise or doubts over legality; you must safeguard yourself thoroughly, (f. 36) and particularly in accordance with local usage. And among the methods of stipulating and applying a written contract, the stringent procedures followed in Barcelona seem to me the best, and all but preclude legal problems.

Secondly, you must consider the person, or rather, the persons to whom you are giving your money: these must not only be able, but also suitable and suited to such commitments, because a litigious assurer can ruin everybody.

Thirdly, you must consider the cost, or the percentage requested, and know how to get it down as far as possible. And the merchant must insure without leaving too great a margin of risk for himself, because no one has ever gone bankrupt from paying a premium, but rather for risking too large an amount.

And to turn to the assurers, we should remind them that they must keep their eyes open for all news from the seas: they must be constantly enquiring and asking about pirates or other ill-intentioned people, about wars, truces and reprisals, and all the things that can threaten a sea voyage. They must keep navigation charts on their desks and be familiar with the ports and the beaches, the distances between one place and another. They must also consider the status of the shipowners and the merchants who are seeking insurance, and the ships, as well as their cargo: these are all preventive concerns. Every ship needs to be insured, because one compensates for another, and if many are insured the merchant cannot but gain overall. And he must do this boldly, because if from excessive prudence he insure one ship and not another, if some misfortune befalls the uninsured ship, there will be no compensation for the loss.

(f. 36') And let these few words suffice on insurance.

Chapter XV On Jewellers

Having dealt with insurers, it seems appropriate, following our plan, to deal with certain individual activities which, for all that they conform to the general characteristics of trading as previously outlined, none the less possess specific features that set them apart, and we will speak first of all of jewellers, undoubtedly practitioners of a noble art. And in dedicating themselves to this craft which depends a great deal on continued practice and an experienced eye, they will have engaged in it since childhood, and will be familiar with the silversmith's skills and know how to handle gold and other minerals and understand the requisite procedures and ornamentation.

They must not only be of good character, honest and trustworthy, but show themselves to be so, given their habitual dealings with gentlemen and the many counterfeits that are always on the market due to their unscrupulous colleagues. And a jeweller must absolutely avoid buying or selling counterfeit items, to maintain himself above suspicion.

The jeweller must also be eloquent and personable; jewellers in fact are continually conversing on level terms with noblemen and women, priests and gentlemen. And this is for sure a noble trade which every gentleman ought to understand.

Chapter XVI Of Drapers and Haberdashers

Drapers and haberdashers, even if they cannot strictly be called merchants, are none the less only a rung below them, in that (f. 37) they must perform the operations of manual workers. And their guiding principle should be to always keep a wide range of merchandise in stock, have a steady flow of customers in their shop and a good name, as well as be able to satisfy the desires of everyone according to their station. They must be steady, reliable and calm, and prompt in naming their price. And they must be sure never to sell one fabric for another, or falsify their goods, because this last is truly an abominable sin, which God will generally punish in the following manner. For these are in fact some things that displease God greatly, as St Augustine recounts jn IIII *Sententiarum*, *distinctio* XV, according to which God sends down afflictions on sinners in five ways.

The first, so that the righteous increase their merit through penance, as we see with Job.

The second, to maintain their virtue so as to resist the temptations of pride, as we see with St. Paul.

The third, to discipline sinfulness, as with Mary's leprosy.

The fourth, to the glory of God, as in blindness from birth.

The fifth, for sentencing to punishment, as with Herod, having a foretaste of hell, to savour here on this earth how he would be castigated in the hereafter. And this last is the fate of fakers and counterfeiters, whom you will never see getting away with their malpractices in the long run.

All other activities must follow the general rules laid out in the preceding chapters.

Chapter XVII On Wool Merchants and Other Specific Trade Merchants

Wool merchants and other merchant-artisans must be above all prompt and diligent, and even when they have employees must (f. 37') also put their own hands to the wheel. Should you come across a lax one, you can call him a failure, for these mercantile trades are a noble occupation for those that pursue them well and diligently, and it is next to impossible to end up poor. For this reason we say that a craft will never fail you when conscientiously managed. The wool merchant-artisan therefore should never rely on his employees, but follow personally every step in the production of his cloth, and monitor each phase in the processing of his wool: he must feel it with his own hands, adjust and separate the threads, wash, beat and comb it, card and spin; make whole cloths, weaving and scouring, fulling and washing, dyeing, ironing and beautifying and finally displaying his product, because he knows that it is thanks in some degree to each one of these processes that a good cloth can be made poor, and vice versa.

And he must maintain a good name in his trade, so that people say: "You can buy X's cloths with your eyes shut", as they say in Venice "Vendramin soap" or "Maestro Bon's sugar" and these two are super-rich on account of their excellent name, known to every class of person.

They must be brisk sellers and keep their stock turning over, handle their affairs with good grace and not waste time, because the lax should surely not only be expelled from the wool merchants' guild, but from the city, as an example to others.

The artisan must answer correctly and decisively to his creditors, and see to it that his projects are realised on schedule. He must neither be nor appear to be a person of no consequence. And as to other considerations we direct you to our earlier chapters, where such matters have been dealt with according to general principles.

Chapter XVIII Things Forbidden to Merchants

(f. 38) Many things are forbidden to merchants that would be tolerated in others, in relation to those attributes of modesty, firmness, professionalism and moderation which a merchant should not only nurture in his heart, but display in his conduct. And the same goes for the trust he must inspire in every sort of person, because merchants are as it were the repository of human treasure. It is no accident therefore that merchants must practice among themselves a sort of religion that if it is properly observed and cultivated more nearly justifies that term than any other. So no-one should be surprised if we insist that the merchant be honest and sober in his ways, and if we deny him what sometimes and in some circumstances is permitted in others.

First of all, we would forbid the merchant games of chance, like dice or cards and others such; and I am not including games that are played in order to exercise the body, like ball games, throwing the caber or spear, running, wrestling and suchlike, because these are pursued for exercise and the demonstration of skill. So much the Civil Law Digest (C, second law) recommends also, and it is particularly forbidden that a man make a habit of gaming out of greed: such behaviour is not only incompatible with the honest life of a merchant, but also a mortal sin, as William of Ockham states specifically; and, in addition to the above considerations, along with gaming, come many other sins such as perjury, lies, profanity, deceit, robbery and the like. And since games of chance know no limits, the merchant (f. 38') who is rich today could wake up poor tomorrow morning (in so far as most gamblers nowadays play at night), and there has never been such a person as a gambler with a clear conscience, for which reason mistrust them. Beware too that you may be obliged to pay back your winnings in certain particular cases, as Aquinas makes clear in IIº, IIº, q. XXXII, if that is you have won off those not entitled to part with assets, such as the mad, wastrels, those under 25 years and above all children, idiots, the deaf, dumb and blind, and those with chronic illnesses, servants, clerics, sons of families without even a soldier's pay, wives possessing no other assets but their dowries, administrators of church holdings.

He who wins from such persons ought to return his gains, not to them, but to their guardians, trustees, masters, to their monastery, their father, husband or church. And if whoever induced you to play should himself lose to you, you should return that too, but not to him, who is unworthy of receiving back his losses: your winnings should be distributed among the poor. The above rule can be found in the Civil Code, *Allearum* and the Digest, and *Lex Ultra*, at the end. And even if one is playing voluntarily with another he is still obliged to return his winnings; this is the opinion of Raymond [Llul] and also to be found in the Digest *C*, *Lex Ultra*, at the end, and the Civil Code under *Constitutione*, *Ioca*.

Secondly, the merchant may not overindulge in either wine or food; and I am not referring to those who drink wine without meaning to become intoxicated, as we read of Noah in Genesis, but to those whom from vice or greed habitually drink wine to excess. For this habit is more abhorrent in a merchant than (f. 39) in other men, for the merchant is a more public person than others; consequently, other men, if they get drunk, can stay at home until they have got over their hangover and avoid talking, so that they are not caught in the act and can secretly deal with their error.

The merchant on the other hand, has to continually appear in public, given the affairs he must give his attention to, and cannot conceal his misdeed. And as wrongdoing it is a source of dishonour to him, but while being a transgression in itself it can also procure him harm for the errors he may commit which may prove very damaging to him. Therefore, to avoid dishonour, the merchant should eschew gluttony, which, apart from the specific harm it can and generally does entail, brings in its wake laziness, dullness of mind, sleep, trembling of the hands and head, paralysed or swollen tongue, impotence, sight-impairment and in the long run many other illnesses, stomach and hip ailments, fevers, gout and dropsy, which are exceedingly troublesome to any man and particularly to the merchant, and about them the Apostle Paul says "Do not intoxicate yourselves with wine, for lust dwells there".

And remember that Aquinas listed five kinds of greed: the first when one eats before the proper hour; the second when one wants one food after another; the third, when one demands refined food; the fourth when one wants an excessive quantity; and the fifth when eats untidily and drinks avidly and without manners. And as Augustine has it, everything should be suitable to the place the time and the person; and we should not censure unthinkingly, because it may well be that a wise man will eat fine food without culpable greed and voracity (f. 39'), while the fool overheat himself with common foodstuffs, engulfed by the vicious flames of greed. And everyone should be content to eat fish, like Our Lord, rather than lentils, like Esau, or barley, like a horse (*distinctio* XLI, *Quisquis*).

The merchant should therefore, for the reasons given, be moderate in his eating and drinking.

Nor should he value food other than for maintaining the body, because, as Boethius says, "Nature is content with little or with the minimum". Nor should we be like those of whom St Paul says "They make a god of their stomachs", with all that follows. Consequently, too much banqueting is bad for a merchant, giving scope to the above errors.

Thirdly, the merchant ought not to act on behalf of others in quarrels and lawsuits, or to seek controversy: if we have already said he should abstain from litigation on his own account, how much more so in the case of others?

Fourthly, the merchant must not keep company with nefarious and evil men, who not only encourage the acquisition of bad habits and estrangement from good behaviour, but can bring one to ruin in any number of ways.

Fifthly, the merchant is forbidden to practice alchemy, because the art of trade rests on seeking out sound and certain enterprises, and safe investments, and not things that can bring about his disgrace.

Sixthly, the merchant ought not to joust, which is a frivolous pursuit, and a source of expense and a distraction, for the merchant who needs to concentrate his thoughts, must not let himself be sidetracked by vain things which may also seriously endanger his health.

Seventh, the merchant must never in any way, either in his own city or abroad, (f. 40) involve himself in smuggling, because this activity is often the cause of utter ruin. Not for nothing is the saying widespread: "Trade in contraband, paid in Neverland".

Eighth, the merchant is forbidden from falsifying the weight or measure of his merchandise, to exchange or sell one thing as another, for this is nothing other than the behaviour of a thief.

Ninth, a merchant should not have too many empty-headed or indigent friends or men that can be harmful to him; and not to develop ties of friendship so close as not to be able to say no on occasions, when a favour is asked of him.

Tenth, the merchant should not be extravagant, for just as avarice is a greater sin than extravagance among nobles and the rich, so is extravagance a much greater vice, indeed should be utterly abjured by the merchant, than is avarice. Thus the merchant must avoid extravagance, because it is totally contrary to the aim of his occupation, which is to become rich, and poverty is the destruction of wealth and annihilates it.

We have now covered the things that the merchant should never permit himself, at any time or in any place, although there are others which ought to be avoided in some circumstances, but may be allowed in others. We will speak next of closing of accounts and a suitable time-frame for their closure.

Chapter XIX Of Seven-Year Balances

Human nature, on which an occupation without any interruption leaves its mark, will eventually become irritated and inebriated, be confused and make mistakes, just as we see with other things, such as a pen which, although having (f. 40') attractive and durable attributes, none the less loses its edge and precision with continual writing, and the same is true of every activity. And we read therefore of the ancient philosophers that, after a period of intense intellectual effort, so as not to devitalise their exhausted minds, they occupied themselves with some light and childish pastime, even playing with pebbles on the beach. And similarly we read in the life of St Paul, who carefully managed the time he spent on each matter, that when he was tired of studying he would turn to basket-weaving or put his hand to other humble work. But what is the point of these human examples when we have that of God Almighty, of whom we read in Genesis: "And on the seventh day God ended his work which he had made; and he rested on the seventh day from all his work which he had made". Not that God needed to rest, but he did so as an example to us, as St Paul states: "For whatsoever things were written aforetime were written for our learning".

It follows, to return to the matter in hand, that the merchant should take a pause from all his activities and trades at the end of the sixth year, and in the year following agree no contracts, but settle his accounts, draw up his balances and realise his cash. And even if, approaching that deadline, good business opportunities should present themselves, he must not take them up, in fact, as we have proposed, he should gather in all his profits because that year is the justification of everything he has done in the previous six. He should further plan and prepare for what he will do in the following year, and in illuminating his mind and resting his soul from daily affairs, he will reap the benefit from his resolution, as Aristotle says (XVIII° *Problematum)* (f. 41): "We generally apply the word 'resolute' only to soldiers, orators and merchants". The merchant should not only be always ready to act when need be, but also to cash up the profits of his dealings, for those who only act and do not recognise the necessity of realising their balances periodically are superficial types who cannot call themselves resolute merchants.

We have insisted on the seventh year, as against the fifth or any other, following the example of our Creator, as the following verse of *Genesis* says: "And God blessed the seventh day, and sanctified it: because that in it he had rested from all his work which God created and made". Which leads St Augustine to explain, glossing this passage in his *Quarto super Genesis,* that God rested on the seventh day, so that we might do the same, and gave us the commandment of keeping the seventh day holy, that is, the Sabbath, so that man might rest from his daily labours, "recognising that he is sharing in the divine goodness". And thus there was established the sabbath day, which etymologically signifies 'ease of mind', according to St Isidore's *Etymologiae,* indicating the suspension of practical work. Thus we, wishing now to follow that greatest of Teachers, eternal and irrefutable, have established a mercantile Sabbath, the suspension of practical work in the seventh year, a most beneficial, useful and necessary decision. Blessed is the man who regularly manages not only to observe it, but also plan ahead for it in good time, because one does it not only to rest, but to collect one's credits, balance everything up and be able to say: "Here is all that I have, plainly reduced to what it is". But those that do not do this (f. 41') you will often find tangled up like new-born chicks in the nest bedding, hemmed in with books and calculations. They are like the apothecaries with their pretty boxes for marzipan, elegantly gilded and figured, but with nothing inside. The merchant should aim for tangible not apparent wealth, and say, "This much I have in hand", because he who feeds on hot air, goes up in smoke.

With this suspension of activities and periodic rest from work we come to the end of our first book. We will continue with the second, God willing, and hope not to bore our readers. It will deal, as we promised in the preface, with religion.

Here ends the first book of trade by Benedetto Cotrugli, dealing with the essence and practice of that art. The second begins with the religious observances befitting a merchant.

Part 2: On the Religion Incumbent on the Merchant

In that we must follow the scheme proposed in our preface, in this second book it behoves us to deal with religion and the devotions a merchant should offer up to his creator; and these observances are very important and necessary to every man, given that, as Lactantius maintains in his treatise *On Religion*: "Man's greatest prize is religion alone". In fact all the other things a man possesses he shares with the beasts: the voice with which it seems that one understands the other, laughter with which one appears to cuddle the other; they are alike in loving their wives, their children etc., (f. 42) in gathering food and storing it for the future, in knowing what is harmful to them and which are the curative plants. In these and many other things the bees seem to be sagacious: hoarding honey, they venerate their king, and arrange and sort their goods.

But although in many, if not in nearly all things men resemble the animals, the animals for sure are ignorant of religion. And so, although I believe that the animals have been given a natural predisposition to preserve life, man's is to multiply it. And since the power of reasoning is at its highest in man, we call it 'wisdom', whose uniqueness consists in the fact that only to man is it given to understand divine matters. Which confirms the truth of Cicero's saying, that "Among all the species there is

C. Carraro, G. Favero (eds.), *Benedetto Cotrugli – The Book of the Art of Trade*, DOI 10.1007/978-3-319-39969-0_5

no living creature other than man possessed of some knowledge of god, nor is there among men any people, civil or savage, that while ignorant of what exactly is owed to god, does not know that it is owing".

We must therefore be devout in our religion: those who do not take in its precepts and give themselves up to earthly things, living like the beasts deny the essence of their humanity. Therefore, as all men are agreed, we must maintain our trust in religion, because man must be eager and willing to embrace religion and learning.

But men often make this mistake: that they either embrace religion without learning, or learning without religion, but the one belongs with the other, and therefore (f. 42') they are led into many errors, and merchants first among them, who do not bother to discover what is necessary to their salvation even while they lay claim to 'possessing a pure faith' or to 'worshipping God steadfastly'. But they do not appreciate that to no man more than themselves is it necessary to know canons, because they have to untangle many knotty problems in their profession. Therefore we will concede them only what Christ said to the centurion, that is, "Follow my precepts", and we have found a number of effective recourses through which, if they follow them, God will surely by means of holy works render them penitent, and consequently, saved.

Chapter I On the Mass

Religious observance has been recorded in every age and in every generation of men, as we have said in the foreword to this second book, but we need to distinguish between the different ways of worshipping God: and thus men have found different means of veneration, by sacrifice or ceremony. And leaving aside the most ancient practices, so as not to bore the reader with irrelevancies, we will begin by considering the more recent behaviour of the Romans, who although they were in all the things they did exceptional, sublime, pre-eminent, very astute and very wise, and have been famous and much praised in subsequent epochs, in their divine observances they were rash, ignorant of mind, careless and led astray, making gods like mortal men (f. 43), liars, adulterers, evildoers, sinners and enemies of God; and they invented numerous absurdities, so that those desirous of virtue and happiness called on the adulterous Jupiter, those who desired knowledge Minerva or Mercury; women in childbirth invoked the goddess Lucina, for pregnancy Rumina, the goddess Cunina to watch over the cradle, for the child's eating and drinking Edulica[1] and Potina, the conjugal gods for weddings, Priapus for consummation; then Neptune for seafaring, the water nymphs for rivers, Mars and Bellona for battles, Segetia for the harvest, for cattle Bubona, for honey and fruit Pomona; the goddess Honoria for those seeking honour, Victoria for petitioners of Victory, the goddess Pecunia for wealth; they called on the god Aescolanus and his son Argentinus to beg for copper and silver; the sick appealed to the gods of medicine Apollo and Aesculapius for good health, and many other infantile deities that I am not going to try to remember here, not least because for any triviality they could create new gods to worship and build altars and sacrifice to.

And since the mighty Romans had long since given themselves over to these abuses and corruptions and wickednesses, it came about that after sacrifices of various kinds suffered under alien laws and customs, the Catholic faith was infused with the true light of the Holy Spirit, sent down from heaven in the form of a fire to the Apostles after the Ascension.

Following the example and the precepts of Our Saviour Jesus Christ the Son of God, in memory of His last Sunday Supper we (f. 43') celebrate the Holy Mass during which the actual body of Christ is consecrated; and every Christian is obliged, on each of the ordained days, to listen to a full mass up until the moment when the priest gives the blessing. And this is laid down *Decretum*, *De consacratione*, I, *Missa*, in the following chapter, and in the chapter *Omnes fideles*. One may be excused only on account of the gravest extenuation, as explained in the above-mentioned chapter, *Missa*; and all those who neglect their obligation to attend mass and prefer vain pursuits deserve excommunication, as in *De consacratione, prima, Qui die*, out of respect for this most important of sacraments, which was prefigured at various times since the origin of man by certain signs and significant rites.

---

[1] Correct reading *Educa*.

And just as the coming and the life of Christ were prefigured in prophecies and ceremonies, so too the priests and the tabernacles, the temples, altars, the sacrifices, the ceremonies the holidays and all that in our condition as servants we owe to God, what the Greeks called 'latreía', all predicted and foretold and signified those things which are the guarantee of eternal life for the faithful in Christ, and which we feel under obligation to fulfil, we see being fulfilled and which we hope to see brought to completion. This is the case of Lamb that is presaged in the lamb of Exodus, when God, wishing to strike at the Egyptians to liberate the Jews from slavery, ordered the Jews to take a white lamb without blemish, sacrifice it and mark the doorframes of their houses with its blood. And when all the firstborn sons of Egypt were (f. 44) slaughtered, only the Jews survived that had the blood of the immaculate lamb on their doorframes.

They were surely not saved because the blood of the lamb had any special properties, but because the lamb prefigured the lamb that was to come: the immaculate lamb was Christ, for he was innocent and just and holy, slain by the Jews and come down to this earth for the salvation of all those who worship the blood, the sacrifice of that precious blood, and the cross that bore that spilt blood. This is what Ezra is speaking of when he says: "This Passover is our salvation and our refuge. Meditate and let this thought rise up in your hearts, because we will humiliate him in a sign, and after that we will hope in him, so that this place will not be abandoned for all time, says the Lord God of virtues; if you have not believed in him and you have not listened to his pronouncements, you will be the laughing-stock of all peoples".[2]

And it follows therefore, my dear merchants, as St Paul says, "The law is made for transgressors", but every day and always it should be your habit and custom to hear mass and to worship this glorious sacrifice and ineffable sacrament, which comforts the soul, illuminates the mind, purges vices, redirects towards virtue, cures of error, reduces the sufferings of the perplexed, eases the taking of the right road, encourages holy works and bolsters the will to perform them; and thanks to the merit deriving

[2] This passage is in Latin in the text. It is now regarded as spurious and would be in the book of Ezra 6, between 20 and 21. Cotrugli probably cites it from Lactantius or Justin Martyr, who both use it to argue that in the Old Testament the Jews omitted passages showing Passover to be a witness for Christ: http://www.biblicalcyclopedia.com/P/passover.html

therefrom, God will demote the ways of (f. 44') vice and dispose you towards what will bring you credit and salvation.

But before attending the mass, the merchant must prepare his heart, so that it be devoutly receptive to understanding. And the mass will protect you from continued sinning and wrong behaviour, it will cleanse you of venial sins through the general confession that a man makes at the mass and the benediction he receives from the priest (*prima*, quaestio I, *Multi*). And when attending the mass the merchant should hold himself with body and mind directed toward God, without allowing himself to be distracted by any other business.

Chapter II On Prayer

We should now deal with prayer and first of all, to take things in their proper order, we must offer a definition of it, which, according to Ramon Llull and Hostiensis, is: "a devout inclination of the mind towards God, which most often, to keep the soul active, seeks expression in oral form"; or, according to Hugh of Saint Victor, "Prayer is a form of worship deriving from penitence", or, according to John of Damascus, "Prayer is seeking from God the things it is permissible to ask for", or again, according to Aquinas (*In quarto*, di. XV), John's definition is perfectly clear: "Some prayers are recited in the mind, others aloud".

Man is obliged to pray in his mind by natural law, which requires him to open himself towards those without which there can be no salvation. And Christ himself, in St Luke's Gospel, ch.18, says "Men ought always to pray"; and John Chrysostom, glossing the saying, comments that *oportet* means here "necessity requires that".

(f. 45) God does not demand of man that he pray aloud, unless the Church ordains it, or it is a penance imposed by a priest for sins committed, as Aquinas prescribes (*In quarto*, *di.* XV); but prayers recited aloud may be added to mental prayer: first, to stimulate the interior impulse to unite oneself with God, because the mind of one who prays raises itself up to God, when through external signs, such as the voice or gestures, the mind follows the path of reason and consequently of the emotions, as Augustine says. And therefore we should dedicate ourselves to praying out loud and with other external signs just as much as we dedicate ourselves to exercising our minds. But should our voices fail us, the mind's impulse may still be expressed by the mind alone; and this is the case with those whose minds and lives are dedicated to God, but without external demonstrations, as David sings in the psalm: "My heart has spoken to you, my face has sought you"; and of Hannah we read in the first chapter of the Epistle to the Romans,[3] that she "prayed in her heart".

Secondly, we add our prayers spoken aloud to pay tribute to God for our debt of all we have received from him, and this should be done not only in the mind but with the voice also.

Thirdly, we add our voiced prayers because the soul overflows into the body with a great outpouring of emotion, as David says in the psalm "my heart hath been glad, and my tongue hath rejoiced". And prayer should be uttered in the manner recommended by Augustine: "Think on and turn over in your hearts what would say with your mouths". And be aware that prayer, according to Ramon [Llull] and Hostiensis, should satisfy thirteen conditions.

The first is that (f. 45') it should be offered in faith, because without faith it is impossible to please God, while the saints " by faith conquered kingdoms, wrought justice, obtained promises" as St Paul writes to the Hebrews (ch.11).

The second condition is that a prayer should be without equivocations: St James's Epistle, 1,6 "Let the supplicant ask in faith and waver not".

The third condition, that it be humble: Ecclesiasticus 35, "The prayer of the humble pierces the clouds" and *De con.*, d. v, *Non mediocriter*.

Fourth condition, that it be properly formulated "You know not what you ask" (Matthew[4] 38); "Ye ask, and receive not, because ye ask amiss" (St James, 4).

Fifth, that it must be an expression of the heart's devotion rather than the mouth's. First Letter to the Romans, ch.1[5]: "Hannah prayed in her heart, but her voice was not heard"; and Augustine too says "What use is the movement of the lips, if the heart is silent?".

---

[3] Rather, *1 Samuel 1*.

[4] Actually Mark.

[5] Again, *1 Samuel*.

Sixth condition, it must convey feelings of unworthiness, like the publican who dared not raise his eyes to the heavens (Luke,18).

Seventh, it must be secret, Matthew 6: "But you, when you pray, enter into your room. ." etc., and, as Isidore says: "Prayer unfolds most appropriately in private places".

Eighth condition, it must be pure, Augustine *On the Psalmist*: "Great is the virtue of pure prayer, it fulfils what is ordained, there beyond the capacities of the flesh"; and Chrysostom says: "No-one can receive the grace of a life in heaven, if he has not been purified of all moral ugliness".

Ninth condition, it should be accompanied by tears, Isaiah 38: "I have heard thy prayer, I have seen thy tears"; and Augustine's gloss on Tobit 4,4: "Prayer propitiates God, tears soften him; prayer soothes him like an ointment, tears spur him to concession".

Tenth condition, it should be considered, the better to approach faith.

(f. 46) Eleventh, it should be passionate as David says in the Psalm "I entreated thy face with all my heart".

Twelfth condition, it must be accompanied by good works, Tobit,12: "Prayer is strong with fasting and alms-giving"; and on the same theme, Lamentations 3: "Let us lift up our heart with our hands". Saint Gregory comments: "The heart is lifted up to God by our hands when prayer is consistent with our good deeds".

Thirteenth condition, it must be insistent, as the man asking bread of his friend (Luke, 11); and as with the apostles continuing to pray and receiving the Holy Spirit.

And remember that of all prayers, the most perfect is that of our saviour himself, that is The Lord's Prayer, according to both St Augustine and Aquinas. It is true that many also use the Office of Our Lady, or of the Dead, or many other offices as their habitual devotion, as well as the seven penitential psalms in remission of corporal chastisement.

I would say that all worship is good in relation to the strength of the good intention moving it, as long as its performance does not induce one to neglect or skimp familiar passages from tiredness or boredom, or from negligence or carelessness, or because one is busy with competing devotions: in fact we must above all observe first precepts with devotion and scrupulous commitment, and fill the rest of our time in other acts of worship, so long as these do not lead us to finding prayer a burden. And effectively it is very difficult for the merchant to dedicate himself to intensive prayer (f. 46') and to do it well; and even if he does manage it and it is his custom to do so, that very habitualness of recitation can cause his prayers to lack piety and zeal, performed dully, and his recital of the psalms to be without due devotion, without awe, without inner conviction, stumbling over and mangling the words, mouthing others, listening and replying in a less than pious manner, often shouting and laughing in inappropriate places unsuitable for prayer, with crude and untoward gestures.

For which reason I say, without wishing to deny anyone their own form of devotion, that to me the most devout and observant merchant is he who, piously on his knees, with his hands raised to the skies, his eyes closed, his mind wholly intent on his prayers, with a sigh in his heart and tears in his eyes, makes the sign of the cross and repeats The Lord's Prayer devoutly, without mangling his words or allowing his mind to wander, and thus avoids appearing a blasphemer when he recites the psalms.

There are three further qualifications necessary to prayer if it is to find acceptance: that it be a request for things necessary to salvation, that it be formulated steadfastly and with devotion. And now, having enumerated the procedures proper to prayer, we will pass on to alms-giving.

Chapter III On the Giving of Alms

The merchant must be generous in extending his hand to the poor and in giving alms out of his own property in proportion to its extent. And if he has nothing to give, he should at least show piety, in accordance with Augustine's dictum: "I have never seen a pious man make a bad death". But if, being rich, he gives no (f. 47) alms to the poor, he commits mortal sin, as in Matthew 25 "For I was hungry and you gave me no food", and Augustine's saying: "Not assuaging hunger, you have killed".

And know that there are seven corporeal deeds of compassion: to feed the hungry, to quench the thirsty, to dress the naked, to house the pilgrim, to visit the sick, to bail the prisoner, to bury the dead. A further seven are spiritual, that is: educate the ignorant, encourage doubters, correct sinners, console the afflicted, forgive those who offend you, bear with the troublesome, pray for all. And these works of spiritual succour are in absolute terms, nobler than the corporeal, except in the case of one dying of hunger: such a one needs nourishing with bread rather than with advice or counselling.

Who gives alms must take care that what he gives is not necessary to his own needs but is superfluous to them, not only out of respect for himself but also out of respect for those who depend on him; because before anything else a man should provide for himself and his own, and give alms to the poor from what he has over. A person receiving charity must be truly in need of help, else there would be no reason for giving it. But insofar as one man cannot go to the help of many, or of all those that are in need, so not every case obliges him to obey the commandment, but only when the sufferer's need is so great that he cannot survive (f. 47') without assistance. In such cases Augustine's saying "Not assuaging hunger, you have killed" is paramount.

If then giving alms out of one's surplus, and, likewise, giving alms to those in dire need are an obligation, giving alms in other circumstances is a recommendation, in the sense that the highest good is always to be recommended. And I say that your superfluity, which the commandment enjoins you to give to those in need, should be given to the poor: in fact, although this surplus, strictly in terms of property, belongs to its owner, it terms of use it belongs to the needy, that is, those who could be sustained by it, as St Basil says: "If you say that all you have comes from God, is God then unjust, who divided to us the things of this life unequally? That you are wealthy while that other man has to beg? Is it, perhaps, in order that you may receive credit for distributing your wealth, and in order that he may embrace his endurance? The bread which you hold back belongs to the hungry, that coat, which you hide in your cupboard, belongs to the naked, the footwear mouldering in your closet belongs to those without shoes, your silver belongs to he who needs it. Thus, however many are those whom you could have provided for, so many are those whom you wrong".

And St Ambrose says much the same (di. XLVII, c. *Sicut*, II.). And apropos of what we have said above, that is alms should be given only out of what is not necessary to you, this amount can only be judged on the basis of what seems what most likely to be the case. And you should not concern yourself with everything that might happen in the future, but you must estimate how much of your surplus is necessary to you, work out the probabilities of the matter, and how they apply to several people. (f. 48) Bear in mind that according to Aquinas 'necessary' can be interpreted in two ways: first, that minimum without which one cannot exist, and this 'necessary' one should obviously not give away in alms. It would be as if someone, pinched by necessity, had only barely enough to maintain himself and his family: giving it away he would deprive himself and his own of sustenance. An exception might be made if the recipient were a a person of particular worth, whose wellbeing would be to the advantage of the church or the state. Certainly to have rescued such a person from destitution would ensure an honourable death for the donor and his dependants, because the common good should always take precedence over one's own.

As to the second instance, we call those things necessary without which a person and those he has responsibility for cannot live adequately in a state appropriate to his condition. To give away such things is a recommendation, not an obligation. And remember that charity should work outwards, as Augustine says in Book 1 of *De Doctrina Christiana*, in this way, favouring our nearest relations before strangers. But on this theme we should also weigh up how much sanctity and how much utility will ensue from an act of charity. In fact an act is more saintly the more it benefits the common good, and this last should be preferred to blood relationship, and is even the worthier for being towards one unrelated.

In regard to the poor, one should always give alms to those who cannot work with their hands (di. LXXXII, c.^{o} p.$^{o.}$) because the civil law prescribes that those who cannot work with their hands but choose (f. 48') to be beggars should be treated like servants of the emperor. The poor man, on the other hand, if given money in arms, can keep them for himself, or indeed give them to another, as Aquinas says (II^{a}, IIe, q. XXXII).

And I will not expand on the subject of illicit gains, on how one should not use these for alms-giving, because this is a matter I shall return to in a chapter on the subject, but will finish here by saying that charity is a beneficial, unique and ideal means for bringing a man to perfect penitence, and consequently to an emending of his ways: in fact tears of compassion which rise up within an honest heart are capable of setting straight the life of a man and helping him to realise the true purpose of his existence.

Chapter IV On Matters of Conscience: What Is; And What Is Not Permissible

Just as Christ replied to the centurion who asked him how to attain eternal life: "Keep my commandments", so one could counsel the merchant. But given that generally speaking merchants are far from devout, addicted as they are to earthly and corrupt things so that it is hard for them to live without sinning constantly, it is well to prescribe preventive rules as an earnest remedy and convert the merchant to right conduct and thus to his salvation. But if a man is to arrive at conversion, no remedy will be adequate if he is still obliged on his side to make restitution for ill-gotten gains: in fact, other sins can be forgiven with a sincere sigh of repentance, but those where there has been some misappropriation (f. 49) can never be pardoned until restitution has been made, because it is written in the sixth book of *De regulis iuris*:"A sin is not mended until what has been taken away has been returned". And we will therefore explain to the merchant legitimate and illegitimate contracts, and we will talk besides only of those that concern chiefly merchants, because to deal generally with the whole subject would require a book apart. We will do our best then to be as concise as possible. And before making any further observation we must establish what usury is.

The term 'usury' covers any gain made on money loaned, either by formal contract or with the mere expectation of gain, see c. 1, 2 c. *Consuluit*, XIIII, q. III, *Si feneraveris*. So when you give money to a friend hoping that he will give you some recompense, even if the terms of your agreement are not explicit, this is usury, whether money or other goods are involved, see XIIII, q. III, c. 1, II, 2 III. This holds not only for cash but for anything that can be given a money value; I am not speaking obviously of other benefits that cannot be valued in cash terms, such as friendship etc. And Aquinas too would have it so, II^{a} IIe, q. LXXVIII, but he also says that if when offering the loan you had no intention of receiving any recompense, but on your money being returned you do in fact receive something, as there was no fraudulent intention on your part, there is no sin: in fact it would have been permissible, even in advance of the loan, to have received something, because lending money should not in any way infringe on the right to recompense.

None the less such a recompense may not be asked for, nor stipulated in any written or oral contract, in so far as it has a money value; unless the consideration be made out of friendship, as it might have been in any case, even if (f. 49') no cash loan were involved.

It is also not allowed to lend a ship to someone with the stipulation that on another occasion the borrower will do the same for you. It is legitimate to do it, but not to contract for it.

It is not permissible for a mill-owner to lend money to bakers on condition that they do not take their corn to be ground at another's mill, for by doing this he will gain more than he offers from the resulting favourable circumstances and deprive the bakers of their freedom of action, in that they cannot go to another mill, where they might receive a better service. Nevertheless if the debtors suffer no harm, no restitution is called for, except to the extent that a value can be put on the freedom to mill their grain elsewhere, when the effort and expense of so doing need also to be taken into account.

Rightly called usurers are those who, on the maturation of a debt, will not extend it without interest to borrowers unable to pay immediately.

Usurers publicly named and shamed should suffer the following earthly forfeits: their wills must be adjudged without validity and void, and they must be excommunicated forthwith; they should not receive communion and their offerings must be rebuffed at the altar; if they die in the sinfulness of usury they should be denied the Church's burial, and most especially those that have entered into usurious legal contracts.

It is not permissible, if you are holding goods as collateral for a loan, to keep any return from their investment: any such gain should be discounted from the original debt.

It counts as usury if you lend grain or wine or suchlike (f. 50) and take in return grain or wine whose value exceeds that which you lent, unless it is unclear whether their value is higher or lower.

If one gives or lends money to one who sets off to trade overseas and the sum owing is increased on account of the risk the lender is subjected to, I say that this is clearly usury, because danger does not excuse a usurious contract: evidently if the lender sought payment for the danger alone, the loan would be permissible, but it is not permissible to seek interest on the loan itself. Just as it is allowed to lend money without interest, so it is possible to insure without interest, see *Extra*, heading *Naviganti*.

What shall we say of those who give away old grain to be recompensed with new grain? I say that if it is done in the expectation of gain then it is usury, but if one does it so as not to lose his grain, and if he to whom it is given can turn a profit on it, then it is allowed, except where the new grain is manifestly worth more.

Is it allowable to receive usurious money? I say that it is allowed to take money from those that gain from usury to satisfy one's needs but it is not permitted to encourage usury. Just as it is permissible for one fallen into the hands of thieves to tell them where to find what they wish to steal in order to avoid being killed, but he himself will have committed no sin when the thieves proceed to steal the money. But if he were to take money from usurers to gamble with, then this is not admissible and constitutes usury, as for any other illicit, dishonest or untoward use of such money.

(f. 50') Is it allowable to take money from a usurer for a friend? I say that if you do it as a favour to the usurer it is a sin, but if you do it as a favour to the one in need of the loan then it is allowed, the more so if, thanks to your mediation, he obtains a discount on the rate of interest.

If one has need of a guarantor in order to obtain money from a usurer, is it allowable that this intermediary seek payment? Some say no, because the guarantor is thus making himself a participant in the usury. Others say that it is allowed because acting as a guarantor does not involve the use of the loan money but is like a pledge received on which I can soon expect a return, but the first interpretation is the more reliable.

Can usury be sought as interest? I answer, following Llull, yes. It is as if a guarantor, standing surety for another, had paid off his usurer's loan, and can therefore reclaim it from his debtor, at which point it is no longer usury but interest, and it is not a question of profit but of avoiding loss. Aquinas deals with this issue, II^{a} IIe, q. LXXVIII: one who grants a loan, may without sin include in the terms subscribed to by the borrower, a provision against any loss depriving him of what should be his. This is not selling the use of money but avoiding loss, and it may be that the one receiving the loan avoids thereby a greater loss than that incurred by the lender, in which case the borrower recompenses the other's loss to his own advantage.

The extent of compensation for loss cannot be set in the loan conditions because (f. 51) no-one can agree in advance on sums yet to be gained and one cannot sell what one does not yet have, and may find all kinds of impediments before having. And the above-quoted Aquinas adds (II^{a} IIe, q. LXII), that anyone holding others' money causes them loss, because he prevents them acquiring what they would otherwise have acquired, and this loss should be made good, not in its entirety but in part, according to the situation of the individuals involved and the activities they pursue.

Can a son-in-law accept, as entitled in law, a dowry from a usurer father-in-law? I say that if he knew the man was a usurer before the wedding, then it is not permissible to accept the dowry, and if he has taken it he should return it, but if he did not know but became aware of the fact later, he may accept it, though it were better he did not. But if the father-in-law also has legitimate assets than it is certainly allowed.

It is not permissible to give livestock to your herdsman in such a way that he cannot benefit from their possession, nor that the master take his portion of the gain and the herdsman his part only afterwards, or that any should benefit from their produce who then die before the herdsman receive his portion: in fact an agreement, to be lawful, should always be equitably divided between the parties, and where it is not, it becomes unlawful.

A contract that requires the repayment of money before its expiry date is unjust, as is one which envisages paying the farmer for his wine or grain a price lower than its future value, which means that you should pay the true value, as indeed for all other goods. But giving money in advance for (f. 51') such goods, paying the future value, is permissible.

It is permissible to make use of another's oxen, paying in corn or some other commodity, except if you were to pretend that the beast had not died in your service and the recompense was owing only from the farmer; the same goes for sheep or goats, when they graze on another's land and there is an element of risk, their deaths should be a risk sustained by all involved.

It is permissible to borrow from an usurer to use against an enemy of your city, when you are waging a just war.

The penalties specified by a contract for an insolvent debtor, are not usury, because there is no usury where there is not fraudulent intent from the outset. But bad faith can be presumed in one with a usurious record. One suspects fraud also when the penalties are protracted for months and years. One must none the less assess the motives of the one not paying, and also when a debtor fails to honour his debt because it is impossible for him to do so, no penalties are permissible.

If you should have been paid by one of your debtors who does not honour the deadline, and to be rid of an obligation and to cover your needs you have borrowed from a usurer and wish to seek a judicial award of the interest you have agreed, you are justified in doing so. Ramon Llull and Ockham suggest a case: It is as if you were to say "I wanted to buy a house or a plot of land which would have rendered ten ducats a year, but on your insistence I did not buy it but lent you the money instead: give me so much, or so much a year, as much as that house would have rendered, taking account the (f. 52) expenses and the risk". This is lawful.

It is also legitimate, if your father-in-law has given you a pledge as collateral for the dowry, for you to use any interest gained on it without discounting it from the capital, because you bear the expenses of the marriage.

If someone forward sells an item at a higher price than the current cash value, and if, having regard to the period of grace allowed to the buyer, he sells it to him at a higher price, I say he commits usury, unless he had good reason to be convinced that with the lapse of time the asset would have increased in value, justifying the premium. And this matter engaged even the ancient writers, who offered only general opinions, perhaps because in those times the availability and practice of forward selling was not as common and necessary.

But we need now to analyse the question in detail, because today the world is so geared to this practice that buying and selling hardly takes place without deferral. And in relation to this kind of contract we need to understand good and bad mercantile practice, the foundations on which it has been built, the circumstances in which it is, or is not, permissible, as we saw in our first book, in the chapter on forward selling. And we call it wrong simply when the intention was improper, as we have said.

But it can be permissible when under the following circumstances you might reason with yourself: “A ship is arriving with a cargo of wool or other merchandise. As a merchant I plan my transaction and commit to it thoroughly the expertise I have acquired in my trade and I decide that this wool will have a certain future value. I buy the whole cargo and, aware of the risk I am exposing myself to (f. 52’), I buy it, say, at fifty ducats a thousand pieces, which may turn out to be more or less than what it is eventually worth according to circumstance, as you know. I take possession of the wool, pay the agreed price, put it in my warehouse and sell it on at fifty-five or sixty ducats the thousand in six, eight, ten months or a year as best I can according to the movements of the market, without exceeding an adequate, reasonable and just price. I sell it five, six or ten bags at a time to the wool-workshops, who in general are unable to buy in cash, or indeed carry on much of their commercial activity in ready money, having in fact themselves to sell their cloth on credit, not being able to find cash buyers, and are therefore compelled to buy for deferred payment themselves”.

In this case all the following elements come together, that is, my own hard work, my capacity for planning ahead: I buy wholesale and sell retail, I take on the uncertainty of gaining or losing, the worry and problems of getting paid, the cost of warehousing, the wages of staff, the restricting of my own liberty of action, in that the money if otherwise employed might have given similar or better results, the choice of the wool and possible warehouse residue, the general diligence involved, the general advantage, shared throughout the city, procured by the buyer, and above all my honest rather than fraudulent intentions. In short, as long as one does not exceed an honest and affordable price, one’s gain is justified.

All this is endorsed by the venerable Brother Antoninus, master of theology and Bishop of (f. 53) Florence, in his *Antonina*; and the same applies if you sell the wool at a lower price for cash, when in need of ready money. In support of all this, I might add a small further justification, which is that it is also permissible to buy a debtor’s obligation at ninety when it is worth a hundred, on account of the effort and hard work that may be involved in its recovery, including possible legal proceedings, and I say that there is much more than we have been able to explain to be said about this question and the others we have touched on above.

When I spoke of buying wool, I specified wool arriving by ship, because I would in fact argue differently for goods that are already in the country and have a known and almost fixed price, which is furthermore not subject to much oscillation, up or down: such goods are not covered by the cases explained above. I would say that in these cases it is better to abstain from marking up the price, and that it is next to impossible to get away with it, not least because you are certain to do down two people, the one you buy from, who paid dearly in the first instance and now must sell for cash, losing God knows how much, and the one who buys from you to sell for cash himself, heading for a loss; and above all you are not going to get away with it when the broker says to you: "I will give it to you after the resale", meaning when that devil-possessed soul rebuys it himself. These kinds of of purchase agreements some call *acivimento* ('acquisition'), others *stochi* ('daggers') others again *strangoli* ('throttlings'). These contracts are never permissible, above all when prompted by fraudulent intentions; many of course try to excuse themselves by saying (f. 53') "I don't know what price these goods will be resold at", thinking to deceive God, while deceiving only themselves.

What shall we say then of those who buy grain cheaply at harvest time with a view to storing it and reselling at a good price. I say that this can be done in five different ways and is sometimes sinful, and sometimes not.

The first is for the common good, as Joseph did: "I will buy the grain now to have a reserve to feed people in times of famine.

The second is to provide for the needs of one's household out of fear that the price might rise, and then to sell the remainder in excess of one's needs at a higher price because that is the market rate at the time.

The third is for charity, that the profits provide for the poor.

The fourth is to practise correctly one's profession of merchant, without provoking shortages, simply plying one's trade; and this is the case when the transaction comes within the normal ambit of mercantile activity from which one makes one's living.

The fifth is for greed alone: he sells at a higher price without thinking of anyone's advantage or need but his own, and to cause shortages. In this way, because he owns all the grain, others are compelled to buy from him at the price he sets. Such a man commits a grave sin, as we read in Llull, Ockham, Innocent and Hostiensis, and Ramon Llull adds that men of this stripe should be forced to repay not any one specific person, but the poor, and particularly in those cases where a group of merchants form (f. 54) a cartel and agree to sell their wares at a certain price, the same applying to all forms of trade.

It is permissible to buy others' debts: if, for example, a debtor owes me a hundred, I can sell that for ninety against immediate payment. It is understood that the buyer will apply whatever discount covers his being out of pocket, how he estimates the risk of not getting paid and the degree of effort required to obtain quittance, especially if he may have to make repeated approaches. But if he calculates his recompense by time, saying "Give me five or six percent a month", then the intention is usurious, and fraudulent.

If it is the community that takes over loans and envisages the application of such and such a percentage of interest per year, that is permissible, being for the common good. It is a case of necessity, which they would avoid if they could. But if another buy up the loans, what we said concerning the debtor in the previous paragraph applies. Remember that sinners are both the man who lends at usury and the man that lends to the usurer, or who does him a favour or gives him help of advice, likewise his agents or mentors. The case of stewards is a different one, who lend and collect usurious money on the orders of their master: these are not parties to the usury, and do not sin, according to Ockham. But if they were to act without being so ordered, they would be obliged to reimburse, even if they had themselves made no profit.

If you have paid interest to a usurer against your will and you happen to come into possession of some of his assets, (f. 54') can you retain the amount he has charged you? I would reply that if such assets have come into your hands by honest means, because you found them, or because you had them from others, there would be no sin and you could legitimately keep back your part. But if the usurer has lent you an asset, then you cannot keep it, and this case should be adjudicated by the courts. It is not that you are obliged to repay, but you must be able to defend yourself against any scandal arising from the situation.

A usurer is obliged to pay himself the interest he has imposed on the debtor, just as if the latter had been obliged to sell his house or something of the kind.

What shall we say about exchanges, which many are mistrustful of, most often because they are ignorant of currency conversion and trading? And notwithstanding what we have said in our first book concerning when and how exchanges are permissible, none the less I say that what determines a reasonable profit is the real exchange, under the prevailing local conditions, taking into account the uncertainty of gain, a true and honest exchange between the parties, without interest, acting only with diligence and prudence in view of the risk and effort taken on by one engaging in an exchange.

No different is our argument for exchanges of a usurious nature, that is not strictly real-time exchanges: say that at Barcelona the exchange rate is fifteen shillings to the ducat, and since payment has yet to be made, you want to put it at sixteen, or something similar. These token exchanges not yet having been paid, cannot be exchanged at a higher price than others, because they are subject to the same risks, the same expiry dates and the same procedures, and above all because more often than not such exchange arrangements which have yet to be realised are set up by subscription (f. 55) by a number of capable men, who would not accept a rate over fifteen. Whereas in this your putative exchange the conversion is a false one: it will be realised on the market at fifteen and then passed on to some courtier, prelate or gentleman, inexpert in the business, at sixteen or even seventeen shillings.

In the same way, when an exchange is prolonged over many days, ten, fifteen, or more, and in view of the time extension an extra interest payment is added, or an additional quarter or half percent over, this is, I say, a usurious exchange and you are obliged to refund the surcharge, in both cases.

Other kinds of exchange are those in which no letters of exchange are issued, nothing is entered in the accounts, and no middlemen or commissions or couriers are paid, but the bare payments and receipts are reckoned up: here too we have a usurious agreement and those involved are obliged to reimburse.

And since many are inclined to distrust the value of the same currency where it is exchanged in different fori at a certain percentage higher rate, I will say not to entertain suspicions, because just as the rate can be three percent higher, so it can equally work out four percent lower. And you will often see that just as currencies can be worth more, so can they be worth less, so that taking into account the uncertainty of gain and the fear of loss, as well as the effort, hard work and expense of couriers, middlemen and commissions, then such contracts are reasonable. And while making a certain profit on money lent will render a contract unlawful, on Aristotle's principle that "all opposites are governed by the same laws", I say that conversely an uncertain profit, with its attendant effort and other factors previously listed, make a contract lawful. These matters, associated with exchange operations I tell you who can understand (f. 55') them, but the material is difficult for those unfamiliar with it to grasp.

Is it permissible to sell something at a higher price than its value? I answer, following Aquinas IIª IIᵉ, q. LXXVII: that to sell for a higher price or buy for a lower price than an item's true value is neither permissible or right, unless the seller suffers some damage in selling his property at its true value; for example, if he himself has great need of it: here one needs to calculate a just price not only according to the value of the asset but to the deprivation endured by the vendor and in this case it is permissible to sell something above its value. But if a buyer does particularly well from a purchase and the seller does not lose out, the former should temper his mark-up, because no one should sell what is not his. Why then do men's laws not prohibit this? I say that human laws leave many things unpunished, and in this case go only so far as to prescribe that if a fair price is exceeded by half or more, the contract is invalid. But God's laws leave no one unpunished, and that therefore under divine law a contract is illegitimate when there is not a just equilibrium between buyer and seller, and if one has gained more he is obliged to reimburse the other if the disparity is clearly damaging: a fair price for things cannot be established precisely, but consists in so arranging things that a minimum increase or reduction does not go so far as to impinge on a just division. And this you will find in (f.56) X q. IIª *Hoc ius*.

If the transaction is inequitable owing to some defect in the goods sold, or conversely owing to some hidden quality, as far as selling something goes, there are three kinds of defect to consider, the first regarding the thing itself, as for example one were to sell watered wine for pure; the second regarding quantity, weight or amount; the third: quality, as in selling a lame animal for a sound one.

Now if a seller intentionally cheats in one of these three ways, he commits fraud and the contract is invalid. If on the other hand the seller was unaware that the goods sold were defective, he has committed no sin, but when the fact is made known he must recompense the buyer. Therefore it follows that it is not permissible to sell alchemists' gold or silver as the true metal, because it is not pure like real gold. If alchemy could really produce real gold it would not be wrong to sell it as such. Conversely, by the same token if someone sells you gold believing it to be copper, your duty is to return it.

Is a man obliged to inform the buyer of a defect? I reply following Aquinas. A seller who puts up a defective item for sale exposes the buyer to loss or even to danger: to loss, if the defect reduces the value of the item and he has not lowered the price, to danger if the defect compromises the safe use of it (f. 56') as when one sells a lame horse for a sound one or a crumbling house for one apparently new, or rotten and poisonous food for good. If these faults are not apparent and the seller does not communicate them, then the sale is fraudulently proposed and the seller is obliged to make good the damage. If the defect is obvious, as for example if you sell a horse with one eye, or if the usefulness of the object proves to be another than what might have been expected, and on account of the defect the item has been sold at a lower price than its market value, then the seller is not obliged to declare the defect, because the buyer is aiming to acquire the object at a lower price on the basis of that defect, and in such a case the seller may reasonably not declare it.

Let us posit a case where a man takes his goods to sell them at a certain place and knows that many others would follow him, but if he were to let it be known he could not sell his wares at so high a price. I would reply in line with Aquinas (see citation above): if the seller sells his goods at the higher end of the market price, he offends nobody, but if he were to announce it to all and sundry, it would be more than anything else an act of charity, but as far as the law goes he is not so obliged.

What should we say of merchants who form a cartel to sell at a particular price and appoint one among them to exercise the monopoly of that product? I reply according to Hostiensis that it would be an unlawful agreement. Similarly if someone obtain the privilege in his city that he, and no other, can sell something – if someone succeeds in obtaining such a charter, he should be stripped of all his possessions and expelled from the city; and likewise anyone conceding such a charter should be punished.

What should we say of those who know of no way of buying and selling (f. 57) except with lies, oaths and perjury? I say, along with Ramon Llull that when swearing to something they lie and perjure themselves, they are stained with mortal sin and obliged to reimburse. If someone out of ignorance declares a falsehood believing it to be true, or even if knowing it false, intends no harm to the other, but is only protecting himself, and is not selling the item at a higher price than he should, such lies can be classed as venial sins; but to swear and perjure oneself is mortal sin.

Some transactions are permissible, others not. According to Llull, impermissible are all those than cannot be performed without sin, such as usury, simony, theft and so on, which are forbidden to all men, see vedi XIIII, q. IIII. Just as some are forbidden because intrinsically bad, others are permissible by their very nature, like guardianship, healing, all the manual arts, the weavers, garment-makers etc.

Can lawful activities become unlawful? I reply, with Llull, that they can be illegal in a number of ways. Firstly: motive, that is when they are pursued with a dishonest desire for riches, not out of need but for contemptible ends; in such cases any activity is proscribed to all, see XLVII, di. *Omnis*, e c. *Sicut*, II.

Secondly: time, that is when they are undertaken on holidays, when one should refrain from working. Likewise, the hour even when decisions are taken, by night rather than day, and the same goes for days of rest.

Thirdly: the kind of person involved, (f. 57') because trade is forbidden to monks and the clergy, as we said in the first book, and as St Augustine wrote (LXXXVIII): "Men are always forbidden to fornicate, but to engage in trade, sometimes yes, sometimes no".

Fourthly: place, as for example the haunts of dishonest and evil-intentioned men (*Digestis, de arb.*, L. *Si cun dies*). Equally the eminence of a place can render trading impermissible, say, if it were carried on in church, for which reason Christ cast out all those who sold and bought from the temple, see Matthew, 21.

Factors are entitled to a just and reasonable commission, but not an inequitable and excessive one, see *Extra*, *De emptione et venditione*, c. I.

We will deal next with theft, even if this does not come strictly within the ambit of trading.

There are two kinds of theft, one the obvious variety, where the thief is caught red-handed, the other where the thief is not surprised with his loot: and it is theft whether the items stolen be small or large, because theft is not a question of quantity, but of the intention of the wrong-doer, see XIIII, q. VII, c. *Ultra*[6]. And this is so when the desire to steal is such that, even if the item is large, he would have stolen it equally. But Aquinas does say (II^{a}, IIe, q. LXVI) that if someone filches tiny bits and pieces thinking their owner will not suffer from their loss, this is forgive-able ; otherwise, theft is always mortal sin and you must make restitution. Even if one has something deposited or pawned with you and you use it, damaging it, then a theft has been committed (f. 58) and restitution is called for.

What should we say of a woman who, before marrying, has committed a theft and the marriage having been consummated, the husband becomes a party to it? Or if, contrarily, the husband were the one to commit the theft and the wife becomes party to it? We might ask ourselves further whether the wife can make restitution from their common assets. I reply, following Ockham, if the husband and wife habitually hold their goods in common and the stolen item is amongst them, the wife can return it even against the husband's will; and even if the object is not there, and the husband has not expressly forbidden it, the wife can reimburse the value of the object. But if the husband has forbidden repayment, I do not think the wife should do so, though were she to, she should not be punished for it.

In conclusion we will speak of the restitution to be made for everything dishonestly obtained, on which subject we have not only *De regulis iuris*, li. VI, as above, and a saying of the glorious St Augustine "There can be no remission of sin where what has been taken is not returned". And restitution will usually be to the person from whom the asset has been stolen, as in illegal contracts and thefts, if you know the person in question, or to his heirs to whom the victim's purloined goods belong by right; or sometimes to one who, while not being the legal owner of

---

[6] Actually: XIIII, q. VI, c. *Furtum autem*.

the goods, has come by them honestly and is making use of them. If the man that had the goods had no right of possession himself but had stolen them in his turn, they should be returned to the rightful owner, and this should be done with discretion, through the agency of a man of the church or some upright citizen.

(f. 58') On occasions the value should be given to the poor, as *de malis ablatis incertis*, that is when the true owners of the stolen goods are unknown, with the approval of a prelate, or on the Church's authority, see *Extra*, di. *Iude*, *Cum sit*, e XII[a], q. I, *Precipimus*. Some say that the same procedure should be followed when an executor lacks a will, when someone surviving the dead man or authorised by him may redirect the amount to pious causes even without the bishop's permission. This is the opinion of the papal chaplain Simone di Marvilla, and of Aquinas.

No restitution should be made to a simoniac, because he has himself has profited illegally: again any money should be given to the poor. There are some who have stolen money, by committing a sin, but may none the less retain possession: such is the case with prostitutes who do not have to return their gains. Some deserve restitution, but not gamblers, unless, say, you have induced Peter to gamble and then won off him: in this case you should pay him back your winnings, but if it were he who had persuaded you and you won, you should not give your winnings to him, but to the poor.

What do we say of bankrupted merchants who settle at ten shillings to the lira, or at a given percentage? We must differentiate: if the creditors have spontaneously written off part of the debt, there is no further obligation of restitution, but if they had no choice, and conceded this unwillingly, you are not free of your creditors.

We have then studied in these chapters the (f. 59) guidelines a merchant should follow. If you follow them as you ought, have no doubt that, thanks to the benefit of the mass and of prayer, which are marvellous things, and of piety, which is most pleasing to God, our Creator will surely award you the grace of dying in repentance and will have you return to his bosom; and with your conversion to the path of penitence you will find yourself exempted from further restitutions to others. As a consequence you will perform a light penance, which will be prescribed by your priest in proportion to the requirements of your soul. All this is to bring home to you that the greater number of merchants, from their bad habit of not making good, will come to die in despair, because restitution does not come easily and sometimes their assets are insufficient to cover their obligations; and even where they are sufficient it is hard for a merchant to make himself poor or to leave his children in poverty. And in the end you will find only a small number of merchants, among many, who make full restitution, because they have entrusted their happiness to riches, not having read what Augustine wrote in that passage from *De Civitate Dei* when he says: "Earthly riches make neither ourselves or our children happy, either because we lose them while we are still living, or because after our deaths they will pass to others who we do not know, or even who we would not want to have them. Only God can give us happiness because his is the true wealth of the spirit.

Therefore, bringing to a close this second book, I urge merchants to study these angelic lessons, and I fervently beseech them to not constrict their souls and (f. 59') minds and make themselves prisoners of avidity, so as to end up obliged to make restitution.

And they should not be surprised by the brevity of the discussion: we have made a point of only explaining necessary and appropriate matters. And let it not be thought the we have proceeded in a superficial manner because we have not continually attached references to chapter and verse: our discussion has been founded throughout on the regulatory corpus of canon law.

Here ends the second book on the art of trade by Benedetto Cotrugli.

Part 3: On the Civic Life of the Merchant

Exordium

Since in our first book we dealt with the essence, the usefulness and the proper exercise of the merchant's trade, and in our second with religion, which is the principal foundation of the righteous life that refines the soul and guides us to our much desired end, it seems incumbent on us now to examine properly, following our programme for what remains to be dealt with, that most commendable attribute that has perfected the life of the men of every epoch, of every condition, whatever kind of existence they led: and that is, the moral and civil conduct of life according to the virtues attendant on human civilisation, a quality essential to any good merchant.

Given that the general run of men, and merchants particularly, who do not acquire their precepts from original sources, are inclined to follow in their father's footsteps, and when their fathers are merchants (f. 60) they become merchants in their turn; and in so far as sons are in the habit of imitating their fathers and failing to equal them, or if equalling them do not surpass them, so the world, deteriorating continually, has become a repository of bilgewater. Wherever in the world merchants are to be

C. Carraro, G. Favero (eds.), *Benedetto Cotrugli – The Book of the Art of Trade*, DOI 10.1007/978-3-319-39969-0_6

found they commit only errors and conduct themselves superficially, without the least evidence of reasoning. In fact, worse still, merchants have reduced the art of trade to mere mechanical activity, and treat the next thing in front of them like monkeys with no logical grounding whatsoever. But their estimable sons, with their elegant manners, should exert themselves not to merely imitate their fathers but to surpass them in every virtue. And were they to behave thus, the world would be an infinitely better place than the one we see. For this is what the ancient Romans did, from whom we have distanced ourselves more than a little, at least as regards all the things we ought to imitate: we read for example of the younger Africanus, son of Aemilius Paulus, in Cicero's account in the sixth book of *De Re Publica*, that he not only imitated his father's wonderful achievements in battle, but outdid him in his glorious eloquence; as indeed many other most distinguished and eloquent men have succeeded in doing, Romans and others, whom we should ourselves imitate as exemplary models of human endeavour.

There were also many others of humbler stock that ignoring the example of their own forebears rose through the nobility of their own genius to pinnacles of glory: as we read of Varro, who was a butcher, and Socrates, sculptor and stonemason, and many others who, born of humble fathers (f. 60'), reached such heights of glory as to take front rank among men.

Therefore, given that the current generation—and this is true particularly of the merchants, following hard on the steps of one another—seems so abased that a virtuous man is hardly to be found, it seems to me necessary, continuing our treatise, to append to this third book what the moral virtues are that a merchant ought to have, and before going any further, we will speak of the honour and dignity of the merchant's calling and then pass on to those virtues.

Chapter I On the Honour and Dignity of the Merchant

The dignity and the honour of the merchant are considerable, even sublime, from many aspects, and four in particular. First of all, in relation to the communal wellbeing, in that profit for the good of all coincides with honest gain, as Cicero has it, according to whom, the nobler souls, for all that they must die, do not hesitate to accept death and endure it willingly.

The prosperity, advantages and soundness of the state derive in large measure from merchants, and I refer as always not to vulgar and plebeian traders, but to those estimable merchants we have set up as paragons in this essay. And this is due to the industry and practice of trade through which food and supplies are brought to cities that are not themselves producers. Merchants also procure different and unusual products importing them from places where they are abundant to places where they are scarce (f. 61); they ensure that there is plenty of coinage, jewels, gold, and every sort of precious metal; they ensure that there is an abundance of work for different trades in city and nation; they cause the land to be cultivated, livestock to abound, they cause incomes and revenues to flourish; they sustain the poor by their activities; through the energy with which they manage their rents they stimulate farm managers to invest; they increase the yield of imposts and excises of rulers and republics by exporting and importing their merchandise to the consequent enrichment of the public and communal exchequer.

Secondly, I would praise the dignity and calling of the merchant in relation to the profitable and honest conduct of his household and his patrimony, because, as you know, the moderate, balanced, solid and well-mannered merchant enhances and adds to his wealth; this is why we are used to seeing a merchant prosper in possessions and property, in riches and furnishings for his residences, in fine clothes for his family, in dowries for his sons and daughters, and consequently in the steady increase and betterment of his social condition through ever more distinguished matrimonial alliances.

He contributes to the advancement of the general public welfare with the splendour and opulence of daily life in his own house, with style and fine manners, prospering constantly, increasing and accumulating his holdings. Conversely, quite the opposite is the case with those who lack this admirable application, hence the proverb, if anything overused, of our forebears: "Sad is the house that is stranger to commerce". If in fact, the farm manager and the gentleman who lives off income, however substantial that may be, do nothing to augment it with zealous commerce, their revenue will amount to much less than (f. 61') it would in the hands of a merchant; and I am not talking only of methods of cultivation, but also the ability, after the harvest, to sell the crop at the most advantageous time and season. And wherever they have children, of either sex, if these want to marry off their girls they will have to sell property, tighten their belts and eventually sell off everything after the death of these entrepreneurs who when alive had not managed through devoting themselves to the art of trade to increase their property and leave a decent inheritance to their children as their father had to them. The patrimony must necessarily be divided among the children so that each gets his share, and even if the first generation do not end up in the poorhouse, to be sure the grandchildren or great-grandchildren will do so, and their house come to ruin. And just as the merchant will better the condition of his offspring through matrimonial alliances, while continuing to maintain his own state, by the same token the poor gentleman, unable to do likewise, must necessarily worsen his standing, slipping inexorably into a humbler condition.

Third consideration: the merchant's state should be appreciated and honoured with regard to his ability to converse wisely. Such exchanges may be practised in public or in private. In private, that is in his own home, where the his upstanding family are thus virtuously engaged; in fact, where money, gold and silver, jewels and like items of value are handled you may be sure you will not find villains, alley boys, hangers-on of every sort, sycophants, thieves, fugitives and gamblers such as frequent the courts of princes, barons and lords, (f. 62) and seek favours from the state, and there every type of low person hangs about, living a loose life, a far cry from what one expects from a well-run household.

And merchants also converse in public, outside their homes, with artisans, gentlemen, lords, princes and prelates of every degree, and all these turn to the merchant because they value his advice; and often these notables will seek him out in his house; and such merchants are not only necessary to them to sustain them and help them with their difficulties (which they are most capable of doing), but also know how to advise them for the best, because the rulers of the states of this world have never understood the financial professions, on which all the nations of the world depend, while the able merchant experienced in such matters understands them well and can give advice and suggest solutions.

Fourth consideration: the good standing of the merchant in relation to trust, both in him and on his part in others. On his side because he looks after others' deposits with complete honesty and pays his debts promptly, as we see every day; and it is often said nowadays that trust is only to be found in merchants and men-at-arms. Generally the faith of others is afforded to them, because neither kings, nor princes, nor prelates, nor any other kind of men enjoy the trust and credit of the good merchant. A merchant's promissory note can be exchanged without problem while those of others only with difficulty, and where accepted they circulate at a much higher rate of interest (f. 62') whoever takes them on; and the merchant's clear and simple handwritten receipt is accepted at face value, while those of lords and other categories of person are not creditworthy without solid legal backing and restrictions.

And therefore, for the reasons given, the merchant can be proud of his remarkable standing. And pursuing our theme we will say that in order to maintain the dignity we have characterised, the merchant must steer clear of all specious adornments of the soul or the body, and should not exhibit the arrogant gestures of robust men-at-arms, nor the unmanly ones of actors and buffoons, but should be austere in his speech, his movements and in everything he does, sustaining as far as possible his proper dignity. And such things will evince a considerable elegance when combined with a handsome figure gifted by nature, well proportioned and in good trim.

So, to preserve such grace and apply it in all the above listed circumstances, the merchant must cultivate a soft, elegant and manly manner of speaking, free of petulance and superficiality without that agitation of mind which, as Cicero says, should never be an attribute of the wise man; and his gait should not be exuberant but measured and austere. And if he follows this course, together with the other recommendations we have proposed in our previous volumes and will add to in what follows, our merchant will attain and maintain the dignity and honour appropriate and owing to his state.

Chapter II On Prudence and the Merchant

(f. 63) For all that prudence is a general virtue and proper to every rank and condition of mankind, it is none the less in some sense more relevant, suitable and proper to the merchant than to other sorts of men, in so far as other things, other trades and professions, subsist and are organised on the basis of particular and firm rules and regulations, while trade alone is conducted on the basis of judgement, of which prudence is an essential ingredient. Prudence is the principal component of integrity and encompasses the differentiation of the good from the bad, and consists in remembering the past, assessing the present and providing for the future, as Boethius says in *De Consolatione*: "It is not enough to see what is in front of our eyes, but prudence must assess the outcome of things". And Tully says: "This is the chief merit of the intellect, to ascertain in advance what may come to pass, good or bad, and what can be done about it, and never be in the position of having to say 'I would never have believed it'". Merchant's errors are liable to be largely damaging or irreparable, and he must therefore keep a clear head, be prudent and ready for everything; he must grasp things without misunderstanding and take decisions prudently and be circumspect in all his dealings, and be prepared to be flexible as called for and arrive at decisions and remedies when misfortunes occur. And from prudence he will derive foresight, caution, discretion and flexibility

And the merchant must be (f. 63') far-sighted: when he is hoping to bring a future project to port he should move steadily towards it, so organising current matters that he will achieve his objective in due course.

He should also be cautious and beware of contrary vices, keeping his eye always on the bottom line. He must also exercise caution in distinguishing the good from the bad, black from white, profit from loss, true from false and reality from illusion and not allow himself to be taken in by apparent good or advantage, as the Greeks deceived the Trojans with their horse, passing it off as an offering to Minerva. Therefore, you who wish to cultivate prudence and caution beware those men who seem good and just, even pious, "who come to you in sheep's clothing, but inwardly they are ravening wolves "or as in St Paul's saying: "Such men are deaf as snakes and advance with crooked necks"

A merchant must also be open-minded and ready to learn himself before instructing others, because "he who knows himself, knows everything". And such wisdom can be attained by reading widely, so I will remind you: whenever you have a spare moment, read. And in this respect you should be alive to two things, as Tully says: firstly, not to assume you know things you do not know, or be tempted to, for this is presumption. Secondly, not to engage with matters you know nothing of and are unnecessary and obscure, neglecting things that are relevant and necessary to ourselves; as for example, neglecting moral philosophy, we might throw ourselves into geometry or astrology. And there are any number of useless and uncultured young men who give themselves up to dancing and courting and banquets and other (f. 64) such delights, ignoring the study of Latin and oratory and other honourable disciplines. For which reason you will find many of our merchants who are proficient at chess, board games, cards, dice, and at fencing, wrestling, playing instruments, dancing, hunting, fishing, etc., and know as much of the sciences "as an ass with a lyre". Such types are indiscreet and uncivilised, abandoning themselves to inappropriate things and neglecting important ones, against every criterion of prudence, or rather that open-mindedness which is its child, which demands instead that the merchant should not only have wide knowledge, but be able to give good counsel to others, and above all to his young and those in a position to learn from him.

Chapter III On the Education of the Merchant

Having next to deal with the merchant's erudition, of what it should consist and how wide it should be, I wilt at the thought of it, because it compels me to think of the infinite: in pursuit of delineating the perfect and complete merchant, I must exemplify the universal man, equipped with the capacity to understand and deal with all types of men.

But to pick out those particular and most important branches of learning without which the merchant can hardly be useful and effective, we will talk of the essential natural sciences that he must perforce master. And those ignorami who refuse to entertain the idea of, or even condemn the cultivated merchant will just have to bear with us. For indeed there are those who profess the greater insolence of suggesting that a merchant should not even be literate.

But I maintain that the merchant, as (f. 64') we have already said, should not only be a good writer, mathematician, keeper of accounts etc., but should be above all well-educated, and a good rhetorician, as this will be extremely useful to him: Latin besides renders a man capable of properly understanding a contract, and merchants make contracts every day; it allows him also to understand the detail of laws, or privileges and everything pertaining to a contract; it helps him to understand the languages of many races, because it is common to many peoples and different ethnic groups like the Hungarians, Germans, French and many others. Latin will also help him to understand properly many aspects of the Christian religion, such as the mass, and the prayers and those things he may like to read for his personal devotions. It will also allow him to hold his own among nobles and men of importance, make him extraordinary (Latin *egregius*—'apart from the herd', 'superior to the crowd')

To be a rhetorician is useful not only because it makes a man proficient in Latin, but also fluent in the vernacular, which also a distinction in a merchant. Latin also teaches him to write letters elegantly, to address nobles and persons of importance in the proper manner; thus, when necessary, merchants know how to write formal missives and open them in the approved manner.

And in so far as conscientious and effective merchants should not be like a common needle, which is a low instrument and useful only for sowing, but should be universal and capable of performing many and various honourable roles, they are for this reason (f. 65) (for in fact, as Cicero says, "We are not born for ourselves alone, but in part for our country, and in part for our friends") sent as ambassadors and emissaries of princes and various lords and signories; and these, were they not familiar with letters and rhetoric, would be like "an ass with a lyre" and "half-men, all but beasts", lacking that excellence of finish that leads to perfection: just as nourishment and food for the body is tasteless without salt, so the soul cannot survive without learning. Which is why Ptolemy says "The man who does not acquire knowledge is coarser than an idiot, inferior to the plants and lower than the unreasoning stones, because he neglects his perfectibility". And Solomon, in The Book of Wisdom, 8[1]: "Therefore I prayed, and understanding was given me; I called upon God, and the spirit of wisdom came to me. I preferred her to sceptres and thrones, and I accounted wealth as nothing in comparison with her. Neither did I liken to her any priceless gem, because all gold is but trivial sand in her sight, and silver will be accounted as mud before her. I loved her more than health and beauty, and I chose to have her rather than light".

And it is proven by the theologians that if Adam had not sinned, there would be a general equality amongst men, because there would not be learning to distinguish them. And wise men have said that domination is of two kinds: the first, that of those who have bought themselves servants, the second that of those who through their education surpass even those who are lords over the servant-keepers.

And Aristides,[2] to one who asked the difference between the educated and the ignorant man, replied "That between the domesticated and the wild horse". And Aristotle said (f. 65'): "That between a live man and a dead one". Diogenes said: "All things are of the gods, and the gods are friends of knowledge, but all the things of friends are shared between them, therefore all things belong to the knowledgeable". And Philip, King of Macedon, demonstrated as much when his son Alexander was born, for he wrote to Aristotle, saying: "You should know that a son has been born to me, and we must therefore rejoice, not so much for the fact of his birth, but because he has happened to be born in your lifetime, so that, living according to your teachings, he may become worthy of the empire". And his son Alexander, having learnt philosophy from Aristotle and hearing that he had published books of philosophy for others, was opposed to this: he said in fact that it would have been a nobler thing that he had not been treated on a level with other men. Also King Antigonus, writing to Zeno, preferred the latter's prestige to that of royalty on account of his great knowledge, and Ptolemy Philadelphus enriched the Alexandrian library by seven hundred thousand volumes. And Zeno himself, who only began to study at the age of thirty, realised as a mature man how much error he had fallen into previously; and this

---

[1] In fact 7.

[2] Properly Aristippus (see Diogenes Laertius, *Lives* II 69).

we have on the authority of Diogenes Laërtius and of Aulus Gellius in his *Attic Nights*.

None the less there is no shortage of ignorant men, wholly without culture, who give themselves over to folly to the extent that they will criticise men of learning; and these are generally coarse and unlettered types, who, resenting their inferiority, espouse the idiocy of condemning the educated; in fact the ignorant are generally bad men, as the Philosopher said: "Every ignoramus is evil". And evil is necessarily opposed to good, which (f. 66) is virtue; thus in this world there is no war and no enmity greater that the ignorant bears towards the wise, or the uncultured towards the cultured. And just as water is ignorant of, and cannot co-exist with, fire, so the educated cannot mix with the uneducated.

And so it is that when a cultivated man stands out from the crowd, he is criticised and despised, or even killed, or crushed and persecuted by the common horde, as we have read of many men, most notably Socrates: although he was judged by all men to be the wisest in the world, and even the oracle of Apollo had predicted his great knowledge, none the less, out of envy for his learning, he was imprisoned by the people and given hemlock to drink, and so died. Likewise Dante, hounded from his homeland, died in Ravenna, and we could cite many more examples, ancient and modern, that it is unnecessary to remember here for fear of boring the reader and also because we have spoken of these things elsewhere in our work and they are not pertinent to our current argument.

And because of the acknowledged excellence of learning the synods of the Christian Church have ordained that the secular clergy should acquire a scholarly culture, in order to distinguish the truth from falsehood and to have access to the theological sciences (di. XXXVII *Cur Ego*). And to this end they have provided us with masters of the liberal arts to be present in certain churches (di. XXXII *In quibusdam, extra et per totum.*).

And the liberal arts consist of Grammar, Logic and Rhetoric; and merchants are limited in their command of the sciences not because there are not numerous other (f. 66') fields of knowledge but because the world is corrupt and so lacking in wisdom that men not only make no effort to learn, and do not even want to learn, but what is worse and shameful is that those who have a degree of schooling are insulted and mocked for it.

And yet it is a noble thing to be a philosopher among philosophers, an orator and historian among orators and historians, a logician among logicians, and not to be ignorant of the Christian faith among the godly, and to be a merchant among merchants and a courtier among courtiers, because a merchant should be the most universal of men and one that has the most to do, more than his fellows, with different types of men and social classes. And this is why, in addition to the already mentioned knowledge and the liberal arts the merchant must also have other practical knowledge of the world, such as one learns more through experience than any other way. Cosmography, for example, which is important for knowing how the world is made up and the names of the nations, regions, provinces and individual cities, but also to understand trading conditions and usages, tolls, the nature of all the merchandise and various things that are transported and exported from every part, because in ignorance of such things the merchant cannot know what is required for each season and place. And he must besides know distances, places, ports, landings, and especially sea charts to understand charters and insurance.

All these things (f. 67) are clearly essential to the merchant, but if we were to speak too of contingent matters, I would say that it can do the merchant no harm to study philosophy, to understand the world and to refine his mind by exploring the world of nature and ourselves, and not least the physical constitution of men, their physiognomy and their character, and it is entirely necessary to be logical: it is hardly unbecoming in a merchant to be able to distinguish the true from the false and to confound unsound arguments and syllogisms, because some men are logic-choppers by nature.

Astrology too would be in some ways an excellent preparation for the merchant, so as to know which years are favourable for the grain or the olive harvest, or other foodstuffs, to anticipate illnesses, wars and suchlike, as the old proverb goes: "Make me clairvoyant and I'll make you rich". It would be good to be a theologian, against those who doubt that theology can provide a merchant with the wisdom to understand canon law and the fundamentals of our faith. Jurist, too: a merchant should not be ignorant of the law, so as to be able to defend himself against fraudsters and safeguard his own interests.

And so *ad infinitum*, we will find that everything a man might know may be helpful to a merchant, because there is no basis or place for the common delusion that learning is to be frowned on. Thus it comes as no surprise to find that true merchants are few and far between.

Chapter IV Where a Merchant Should Place His Trust

Self confidence means security and the capacity for action, and it is an attitude entirely consistent with the merchant's character, because cowardly merchants are unlikely to prosper, nor should they be so bold and reckless as to go beyond what is reasonable, because too (f. 67') bold or headstrong a merchant is dangerous, particularly when he exceeds his limits.

He must risk within reason, and conduct his affairs with courage trusting in God and good fortune: the business of the entrepreneur, properly understood, should be rational and accomplished with dedication and discernment, without levity, after which he is in the hands of fortune.

And the wise are always inclined to prefer negative outcomes after rational preparation, to positive ones that come about quite irrationally, whereas the crowd, on the contrary, will judge a man only by results and can only say: "go home" or "that's what it seems". And wherever they see a rich man they judge him reasonable, and the poor foolish, certainly in our homeland, where it is a habit derived from the Bosnians, who like the Manicheans, honour the rich and readily entertain them in their homes, and dismiss the poor, claiming to follow the manifest will of God or fate.

And therefore in all circumstances, and especially in times of misfortune, the merchant should be confident and bold, and the more that fate buffets him the more he should face it with strength and resolution, because ill fortune has a habit of punishing above all those who turn their backs and flee, rather than those who put on a brave face. Which is why Virgil sang "Fortune favours the bold and rejects the timid".

Chapter V On the Luck of the Merchant

It certainly also behoves the merchant to be lucky, no less than the doctor, of whom Avicenna says: "He must perforce (f. 68) be fortunate". And this will be demonstrated only by experience, as we see conscientious, moderate men, disciplined in all they do, whose destiny is a history of failures, while conversely we see callow, reckless and more or less irrational and ignorant ones whose affairs are crowned with success.

And this cannot be put down to deserving behaviour rewarded by God, but it seems that fortune is simply a friend to them, and I think this is something we carry with us from birth, in that our bodies are ruled by celestial forces; and just as we see that some are naturally of one physical type and others of another, one is inclined to soldiery, and another to study, and so on, some will be luckier in certain endeavours than others, which is what the Stoic meant when he said: "Fate guides us, let fate have her way".

Chapter VI On the Merchant's Integrity

As we must now deal with the integrity of a merchant, we will say immediately that as the merchant needs to establish private and public relationships of every kind, it seems to us that he must be consistent in his behaviour, the opposite of which would mean being a superficial and unreliable cipher.

He should be a man of equable temperament, upright and reliable, so that his word can be trusted and the currency of his promises undoubted and never fall short. In fact he should be especially punctilious in respecting his promises and any financial engagements he has entered into, and hold to his agreements.

Money should not be his primary concern, as in the story they tell of that glorious prince of merchants, Cosimo de' Medici: having been asked by a foreigner (f. 68'), who seemed a respectable and trustworthy person, for 300 ducats, which this man claimed to have deposited in his bank, but which there was no trace of in the accounts, and was in fact a complete invention, did not Cosimo take him by the hand and see that he was given the money, not wishing his reputation for honesty to be damaged or sullied in a any way. He thereby demonstrated that the honesty and trustworthiness of the merchant must be established and maintained more keenly than riches. And this degree of integrity can hardly be demonstrated except by being put to the test: and it seems to me that we can confidently call honest only those who have taken deposits secretly and although being in a position to deny possession have handed them back without hesitation or shilly-shallying. And the higher the sum in question, the more honest they can call themselves; in fact if the amount is large some scruples are to be expected, but if small one will think nothing of it.

And mark that one must not only be upright in one's actions but also firm in spirit and a man of unimpeachable morality, who has never allowed the thought of dishonesty to sully his soul. Consequently one should never extend one's trust or credit to bankrupts, least of all those who have failed through iniquity, because "whoever has been wicked on one occasion, one can presume to be wicked always", *De regulis iuris*, liber VI. And such can be considered ignominious wretches, and merchants in name only.

Chapter VII On the Merchant's Diligence

A merchant should show exemplary diligence and dispatch, which are the progenitors of wealth, for all that Christ said to the apostles "Therefore take no thought, saying, What shall we eat?". Christ, as Chrysostom explains, said this in the context of man not despairing of the (f. 69) Grace of God, trusting more in his own efforts than in the goodness of God, who dispenses all bounty, as in St James's saying: "Every gift and every perfect reward comes down from on high and emanates from the great Father of Light". This is directed at the lax, whose sloth is numbered among the mortal sins. And the diligence of which we speak must be applied not only to the projects a merchant is currently pursuing, with due address and solicitude, but also the business he has successfully concluded and must not fail to follow through: this second case is the more crucial, because in the first merchants risk only gaining little, while in the second they can bankrupt themselves.

And you may be sure that when you see one whose transactions fail through negligence, it is unlikely he will ever prosper. And in this, as some of you will know, I have already proved myself clairvoyant, in particular in the case of a fellow citizen who appeared scrupulous and diligent enough, who asked me to keep an eye on his warehouse and gave me the keys. I went to inspect it and it was awash with water because it was raining and there were holes in the roof; straight away, for all that he was a well-respected person, I said that he would soon be ruined, and I was right. Diligence therefore, in both the above situations, must be cultivated by the merchant.

And I am not talking of those clowns, who seem physically very busy, but are actually disorganised, and all their agitating of their hands and feet and running about is the result of weakness of mind, not natural impulse.

And application should be an attribute of the interior man, from which all mercantile aptitude stems, while promptness in manual things is appropriate to children and those who work with their hands. And the merchant should be diligent with his pen (f. 69'), both in writing up his activities in his notebooks, and in answering letters: no letter should lack a reply, however tiresome, because every letter contains something of use to you, either now or in the future. And this precept will not let you down: as Tully[3] says, there is no book so bad you cannot get something good from it, just as there is no letter which might not bring you some advantage, directly or indirectly.

Chapter VIII On the Merchant's Fluency of Action

A merchant should be fluent in his operations. And acting without awkwardness is always the sign of a balanced and well-organised mind; and every time you see someone writing with difficulty, praying in a forced

[3] Actually Pliny the Younger.

fashion, or generally doing what he has to in such a manner, you can surely say that he is inexpert in the matter, because facility derives from a good brain which has accustomed itself to the procedure in question and does it easily, without awkwardness. None the less there are always some who make more of a to-do about the hundred ducats they have invested in some particular merchandise, than others who have invested a thousand.

Some write as if the letters flowered in front of them with a rare elegance, while others sweat over a bill of exchange, and all this derives from the aptness or otherwise of their natural talent; and the philosophical explanation is ready to hand: "No harm will come from good habits" as Aristotle says. And in this respect a degree of gracefulness behoves a man: there are those in fact gifted with grace in some procedure and it seems that everything that issues from their hands is elegant and precise; while those who lack it labour to achieve a lesser result.

Chapter IX On the Merchant's Shrewdness

(f. 70) The shrewdness of a merchant, or his cunning, must be employed in moderation: he should neither hurt others nor allow himself to be got the better of, but manage to intuit where deceit and falsity lurk. And if a man is credulous or lacking in reasoning, he should not take up trade, because in this profession nowadays there are a thousand snares, frauds and deceits. And this guile, which is linked to fraud, should not be used even to a good end: "But we have renounced the hidden things of dishonesty, not walking in craftiness, nor handling the word of God deceitfully" (*2 Corinthians*, 4).

None the less it is as well to understand subtlety, so as not to be deceived: "To give subtelty to the simple" (*Proverbs*, 1). For from this subtlety, as St Thomas has it, derive fraud and deceit, and cunning tends to the bad, as the Philosopher says (VI° *Ethicorum*). And therefore Christ counsels us: "Be ye therefore wise as serpents", that is, do not let yourselves be seduced, "and innocent as doves".

And this as far as his actions are concerned, for within himself the merchant must always be virtuous, innocent and pure in heart, without even contemplating trickery, still less practising it.

Chapter X On the Civility of the Merchant

Since the merchant must be, more than the general run, a universal man, who contracting public and private relationships in the pursuit of an active life, must be full of civility, because in being a merchant he should not be detached from such things as belong to the public and the private life; he should be companionable, measured and full of piety and civility, as you will gather here and there in every part of our treatise; none the less there are some (f. 70'), indeed many, who make gold and silver their god, and pay no heed to their parents, their friends, or to seeking the best for their country, who do nothing to settle their sons or even their daughters; they have dedicated themselves to just the one goal, and in every other civil situation they appear loutish, interested only in accumulating money.

Such people should, on account of their avarice, be ejected from human society, like Crassus, and liquid gold and silver be poured down their throats saying: "You were thirsty for gold—drink it!" This is the avidity that is called, as St Thomas says, "insatiable desire for possession"; and it goes against charity towards one's neighbour, love of country and of God, and it has always been the case that any one who hoards in this way commits mortal sin.

A merchant should be urbane, moderate in regard to money with country, friends, children, parents, wife or servants, in fact, to each according to his position, and to the time and place, but also not denying himself his due: many in fact, being wrapped up in their own greed, in the end bore even themselves with their infinite, insatiable craving. These can be equated with the most brutish creatures, and I myself have known not a few.

Chapter XI On the Merchant's Sense of Fairness

Fairness, according to St Augustine, is rendering to each what is his, and this is a virtue that embraces many others. Therefore a merchant should always be concerned to render to each his due.

You should, without hesitation, point out when the other party is deceiving you, either miscalculating or speaking in an ambiguous manner during negotiations (f. 71). You should not forget what happened to that friend of yours: with the contract signed and the goods taken home, he realised that his partner had made a mistake in his accounting and the result was not just a ledger error but a real and irrevocable loss costing him three hundred ducats. Your friend called on him and returned the ducats to him, and the other had not even realised. A merchant's sense of fair play requires that he act in this way: uphold fairness towards others, not only in obvious matters, but also in concealed ones; and if you do not do this, I cannot call you fair.

You must be fair not only in managing money but also in delivering judgements, because it usually falls to merchants to be arbitrators; they must be ready to administer justice even on holidays, as and when men need them to, curtailing deferments, disallowing excuses, pointless appeals and deferrals; they must reject the disputations of lawyers and attorneys, put a limit on the proliferation of witnesses, but still collect necessary and legitimate evidence, resolving disputes simply and to general agreement, without the brouhaha and formality of a full trial, but respecting the essence of the truth. And all this is envisaged under the law *de iure et verbo, Si sepe, in Clementinis*.

And you must proceed carefully, because a man's capacity for judgement is easily corrupted in one of these four ways, that is, through fear, cupidity, hate or love, as we read in the axiom: "These four things, fear, hatred, pleasure and riches, are wont to corrupt the upright thoughts of men" (XI, q. III, *Quatuor*).

Chapter XII On the Steadfastness of the Merchant

A merchant must be steadfast in facing up to the both the reversals of fortune and the injustices that he may often (f. 71') be subject to. For this reason they used to say that the merchant must have four attributes: an ass's back for steadfastness, a pig's snout for sobriety, and a merchant's ear for patience and tolerance.

And note well that superficial and impatient merchants cannot be even considered merchants: a perfect example would be a blabbermouth, because generally blatherers have lightweight minds that fly away from them, and they all have a touch of madness.

Fickleness is a typically female fault, while steadfastness is a male virtue; furthermore, the merchant must always be steadfast and firm in his resolve, and not changeable and frivolous, as Seneca says in a letter to Lucilius: "The first indication of a sound mind is the ability to stay still in the same place, content in one's own company".

He must also be steadfast before the vicissitudes of fortune, as Boethius says[4]: "It is a characteristic of a strong and steadfast mind that it's possessor is not unsettled by adversity, nor will get above himself in prosperity".

Chapter XIII On the Presence of the Merchant

In virtue of the dignity that comes with his position, a merchant should also have presence and charisma, because these contribute greatly to his authority, particularly before foreigners who may turn up unexpectedly at any time. Bear in mind that authority and distinguished looks are the outward signs of the integrity within. Thus Aristotle, writing to Alexander, in tracing the most perfect natural physiognomy of a man, defines his idea of charisma: it must be evident in a man's face, in his voice and gestures, his good looks and poise, with which the Genoese are naturally gifted. And so, just as a calm demeanour and good looks are indicators of one

[4] Probably Cicero, *De officiis* I 80.

with an orderly mind, equally their lack in superficial men is an indicator of instability and frivolity.

And again when you see men who are careless with words, gestures, in voice and countenance, you will immediately know them to be weak-minded (f. 72); consequently and above all, when you see such men with their hats only half on their heads, “Since altars smoke”.[5]

And furthermore those who wear their hat or cap tilted over the eyes are arrogant and irascible; those who expose their foreheads and let the cap cover their neck are vain or in love; those who wear their headgear over one ear are extravagant, superficial, weak-brained, quarrelsome, presumptuous, boastful and without substance, and mostly talk nonsense and at length. Those on the other hand who wear their hats well set on their heads, centred, almost like a crown, are men with orderly minds, full of authority and modesty, “because virtue is an elective disposition that clings to the median”, Aristotle, II° *Ethicorum*.

Chapter XIV On the Merchant’s Generosity

We will next talk of the merchant’s generosity, and we will say that generosity is the virtue that distributes favours, which as affect we call benevolence, as effect, beneficence. This virtue consists in the giving or returning of assistance, so the merchant must be ready to remunerate with favours those from whom he has received them, and award them to others where it seems to him necessary.

As Seneca says, it behoves us not to be hard-hearted in this remuneration. None the less, my merchant, it is fitting that you distribute largesse generously, but not over-abundantly, and above all avoid doing so unnecessarily, as this is a virtue more appropriate to lords and men of importance than to merchants: in fact, just as it is the duty of lords to give, so it is that of the merchant to accumulate and hold on to wealth, for this is the goal of the merchant. But he should always be ready to return favours promptly, because (f. 72’) just as the merchant should pay

[5] “Quod altaria fumant”, in Latin in the original, is a citation from Vergilius, *Bucolica*, Egloga 1, that had become proverbial to show a spiritual emotion.

all his creditors on closure, without deferment, so he should return to everyone the favours they have given, without delay. In fact it is a sign of ingratitude to sit on a favour, and likewise to refuse to recompense those who have hesitated a good deal before helping you. One who has only offered tardily has clearly done so with reluctance, and the longer you delay the more gratitude you forfeit, and many would rather have you say no speedily, rather than receive a favour grudgingly given.

And be sure that the favour you do to one does nor entail doing harm to another, because what favours one person while harming another, is not a favour but fawning. And therefore, as Seneca[6] says, "One should try to practice a liberality that benefits many but harms no-one", not like that great multitude of merchants who engage in all kinds of usury and then build churches and hospitals.

Otherwise, when you do a favour, do not criticise the beneficiary or rub his nose in your generosity, for by doing so you will lose the merit of it, as Tully[7] says: "O arrogant pride, one can accept nothing from you, because you corrupt everything you give". When someone asks you for help, you should not refuse them with weasel words or some quibbling excuse, as Antigonus did, when the Cynic asked him for a talent, replying "It is more than a Cynic should ask for". And when the Cynic asked him instead for a denarius, replied "You cannot ask for anything that suits you". These were petty replies, as he could well afford either a talent or a denarius, being a king.

Alexander did the opposite: when he had given a whole city to a poor man who asked alms of him, and the man had said "Sire, a city is not suitable for me and my low estate", Alexander replied: "I was not thinking of what it is appropriate for you to receive, but of what it is appropriate for me to give".

And (f. 73) be sure, if you have done a favour to an ingrate, not to complain about him, because if he does not behave as we had hoped, that is because we are different from him, a we showed by giving in the first place.

---

[6] Rightly: Cicero, *De officiis* I 43.

[7] Rightly: Seneca, *De beneficiis* II 13.

Let the merchant be open-handed in his giving, and not rigid in expecting something back. See to it that others are always in your debt rather than you in theirs: if one proves ungrateful he does not offend me, so much as himself. And we were able to observe, thanks to my long acquaintance with his court, how that divine and glorious prince, Alfonso King of Aragon, such was his great generosity, never allowed himself to be outdone in courtesy. And therefore, out of his greatness of soul, he was wont to raise up men of low condition and make them officials and functionaries of his kingdom, so that his liberality was reflected by them, since none of these beneficiaries could claim to have earned their position through their own merits, but only through the great generosity of their sovereign. And, from his commitment to this virtue, he preferred to reward those who were worthy of it, rather than those who seemed to him born and shaped for preferment, and many who failed to understand this would censure him for it. And I never failed to note his inexhaustible thirst for generosity, which came quite naturally to him, so that he was himself generosity in person.

And your own generosity should be different with those who are cast down by fortune and are in need, than with those who are already well enough off but wish to do even better. And it is better to reward the good than the rich, because the rich do not require favours, hence the saying of Themistocles: "I prefer a man in need of money to money in need of a man".

Chapter XV On the Merchant's Composure

Tranquillity of mind is a virtue that becomes every sort of man, but a merchant above all; and all composed people, (f. 73') you may be sure have a good physical constitution and a good disposition of the positive humours, and consequently they are happy, joyful men, in peace with themselves and with others, friends to all, not envious or calculating or prejudiced, nor vindictive, nor suspicious, nor avaricious, not usurers nor wicked men, all evil inclinations that you find in constantly gloomy types, with low foreheads, eyes always fixed on the ground.

These are the most vicious of men: they are always thinking the worst and doing harm, and they are extremely covetous in relation to others, both for themselves and their families. You should beware even of conversing with them, as among other things they are liars and charlatans; just as on the outside they seem always pained and melancholy, so on the inside their hearts are sly, and in many places men on of this type are extremely unwelcome, like in France, Germany, Hungary, etc., where they are always laughing, joking, singing and dancing and melancholy types are ill thought of and those peoples avoid having to do with them.

I say to you that servants of God, merchants, gentlemen, men-at-arms, nobles and men of other ranks should be entertaining and joyful and tranquil in their minds. You can be sure that a merchant with a confused and embittered soul will not, and cannot, give good advice and take sound decisions, because this disposition increases evil humours and suppresses the intelligence and the phlegmatic humour, and dulls the wits. Let the choleric humour and high blood play their part, and be cheerful and calm in the face of prosperity and adversity.

Men of this sort will live long and well, and decide on all matters clear-headedly. And you knew my forebear, Stano, who at ninety-six years old (f. 74) got by chance a bad hernia. I took him to the doctor, who was amazed at his age, given that he was so flourishing and happy that he had not a line on his face and could pass for a man of forty. When asked what had kept him in such a florid state he replied: "Notwithstanding the many and various misfortunes that have befallen my children, I have never allowed myself to be disturbed by them, nor allowed myself to be idle; and another thing: I have never risen from the table glutted". Thus the doctor was able to see that the composure afforded by well-balanced mind had prolonged his life.

And every man therefore, from his earliest youth, must take good care not to acquire a negative attitude, for as Seneca says: "What has become once and for all rooted and innate, can at best be attenuated, but not completely expunged by ingenuity".

Chapter XVI On the Merchant's Modesty

Turning next to the modesty and uprightness of the merchant, we will say that it behoves the merchant, more than all other men to honest and thoroughly upright: just as in his enterprises and his day-to-ray activities he must excel above other men, so he should excel in modesty and personal honesty.

I say that in his home as much as outside it, equally with his parents, his friends and companions, as with his children, his wife, his servants male and female, and lastly out in the world of men, the merchant should behave like a young damsel or a monk. And the Romans would live by the same rule: even fathers would not take their sons with them to the baths, as Valerius Maximus narrates, to avoid displaying their nudity before their children. And the same goes for many countries today, and the least respect for proper behaviour we find in Italy, where they not only regularly (f. 74') go to the baths with their sons, and mothers with their daughters, but the men think nothing of appearing in front of their fathers and sons, even women, without their trousers and in short tunics; but they also have an unconstrained manner of using certain loose and low expressions, and in some areas references to parts of the body which it is shameful to name.

In as far as this goes I must praise our own language which, as you know, makes use of nothing untoward, nor indeed expressions blaspheming God and his saints, and if it is absolutely necessary to name something shameful we decorously use the cleanest of synonyms, so that 'pants' become 'underclothes' etc. Among the Italians only the Genoese avoid immodest speech, never using an inappropriate word. As Dante said of them "Ah, the Genoese! Perverse[8] men with their beautiful manners and full share of flaws". He allows them their good manners, which are advantageous to the merchant, who should be calm and polite in his speech and movement, in conversing with others and all the other practices of human society, taking their example from that noble Caesar, who even on the point of death, stabbed twenty-three times, covered his private parts so that they would not

[8] Actually *diversi* = 'different', that is 'inhuman'.

be displayed to all men. And praising him, Valerius Maximus says: "O Caesar, even dying you showed how we should venerate our decency".

Chapter XVII On the Praiseworthy Personal Attributes of the Merchant

Now that we have spoken on the particular virtues a merchant should have in relation to his public life, we will next talk of the praiseworthy attributes a merchant should have in himself. Above all, he should be a sociable man and adroit in conversation, at least with the (f. 75) good, rather than the wicked; he should be amiable and benevolent, fashioned pleasingly of human clay. Her must be agreeable with all, and, especially when buying and selling, cheerful and good-humoured.

He must be splendid, as the aspiration to glory tends to make a man morally pure and contemptuous of vice.

He must be chaste, lying only with his wife, because coitus ruins both the pocket and the person, and diminishes the intellect. And I know from the account of Angelo de Conti that a certain gentleman in Venice married and died in the same year. As the doctors were unable to identify his illness, they performed an autopsy: in his skull there was no brain at all, from which they deduced that his death was caused by coitus. Which is why you will find many lunatics and brainless types who have given themselves entirely to the pleasures of the flesh.

He must be regular in his gait, without waving his hands and feet about and making his person ridiculous, as many have the habit of doing, all of them superficial men with no depth to them.

He must be morally solid and mature, without any superficiality.

He must be able to get on with every sort of person, to engage with the great and the small, with gentlemen, lords, and men of standing, but equally with artisans, peasants and porters; and conversely he must not be irascible, vindictive, arrogant, argumentative, fickle, a buffoon, empty, spendthrift, without substance, a drunkard or a glutton.

Finally many a vice, which would be just about pardonable in others, to the merchant is never so, nowhere and in no circumstance.

Chapter XVIII On the Merchant's Temperance

In concluding this book we will speak of temperance, which is the highest of virtues and brings (f. 75') with it many others. First of all it must be measured against both prosperous and adverse circumstances, a variation which a merchant will experience more often than others, indeed almost continually: in prosperity one should not exult, nor in adversity be cast down, as we have already said, following Boethius.[9] And every temperament should find its proper mean, which is where virtue lies, as Aristotle in IIº *Ethicorum* says: "Virtue is an elective disposition that clings to the median".

Secondly, the merchant should be moderate in his eating and drinking, for the end of such excess is drunkenness, which is much more damaging to a merchant than to others, because a merchant is a more public person than others, for they, having debauched themselves, can avoid meeting with anybody, and get over their hangover in private, whereas a merchant must continually appear in public and cannot hide his state which, apart from being dishonourable, can also be harmful to his accounting, his buying and his selling, because he may make errors that could be very damaging to him.

A merchant should therefore avoid eating too much and above all drinking too much, because it is an affliction extremely harmful too him, for as well as the disgrace, which one should steer well clear of, listlessness will follow, dulling of the brain, drowsiness, swelling of the tongue and eventually any number of infirmities, like gout, pains in the sides or the stomach, fever, dropsy, leprosy and many other diseases highly troublesome to any human being, but to a merchant more than most. And of this affliction, the Apostle says: "Do not intoxicate yourselves with wine, for lust dwells there". And among doctors they say: "Gluttony has killed more than the sword". Aquinas listed five kinds of greed: the first

[9] Again, probably Cicero, *De officiis* I 80.

when one eats before the proper hour; the second when one wants one food after another; the third, when one demands refined food; the fourth when one wants an excessive quantity; and the fifth when eats untidily and drinks avidly and without manners.

But remember that Augustine adds that everything should be treated reasonably, that is, bearing in mind what is suitable to the place the time and the person; and we should not censure unthinkingly, because it may well be that a wise man will eat fine food without culpable greed and voracity (f. 76), while the fool overheat himself with common foodstuffs, engulfed by the vicious flames of greed. And everyone should be content to eat fish, like Our Lord, rather than lentils, like Esau, or barley, like a horse (*distinctio* XLI, *Quisquis*).

The merchant should therefore, for the reasons given, be moderate in his eating and drinking. Nor should he value food other than for maintaining the body, because, as Boethius says, "Nature is content with little or with the minimum". Nor should you be like those who, as St Paul says "make a god of their stomachs and find glory in carousing", because no good can come from gluttony, but every sort of shameful activity and debilitating lust.

Thirdly, a merchant should be measured in his speech and not talk too much; in fact talking too much is not only reprehensible in all men, but chiefly in merchants, in that for others it is inadvisable in relation to their good standing, but to the merchant also in relation to his profits. Verbosity has in fact very often cost a merchant dear, because it cuts off the possibility of his partners giving you advice, which will end up by harming him, (f. 76') if not straight away, then eventually. For keeping silent never hurt anyone, but talking has harmed many.

It is true that a prudent man should not remain silent always, but should speak at the appropriate time and place, as the circumstances require, and above all bearing in mind five things. Firstly, you must consider well what you have to say, because you should be wary of saying things unconnected to the preceding conversation, or irrelevant, vile, vain, obnoxious or dishonest things, unworthy of your station.

Secondly, you should understand when not to interpose your opinion into the conversation of others; rather than interrupting, wait until it seems to be your turn, because at the right moment your contribution will be listened to and taken into consideration. You should not behave as so many do in our country, seven of whom will talk at the same time and everyone grasps what they can.

Thirdly, you must be aware of how much you are talking, because you will have to end your speech at some point. Do not be prolix, leave room for others, do not be always wanting to speak yourself, for that is how animals behave. And when you do speak, do not let your prolixity get away with you, starting from the creation of the world to narrate the history of Troy, as Cicero[10] puts it. Your argument should be clear, lucid and brief, but not so brief as to be obscure, as the poet says: "If I struggle for brevity, I end with obscurity".

Fourthly, you should consider to whom you are speaking. This means you should not always answer everyone, nor be influenced by their station, but you should always try to respect others, because this is decorous and costs you nothing, and the honour you do to another reflects on yourself, as Aristotle said: "Honour belongs to the honourer" (f. 77).

Fifthly, you should know how to speak. This is a large subject, and as Cicero has taken the trouble to write a book on it, I will not expatiate to you here, not least because I have already said that a merchant should study rhetoric, but I will say a few words for the uninstructed, many that they are.

You must present your address with as much charm as you can, both as regards your voice, your appearance, your gestures and your reasonableness.

Voice: you should be soft-spoken, and according to the gravity or otherwise of your material, modulate into harsh, pitying, proud, delicate, etc.

Appearance: you should not move your head about, nor your eyes, mouth, hands or feet, but keep still and let just your tongue work, giving your other members a rest.

Gestures: in facial expressions, movements of the mouth and other gestures that accompany speech, some men are naturally more graceful than others, but a man can mould his nature and show himself to be of benevolent stuff and as agreeable-looking as he can manage.

---

[10] Actually Horace, *Ars poetica* 25–26.

Reasonableness may be accompanied either by a winning or an austere manner, because moderation of speech and earnest reasoning are attractive attributes in mature men, and even more so in the young, and they are rare indeed those who are knowledgeable, as Petrarch says: "Rare are the types of men who are gifted with knowledge at a young age", but blessed those few to whom such a talent is given.

Sixthly, a merchant should also practise moderation in his trading, that is, in his buying and selling, in his shipping and in whatever way he chooses to pursue his calling, because whenever you come across superficial souls, avid for enterprise, who want to catch every bird on the wing, you may presume them close to ruin and should avoid becoming embroiled with them. Pay attention rather to those that act with restraint, that is within the limits that they feel their assets will permit, and moderating (f. 77') their activities. And when they come to propose their projects to you, do not refuse to examine them closely and put yourself to realising them, but agree only to those that your business can digest, and do not fill your stomach with the risk of failure and ruin: these things you will learn with experience.

Seventhly, the merchant should be temperate in love and friendship. Ours is an occupation that is not compatible with too many friendships with men or women, fleeting or intimate, as with women, priests, friars, wanderers, lords and poor men, or men who when they owe you cannot pay. For if someone becomes intimate with you, you are obliged to help them, and if you do so, you will lose by it. If you help him, you will make an enemy of him, because at when settlement day comes, your or your employees' promptness in requesting it will weigh on him and turn him against you. The merchant therefore should have many acquaintances and few friends, even if the term 'friend' is one we use too freely, because one finds very few true friends, though many call themselves such, and would be more appropriately called 'acquaintances'.

Try not to accept others' money as security, or to make loans: it is better to blush once than blanch a hundred times. And so, now that we have added temperance to the other virtues and other accomplishments enumerated in this work, those who have followed us thus far will truly be able to call themselves merchants.

Here ends the third book on the art of trade by Benedetto Cotrugli.

Part 4: On the Economic Virtues of the Merchant

Exordium

(f. 78) As we have now dealt with the material of our first three books in accordance with our design, we will follow them with a further discussion, in this fourth book, on the manner in which a merchant should conduct himself with regard to the economics and administration of his household and family. And this is no less worthy of a merchant's attention than his public life, following the saying of Valerius Maximus: "Of what use is valour far from our country, if we live badly within it?" And likewise Aristotle held that the father in every house should be regarded as "king of his household", because just as a king must govern his realm, so the father of a family must govern and have care of that family. And no small care, because many, from neglect, have incurred great shame and contempt, so that it were better they had been killed. For the same reason, Ockham would have it that, just as a father should be governor of his family in spiritual matters, he should also discipline their behaviour. And if he does not do this he is worse than the infidels. Hence St Paul's saying (1 Timothy, 5) "But if any provide not for his own, and specially

C. Carraro, G. Favero (eds.), *Benedetto Cotrugli – The Book of the Art of Trade*, DOI 10.1007/978-3-319-39969-0_7

for those of his own family, he hath denied the faith, and is worse than an infidel"; *di.* XLVII, *Necesse est.*, and the chapter *Quantum libet*. And on the same theme we learn from the Philosopher in *Economicis*: "It is incumbent on every living man both in private and in public to show a proper care towards all, to gods and to men, but particularly towards his wife, his children and his parents".

And therefore, just as we have already said many times that the merchant should not dedicate himself (f. 78') to a single endeavour because he will become no more than a crude instrument useful for nothing else, so I say that he should not be intent on merely accumulating money but must look to the running of his family and acquire houses and possessions, because he can never know what fate might have in store for him. Indeed it is an essential good that he have a house and assets, as Aristotle says, citing Hesiod's pronouncement according to which the father of a family should have a house, a wife and an ox to plough his fields. And therefore I call the merchant who has nothing but money a gambler, because should he lose his cash, which is something we see often enough, he will have to dig ditches.

Therefore the merchant, while he is steadily making money, must set aside some part of his profit and invest it in solid things, because, my dear merchant, every rational man must do all the things he does with some end in view; but if your only aim is continually piling up riches on riches, so that if you lived for a thousand years you would accomplish nothing else, I should think you an animal, a beast without a brain, and no man, and your accretions would be those of the rich man "who was buried in hell" (Luke, 16) for as the Evangelist says: "It is easier for a camel to go through the eye of a needle, than for a rich man to enter into the kingdom of God, etc." because you are rich only in your infinite greed.

The merchant, as you know, must practice his trade to meet his needs, but he who does this in the manner we have said, is always in a state of sin, as Alexander of Hales has argued; and at times it can be best to retire (f. 79) from the game at its peak, without seeing the matter through to its end, as you will often wish to do, but may not be able to. Therefore stop on the crest of the wave and do not wait until the last moment, which may even bring you to poverty.

Chapter I On the House

The first condition the dedicated family man should respect is that the house which serves as their habitation should reflect well on all of them, and that house should meet the following conditions. First, it should be conveniently sited near the places where his business is conducted, at the Rialto in Venice, in the West generally the *Loggia*, in Florence, Naples and many other cities where the banks are, in Milan at the *Tocco,* in many other places the main square; and this adjacency is for the convenience of the merchant, because often he must go there, or send someone, at all speed, for sometimes not to act speedily will lose him the tastiest morsel, not least because it is common practice among merchants to snatch such morsels from their fellows' mouths.

Second, it should have an entrance worthy of your standing, for the strangers that come visiting who know you only by reputation: a handsome house will earn you much credit.

Third, it should have on the first floor an office space suitable for your needs and welcoming, with places to sit on every side, and sufficiently secluded not to upset the household with the frequent presence of strangers come to reckon up with you.

Fourth, it should have a spacious and bright dining-hall, so that in the summer the closeness of the air will not drive you out to the country, which is the ruin of all business and a general forfeiture of gain.

Fifth, it should have (f. 79') well-decorated and orderly bedrooms, suitable to your station, without excess.

Sixth, it should have an ample and well-lit kitchen to make meals near to the room of the servants.

Seventh, it should have storerooms on the ground floor, such as cellars for wine, depositories for wood, stabling for horses.

Eighth, it should have further storerooms on the upper floors, such as granaries for corn, larders for bread, cheese, preserved meats, vegetables and other provisions, and all under lock and key.

Ninth, it must have separate rooms for the servants so that they do not mix with the women of the house, without ready access from one part to another.

Tenth, it should have latrines or water closets for the hygiene of the household, and facilities for throwing out dirty water.

Eleventh, there should be water in the house and washrooms so that the servants do not need to leave the house to wash or for other reasons.

Twelfth, it should have open spaces that receive the sunshine, where the washing can be dried; good solid doors, and secure locks everywhere; and whoever delights in literature should not have to keep their books in the common writing areas, but should have a little desk of their own either in their bedroom or at least nearby, where they can study when they have spare time, which is a most honourable activity and worthy of glorification.

Chapter II On the Villa

The head of the household should besides have a villa in the country, or, if he possibly can, two villas of different types: one to generate profit and income and maintain the family, and in this case you need not worry how far it is from the city, as only its profitability concerns you; none the less these holdings are useful when the metropolitan air is dangerous and infected, and the further off they are, the better they serve this purpose. The second villa (f. 80) should be for the pleasure and refreshment of your family, as long as you do not go often yourself, because frequenting the countryside distracts men from their business; and this villa will also help you realise the aims to which this work is tending, as we will make clear at its close and conclusion.

The first villa-farm is useful to the merchant in so far as it represents income and not outlay; the second, used in moderation will allow him to revive his spirits and make him more alert in his dealings. In both cases however, make use of good managers and do not be constantly checking on them, because in the long run, when the time for your retirement comes, you will make up for it.

Look to your business interests while you are in your prime, because the earth is our mother and dedicating ourselves to her we gain such a kind of wealth that almost takes us out of ourselves and little by little we abandon all other activities which become burdensome to us, which is why Virgil sings of "Happy harvests", because they make a man truly happy. And if you have the means to allow you to buy more villas, buy them for profitability and not for show, as I would always advise in or outside the city, and now you know what you need to know of this word 'villa'.

Chapter III On a Man as Administrator of His Household

And as we have dealt with the administration of the life of a household, it seems natural to speak next of its administrator, who should first of all be a man and make himself obeyed by his wife, his children and the rest of the family, servants included, which is why they say: "It is a sad house where the cock is silent and the hen crows". See to it that you are a cock (f. 80') and not a hen, that you wear the trousers, and that your conduct seem, on occasions, to be fearsome, even if you are not so, and otherwise pleasant, so as to live cheerfully and render your house cheerful; and above all you must take care that your family not know your true nature, for as soon as they know it, you are undone. And for this a degree of sagacity will be necessary, indeed I who write to you am unsure if I have enough.

You must be respectable, mannerly and honest and see to it that your family learn correct behaviour from your example rather than your instruction, as one learns better from actions than from words.

Rise earlier than others in the morning and go to bed later, and amuse yourself every fortnight or so by inspecting the whole house, checking every corner, above and below, including where the servants sleep; and pick up on every omission and always find something to straighten out or have another adjust, so that they will fear your unannounced visits and keep things tidy.

None the less, to some are given many gifts, almost by divine intercession, both in regard to management capacity, and in regard to their outward appearance, which in exceptional cases owes much to the heavens, as Pacatus Drepanius said, addressing the emperor Theodosius. It is certain in fact that a handsome appearance in one who governs a household confers a certain authority on him in front of his family, no less than the handsome aspect of an emperor, as Solinus says of Alexander of Macedon, who showed in his countenance the integrity and nobility of his heart.

Similarly, Augustus was superior in appearance (f. 81) to other men, high forehead, smiling eyes, bright cheeks, whose rosiness beguiled all who saw him; nor were the general lines of his body without majesty, so that he earned the goodwill of well-disposed men no less from his attractive appearance than from the doctrines of Aristotle and Callisthenes, his teachers. And we read similar things of Hercules, of Caesar, of Trajan and of many other noble and excellent emperors and caesars. And if your bodily proportions are not ideal, you must do your best to overcome nature, just as many have acquired by ingenuity what was denied them by nature, as is gossiped even of Aristotle, though I can no reliable written confirmation of this.

And when necessary, you should reprimand your family with harsh words, appropriate to the place and time, and with the stick on occasion, but without losing your temper: do it to educate and not in anger, as we read of Plato who said to the servant who had erred: “I would strike you, if I were not angry”.

And we will leave here our discussion of a man in his house to proceed with the rest of our work, and speak instead of the merchant’s clothes and finery.

Chapter IV On Clothes and Ornaments

The first clothes were to be found in our Earthly Paradise, made simply of sheepskin, to cover their private parts when our ancestors first knew nakedness after the Fall, as we read in Genesis. At that time they made knee-length garments to clothe themselves, which is a habit still followed in some places. Then, gradually, superior apparel (f. 81’) was created for various solemn ends: the Romans wore the toga, those at least who were of honourable status and entrusted with the administration of the state; knights and citizens wore gold rings, freed men silver ones, slaves iron, as

Isidorus Hispalensis describes in his *Ethimologiarum*. Then, as the Paduan Livy relates, when the Romans were defeated in Puglia by Hannibal at Cannae, the Roman women went to the Senate carrying their jewellery in their skirts, giving everything towards avenging that defeat. In their honour a public law was passed permitting women to wear gold and precious stones as much as they wished.

With the passage of time, as happens in many other areas, modern men have abused and corrupted every distinction of style and dignity, so that one can no longer tell the plebeian from the gentleman, the merchant from the lord, indeed, which is worse, counts and lords have now moderated their dress and reduced it to the appropriate minimum, while the plebs have given vent to such sumptuousness and refinement of dress that they might seem counts themselves, did not their natural appearance betray them; not for nothing does the well-known Illyrian proverb say: "If the goat claimed not to be a goat, his horns would give him away". And if you look at a plebeian couple, got up in their finery, their very clothes seem to accuse them: the more sumptuous they are, the more their wearers seem apes in fancy dress. Whereas when you see a gentleman in a simple cape or a lady in a *dobletto*, you will still observe their (f. 82) nobility. And it seems that, while rich ornamentation does nothing for the presumptuous plebeian, the modest look well in everything, as we have seen in the previous chapter and elsewhere in this work.

Good looks are a great gift from Heaven, and are the first grace a man receives, being fixed from the moment of conception, whether by the will of Heaven, or from heredity, God being always the first cause. And if our modern world is broken and corrupt, it is because, just as the brute beasts must behave each according to his kind, so should men observe their separate distinctions, and give to each his due, as good order requires.

For which reason many merchants are deserving of censure who have introduced inappropriate practices into many countries, and into Italy in particular, whereby they dress more sumptuously than counts aspire to, or kings even. Certainly in our own times two princes have condemned such abuses, the Emperor Sigismund of Luxemburg and my own divine lord Alfonso, King of Aragon etc.

And to make myself clear I will speak of the second, who wore clothes of light wool, brushed silk, black damask and only very rarely smooth velvets, usually preferring plain woollen clothes, which became the fashion not only in the fortunate city of Naples, but throughout the kingdom, and in a large part of Italy, so that it seemed to me a general demonstration of sobriety to see all those gentlemen with such tunics and with silk slippers and cloaks of light cloth, particularly those of moderate length. I am not speaking of certain pea-brains (f. 82') who exaggerated with ultra-short costumes. His divine majesty always wore his below the knee, which seemed to me a sure demonstration of humanity, mildness, good manners and modesty. But I know and have seen, for I have travelled to many places, in Italy and elsewhere, which I will not name so as not attract censure or to irritate anyone, that in many esteemed cities they dress in a manner deviating completely from every accepted usage appropriate to the public or the private man, that is, everyone from gentleman to jester and labourers too, dress up from head to toe, and, not content with that, sport also great capacious sleeves. And these costumes are from the thinnest cloth, or silk lined with pine marten, sable, taffetas, gossamer silk, and other luxurious linings; and I tell you that they weigh many pounds and then when those sleeves are humped on the shoulders the wearer seems a *portatore* as they say in Florence, or *fachino* in Venice or *bastagio* as we say, in short a baggage carrier or porter; or else a seller of women's clothes, as women are wont to wear such things, which suit them, and they find it harder to do without vanity and luxury.

And having seen so many people in so many different guises, and having studied law and men's rights, and having mused on the contrast between people and their distinctiveness, I believe I have seen donkeys saddled as racehorses, I have seen Sir Fog: as Boccaccio had it, "Porcograsso and Vindaciena",[1] because we are a long way here from civility and moderation, this is not genial, earnest, modest, human behaviour, (f. 83) nor observant, religious, magnanimous, measured, wise, diligent, moderate, benign, but against all morality and good practice, since a man in his sober and civil dealings should never exceed the moderation appropriate to our nature. I am not saying that no one should ever dress with any

[1] The citation is from the novel about Simone, Bruno and Buffalmacco, the ninth in the eigth day in Giovanni Boccaccio, *Decameron*. In Boccaccio's text, it reads "Porcograsso e Vannacena" (literally, "fatpig and gotodinner") and is a gross mispronunciation of the names of the philosophers Ippocrasso (or Ippocrates) and Avicenna.

show of dignity, but it ought always to be done in moderation, because if princes wear damasks and velvet, you have no reason to wear sackcloth.

I would add that there are many (and God knows that I speak the truth, because I have seen them) who own nothing but what they stand up in and their household furnishings, and who live on what they earn day by day. For this reason, my dear merchant, dear citizen, I tell you that light clothes should be enough for you, of any colour but scarlet, which is reserved for doctors in token of their office, and for women on account of their delicacy, for which we pardon them many things, and for knights on account of their position. Any other colour will be seemly on you, barring yellow or bright blue or other such frivolous or buffoonish hues. Because just as dark colours are indicative of seriousness, so bright colours are indicative of frivolity and madness. Dark colour is a sign of a serious and reliable man, as nature dictates.

I am not saying that velvet or damask coats are not entirely suitable, but go no further than that. Do not get yourself up in silk, or you will look like a monkey in fancy dress or a king bee. Make it your choice to dress cleanly, simply and elegantly, because it is certain that two external things reveal the inner man, as Seneca (f. 83') said: "From outward actions we can judge the inner inclinations", that is, dress and effective deeds, because whenever you see one decked out in frivolous colours, or with quarterings and fringes and excessive ornament, you can be sure his soul is likewise fancily caparisoned.

And those belonging to a faction will wear the uniform of that faction, and those who inherit none from their predecessors will seek new ornaments. Whereas those who dress with moderation have well-balanced souls. Similarly those who when building divide their houses into a warren of little rooms and corridors, have convoluted and fragmented souls; and those that put up solid and stable buildings have stable and solid souls, and so on.

For myself, I admire a cloak that does not exceed a proper length, below the knee that is, and a tunic that is comfortable and not overflowing heavily and inappropriately at the sides: you must be master of your clothes and not they of you. I favour black, or a deep red cut with a darker red, soled hose or shoes, as appropriate.

As far as the head is concerned, think first of your health and wear sensible hoods or caps or berets, because a host of illnesses derive from ill humours from the unprotected head. Pay no attention to the crowd, but look after your own life and health, and avoid above all what can be harmful to you. And you, you idiot, with your long wide sleeves scraping the ground: not content with seeming a priest of Hercules, must you wear sleeves so heavy you must carry them on your shoulders? Between you and a maniac the only difference is this: the maniac is mad all the time, and you only on holidays, when you pile your finery on your shoulders.

And if you want to understand what is reasonable, imagine (f. 84) if it were only you to parade in front of the populus got up like this, and you had no other like-minded dolts for company, how all the children would run after you, and you would seem a hawker of women's dresses. And I don't want you to take Pyrrhus[2] as an excuse who dressed in the clothes of his beloved Deidamia: he did that in the throes of love, which is blind. But for you who are a merchant and not in love, it is not seemly, because these are women's clothes by ancient tradition, and it may be there was one who for love of his beloved began to do this, and others followed him, one after another, like sheep, in defiance of all taste and good sense. And that is enough on the subject of reasonable dress for the merchant.

Chapter V On Tableware and Furnishings

Massaria (tableware) derives from 'excess', because in many parts of Italy, and Venice in particular, *massa* means 'too much'; but the merchant should not burden himself with an overabundance of tableware and furnishings, but should have only the amount necessary for his use of them, according to his economic possibilities. There are many who take such pleasure in their furnishings that they dedicate all their time and money to them.

And if, from some particular compulsion, you cannot avoid a degree of abundance and excess, choose silverware and other goods whose value can be realised if necessary. And, as I have already said, the merchant

[2] Properly Achilles.

should have sufficient ornament in his household, which should be clean and tidy and well organised, because many foreigners (f. 84') will call on a merchant's house in the course of their business which takes them hither and thither.

Chapter VI On His Wife

Although we have already written an autonomous work on the theme *De Uxore Ducenda*, dedicated—as you will know—to Messer Volce de Baballio, in which we have discoursed at some length, in the Latin tongue, of all the matters in which a wife should obey, of her duties, of the education of her children, and of all the instructions that ought to be followed by each member of the household, we will none the less, in so far as this chapter requires us to touch on the same material, make a few further observations. The philosopher Theophrastus wrote a book *On Marriage*, in which he maintains that a man who wants to take a wife should be wise, rich, healthy and young and that these are the necessary preconditions for marrying. And if these, or some of them, are not present, he should not take a wife.

And similarly the woman should be comely, well-mannered, of respectable parents; and I have not said rich, unlike the majority of today's young who look for wealth rather than a wife and then find once the knot is tied they do not get on with her at home. There are then three qualities one should seek in a woman: the first is that most honourable of qualities which is virtue. The second is assets, being a dowry or inheritance or wealth: these you should not seek but if they come together with a dowry of honest virtues, I would certainly not say they are to be discounted. The third is the quality that delights the eye, that is, beauty, which is a gift of God to its possessor: but beauty fades with (f. 85) time, because all women become old and ugly, and if you have chosen a wife on account of her beauty, when that passes, so will your love, and the same is true of her assets.

But virtue, the first quality I cited, which I called the most honourable, lasts forever, and lives as long as its possessor, and never fades. This is the endowment and dowry you should wish for, as Seneca says: "The honesty and loyalty of a wife, her modesty and manners are what should give pleasure to her husband: the only lasting qualities are those of the mind and the spirit, which owe nothing to outside influences: whereas each passing day gathers in the flowers of beauty".

Be careful therefore and choose well, and take for a wife a woman who has a dowry of the spirit, that is, virtue, which, as Cicero said, is not annihilated by fire or by shipwreck, nor by any turn of fortune, and do not confuse a transitory good with a permanent one.

A woman should be prudent, steady, sincere, patient, studious, human, modest, compassionate, devout, religious, generous, equable, demure, diligent, sober, abstemious, wise and industrious and constantly occupied with work, because there are two things that often cause a woman to go astray, idleness and poverty; and both these things can be avoided by keeping active because while a woman is working, first she is not idle, which can lead to romance and venery, as Petrarch says of the preconditions of love: "fed by idleness and human lust". And St Jerome: "See that the devil finds you always busy, etc." Secondly, as long as she is working she will not end up in poverty and will always be in funds; and it is surely one of the things most (f. 85') necessary to a woman that she always has and keeps at something to occupy her hands, and therefore even the Emperor Octavian had his daughters learn to spin, weave and sew and other womanly skills, with silk or gold or flax; and when asked why he did this, he replied that for all that he was ruler of the world, he could never be sure that his daughters might not one day be in need, so he insisted on this so that they could always earn a living. Besides, while they are vulnerable, they should always be occupied to preserve their good name.

A woman should attend to her appearance, according to her station, both in regard to her clothes and jewellery and in keeping her body neat and clean, but in no circumstances should she paint her face as they do in many parts of Italy, in Greece and in Catalonia. Thanks be to God that this is not done in our city, as it is forbidden and a sin that goes beyond many of the word's dishonesties. And if you have the misfortune to come across a man who makes up his face or hair such as I have seen, avoid him like a demon from hell: he might have all the wisdom of Solomon, but he will prove be an idiot none the less, according to Ovid's saying: "Let young men that get themselves up as women steer clear of us". And

Martial Cocus,[3] writing to his friend Licinus[4] who anointed his grey hair to dye it back to black: "To pass yourself off as a young man, Licinus, you have now dyed your hair; from one moment to the next you're a raven from having been a swan. But you won't put it over everyone: Proserpine knows you're white, and she herself will strip the mask from your face". Avoid therefore mixing with such men, for they have no wisdom or brains in their heads. And when a husband and wife are both quarrelsome, they will never be at peace or lead tranquil lives.

When a merchant takes a wife (f. 86) he should admonish her from the outset and establish the manner and rules of their life together in the first year of marriage; and he ought not to loosen the reins but keep a good grip on them, and not allow her to win in any disagreement, and caress her regularly and with a delicate hand as you would a hawk, so as to train it to your will.

See to it that she loves you, but also fears and honours you, and do not stoop to an excess of harshness, as Aristotle insists in his Politics taking as example the continual administering of a medicine that ends up becoming just another foodstuff; likewise continual criticism can become a fixed thing and no longer corrects effectively and ceases to be teaching, becoming a joke and a game.

And make sure things do not get to the point that you have to raise your hand against her, for as soon as you lay a finger on her you will be in difficulty. Be aware that women have different natures: for some kind words are best, and these will be noble creatures brought up with delicacy and grace by their fathers at home. Harshness would be pointless with them, because their very nature is disdainful of harsh words or blows. And, given the nobility of their characters, you will rarely find that they do not fear and honour you, for in them a good upbringing and the best manners are united: lucky the man who has found one such, because in the majority of cases they are a treasure.

There are others who need to be cowed with a frown, and these are by their natures shrinking and timid: there tends to be little substance

[3] The Latin poet Martial (Marcus Valerius Martialis) was known in the Middle Ages only through anthologies including some of his epigrams, and sometimes cited as Martialis Cocus, as Cotrugli does here.

[4] Actually Letinus.

to them and they are unintelligent and learn with difficulty. And such women must be educated with a degree of cunning, you must give them freedom and encourage their initiative, encourage them with loving caresses, and loosen the reins a touch, as a horse-breaker will when he wants a yearling to walk on, which he does by easing the bridle; and you must lead them at the right moment and place, not neglecting the spur, and this requires (f. 86') considerable finesse, as you will know who have done it. And these are women who have lived in their father's houses in a state of fear with no sort of measured or sensible education, and I tell you that the younger ones need to closely followed if they are to become able, reliable and wise.

Some are proud and fractious and in their father's houses they have been brought up in a squalid and disorderly fashion and roughly, rubbing shoulders with the servants, from whom they pick up any number of bad habits. These, as soon as they have arrived at their husband's house, believe themselves transferred from a prison to a castle, and with their overbearing and arrogant ways they think themselves great ladies, like slaves suddenly given freedom, they seize the reins and give orders haughtily. These need to be severely admonished from the outset and threatened with slaps; they must be made to show affection and threatened with disdain, and finally, if they will not be corrected, you may fall back on the stick, but this should be the very last resort.

And if ill-luck should force you so far, keep it hidden, so that it remains a secret, because there a few things more deleterious to a man of a certain standing than being known to beat his wife, for women are delicate and inferior creatures, defective men, as Aristotle says; for nature always tries to produce a man, but sometimes, due to an innate defect or from some frigidity on the man or the woman's part, a female is produced instead, which he calls 'a failed man'.

But since she is an inferior creature and lacks the physique to get the better of you, it is a cowardly thing to raise your hand to her, and you will be considered a poor sort of man if you do it without a serious motive; in fact he is truly not much of a fellow who cannot with proper discipline bring a woman (f. 87) round to appropriate behaviour, because a woman is just what a husband makes of her. And if she sins, the fault is the husband's and not hers, which is why the Church inflicts a severer penalty on a man who kills his wife than on one who kills his mother.

Others are women of little intelligence, and superficial; they would like to do better, but in their fickleness they forget and cannot remember things, and these have been brought up since infancy without any education. It is essential for the memory that it be put to work in learning, as with use memory will strengthen and become more useful. And many have criticised me because I have had my daughters learn Latin and recite many lines of Virgil from memory. I do this not only to make them perfect Latinists and rhetoricians, but to make them sensible, wise and with good, sound and healthy memories; and these are virtues that, to the wise man, constitute the best of dowries: lucky the young man who meets them! Lastenia and Axiotea even dressed as men and went to hear Socrates, and became themselves philosophers anxious to inform themselves of the classic teachings. By contrast, those with little brain can only be redirected with the greatest difficulty and need constant, almost continuous correction, and they need to be put alongside a respectable matron, who can impress on them her own comportment and train their superficiality to responsibility.

And others are slow-witted and half-asleep, dull of intellect, fat in body, somnolent and unkempt, all flesh and no spirit. These have lived in their fathers' houses in complete freedom, without having to think of practical things, in foolish company, where they thought of nothing but stuffing their faces, and remember too that there are places where the women habitually (f. 87') eat soup with malvasia in the morning and then continue to sit down to such meals throughout the day. Young men, beware, beware, beware!

A woman must absolutely be sober, and certainly in this respect I must commend among Italians the women of Rome who never drink wine. The Neapolitans likewise drink very soberly and never during the day; and if they are thirsty, they drink pure water, both during weddings and banquets and in their own homes. The Spanish too are fine women who never drink wine, which I greatly commend, and this is a habit derived from the ancient Romans among whom Valerius Maximus even writes of women who drank furtively and were killed for it by their husbands. And these carnal, inebriate, sensual and stupid women need to be firmly corrected and made to be abstinent; they must be dissuaded from eating greedily and continuously, rendered obedient and encouraged to fast, to break the habit of constantly consuming soups and broths, which fill the head with humidity and cause sleepiness and memory loss. They must be kept too from bad company, particularly from those who encourage their shamelessness.

But if, as Aristotle recommends, you take a sixteen year old wife, you being, say, twenty-eight, you will be able to shape your woman to your will and she will be exactly as you have made her. Do not take one any younger, because the Philosopher tells us that at these ages men and women are at their best, and will produce perfect children. And when you have established her in you house, put her to the test judiciously, and if she proves reliable, entrust her with your money and your possessions, because the more trust you put in her the more faithful she will be.

Show that you respect her and see that all your household do likewise, as when they have seen the honour you do her, they will honour her themselves, because, as Livy recounts, (f. 88) such honourable recognition was afforded to women earlier than to men. In Rome when Lars Porsena was besieging the city to depose the last of the Tarquins, he had reduced the city to such a state that he was able to demand a hundred virgins as hostages; and so much he obtained given the dire straits of the city. But Cloelia, a noble matron in charge of the virgins, once Porsena had lifted the siege, swam with a group of them across the Tiber by night, and brought them back safely to Rome. And the women of the city were also honoured officially and paraded the streets, as Valerius Maximus narrates in his chapter De Pietate, after Coriolanus, exiled from Rome, had led an army against his homeland and had the city on the ropes; numerous embassies of senators, kinsmen, priests and augurs of the epoch intervened to no effect. Eventually his mother went to him, accompanied by many distinguished women, and with her reproaches managed to put an end to his invasion and lift the siege. But we find few such women nowadays, even if all have earned our eternal respect on their account.

As to the rest, take care not to encourage your wife's wantonness from the outset, because you may come to regret it. Engage in coitus with moderation, because this will encourage good behaviour in your wife, the most favourable circumstances for procreating children, and a more perfect and understanding love.

And you should speak to her in one way in public and in another in private: in public in a respectful and straightforward way, discreet in both speech and laughter, and in private in a pleasant, loving and reasonable manner.

Do not give her cause for jealousy or suspicion, return her love fully. Do not (f. 88') be urgent with her, treat her as a woman and not a whore and do not expose your private parts to one another. With great temperance you will live decently in word and deed, with faithfulness and moderation, and the more you live reservedly, the more you will mutually sustain one another in love and desire. And in this way each will be able to nourish the other in their ill-luck and distress, because otherwise it would not be true wedlock and intimacy.

Do not attempt to know everything about women's matters, and if you know where she has read or heard things, pretend you do not and under no circumstances bring the subject up.

Live continently and remain faithful to your wife, for this is a commandment, as St.Paul says, "Do not betray one another, etc." and following God's will in this, just as you do not betray your wife, so will she not betray you, and as you do not steal others' wives from them, so will they not steal yours. And therefore, as Aristotle says, out of respect for God, before whom you swore to be faithful to your wife, you must keep your promise, and those who do not honour it, dishonour God himself. In fact it is a great compliment to a reasonable woman that she sees her husband keeping himself chaste and not thinking of other women but of his own before all the rest and remaining faithful to her, and she too will be that much more inclined to behave the same toward him when she sees how she is loved constantly by her husband.

The wise man then should not neglect to honour his kinsfolk, his children or his wife, and by giving to each his due show himself just and god-fearing; no one accepts gladly being deprived of the respect that he feels his due, nor will a man be content (f .89) when many things are given out to others, that he is deprived of what is his due, even when he has little, and nor does anything belong to his wife except what her husband can give, his steady respected and faithful company.

And a man should not distribute his seed anywhere he pleases, because children like those from true marriages will not be born from underhand and wicked associations; the outcome will be that a woman will be deprived of her honour, his children will be offended and he himself will reap dishonour from it. And Ulysses having an honourable attitude towards Penelope, even when he was far away from her did not transgress, whereas Agamemnon out of love for Chryseis sinned against his wife Clytemnestra who repaid him by behaving similarly with Aegisthus, because this is what God promises, as our moral Philosopher says: "A crime will pursue its author". Thus Ulysses, for all that the daughter of Atlas begged him to remain with her, would not betray the love of his Penelope; and although Circe promised him many things, he replied that he wanted nothing more than his own homeland, barren and untilled though it be: and so he kept a firm faith with his wife, and deservedly received the same in return. And the poet Homer goes on to declare that there is nothing better in the world than a husband and wife administering their household in common accord.

You should nurture a perfect love together, because matrimony was instituted, according to Aquinas (IIII di. XXVI) for the procreation of children, which would have been necessary even had Adam not sinned; matrimony then was instituted by God before Adam's sin, because he created woman from the rib of man to be company for him, saying to him "Be ye fruitful and multiply". And Adam said (Genesis II) "This is now bone of my bones and flesh of (f. 89') my flesh", and he was inspired by God to pronounce these words in recognition of this new institution of God.

But in so far as matrimony constitutes a remedy against the affliction of sin, it was instituted at the same time as the laws of nature; but there are some who believe it was instituted along with the laws of Moses. And in the sense that it symbolises the union of Christ and the Church, it can be said to have been instituted with the New Testament, according to Aquinas (and see XXXII q. II). But remember that there are two fundamental reasons for the institution of marriage, to bring up children in the praise of God, as in the first book of Genesis "Be ye fruitful and multiply"; and to avoid fornication, First Corinthians, 7: "Nevertheless, to avoid fornication, let every man have his own wife, and let every woman have her own husband", and this is to avoid sin.

And there may be all kinds of other reasons to contract marriages, to bring about peace, for beauty, wealth, etc.: and these, even if they cannot be said to be exactly according to the will of God, none the less, though the marriage be made for one of these reasons, it is enough that your intention to contract it is expressed publicly, see XXXII *q.* II, *Deuteronomi* XXII[5]: "And if thou seest among the captives a beautiful woman, and hast a desire unto her, that thou wouldest have her to thy wife; then thou shalt bring her home to thine house". And according to Ramon Llull, the obligations of marriage are fundamentally three: faithfulness, children, and the sacrament, see XXII q. II, *Omne*.

As far as faithfulness is concerned, it should be independent of either of the others; as to children, the couple should love them, help them and educate them piously; as to the sacrament, the marriage should not be dissolved. Even if sometimes a physical separation (f. 90) has to be made, by mutual consent, for religious reasons, or to avoid fornication, none the less a marriage between faithful parties, once properly contracted and consummated, is indissoluble until death.

And the above three things are so fundamental that anyone who prejudices any of them, vitiates the marriage contract. Thus, a husband, having contracted a marriage, is no longer the sole ruler of his body, which belongs to his wife, nor she of hers, which belongs to him; but neither should rush, as soon as the ink is dry on the marriage contract, to fulfil their matrimonial obligations, but allow themselves a pause of two months, as Aquinas suggests (III, *di.* XXXII) for three reasons: one, in case one of the two should decide for the religious life; two, to prepare for the ceremony; and three, in case the husband is not in agreement on the date, and wishes to postpone it. According to Ockham, it is mortal sin to come together with one's wife before the nuptial blessing, which should be conducted in the appointed place. But if the wife has reason to believe the husband wishes to consummate the marriage, then the sin is forgiven her, except in such cases where there are clear indications of deception, such as extreme differences in class or wealth.

They should then reciprocally fulfil their conjugal obligations in accordance with the rights one has over the other by virtue of their sacramental

[5] Correct reading XXI.

union, as we have said above. You are excused only by illness, in so far as the wife cannot claim power over your body if she does not keep it healthy, and if a claim goes beyond what is reasonable, it is no longer a claim but an extortion.

Does a man sin if he becomes unable to fulfil his conjugal duties? I say that if he finds himself (f. 90') in this state due to having abundantly fulfilled them in the past, then the wife has no cause for insistence.

If he is prevented by some other factor, such as moderate self-discipline etc., then he commits no sin, but if his motive is improper, then he sins. And if the wife should fall into the sin of fornication, this cannot be blamed in any way on the husband, who should none the less do his best to see that she controls herself.

Can the conjugal act within matrimony be sinful? I say that if the couple come together to produce children, this is not sinful but meritorious, First Corinthians, 7: "If a virgin marry, she hath not sinned"; Genesis, 8[6]: "Be fruitful, and multiply, and replenish the earth". If they come together to fulfil their conjugal obligations, here too there is no sin, again Corinthians 7: "Let every man do his duty by his wife". If they do it out of desire, as they could otherwise not contain themselves, then the sin is venial, St Augustine: "The sin of incontinence consists in a man lying with his wife beyond the necessity of procreation, but a benefit of marriage is that this becomes only a venial sin, on account of the nuptial bond".

And remember that according to Aquinas, when a man takes his wife for pleasure, as long as this remains within the ambit of the marriage, that is, he would not go with another in spite of his desire, then he commits a venial sin, but if he goes further, that is, he would do the same with a woman not his wife, then he commits mortal sin, because he behaves like an adulterer or passionate lover with his own wife and nothing could be worse than to love a woman as if she were an adulteress, see XXXII, q. IIII, *Origo*.

And if he lies with her for the sake of his body's good health, he is not absolved from sin, because he seeks good health through something not (f. 91) intended for that purpose, as if he were seeking good health

---

[6] Instead of 9.

through baptism, as Aquinas argues in IIII, *di.* XXXII: a husband is obliged to fulfil his conjugal obligations not only when his wife expressly asks him to, but also when she makes herself understood through certain signals. This need not be the case with the man's request, because women are usually more bashful than men about requesting conjugal rights.

The man should not scold a wife who does not ask for the performance of his conjugal duty, unless for some reasonable motive, and he should not himself ask with persistence, for the ill effects that may come of it.

On the established holidays and fast days neither should ask the other for the performance of their obligation, but if you are asked you should perform it, First Corinthians, 2: "You should not abstain by mutual accord, or temporarily". In fact during the days of processions and fasting you should not come together, because then one must abstain even from permitted things in order to obtain what you are petitioning for. But one suffering from concupiscence or impatient with the liturgy or the Church's exhortations, who does it none the less, commits only a venial sin.

But one should in no circumstances either ask or concede the fulfilment of marital rights in sacred places, for this is a different matter from the times when it is forbidden.

During pregnancy, if there is no risk, one can ask without mortal sin, because marriage is not only a duty but also a balm. If there is risk, one should neither ask nor allow.

During the menstrual cycle it may be natural and regular, and thus without (f. 91') sin, because otherwise the husband would have to always abstain. If it is a natural thing, as it may be, the wife is forbidden to seek absolution from the obligation; but if the man is insisting, we need to distinguish: if he asks and is aware of the fact, the wife may pray him to abstain, but not so persistently as to drive him into other reprehensible amoralities. If he asks, without knowing, then the wife should prudently cite some indisposition. If he continues to insist in any case the wife should perform her duty. It may not always be wise that the wife reveal her discomfort to the husband, for fear of putting him off, except when she is confident of her husband's good sense.

Unnatural union with a woman can occur in two ways, by ignoring either the proper canal or the natural procedure. As to the first, it is always mortal sin because it entirely frustrates nature's intentions. The second case may not always be mortal sin, as some maintain, but is for all that an indication of mortal concupiscence and becomes the more sinful the more it departs from natural practice. None the less, it may be without sin in so far as the body agrees with it; and can be excused, according to Ockham, in the case of illness, or if pregnancy would be dangerous.

If the woman commits adultery does she lose her conjugal rights? I would reply that according to Ramon Llull it would seem yes, at least as far as the judging of her soul is concerned, because sinning against the law undermines the (f. 92) marriage, and she can therefore ask only after the fault has been corrected; none the less he should absolve her, just as he is obliged to restore rights to a a wife who has given birth, but she may not ask it.

Finally, out of respect for their declared obligation of living decorously and in a good loving relationship, they should be faithful and sustain their faithfulness and where this is so, conjugal love will be solid and lasting, as we have outlined at greater length in the work mentioned at the outset. We will move on now to speak of caring for and educating one's children.

Chapter VII On His Children

Nature teaches us to love our children because they are our own work, as Aristotle says: "Anyone will love their own work, like poets and parents"; and Virgil: "In Ascanius we see every degree of care for his beloved father". And the Greeks therefore derived the word *filius* from *filos*, meaning 'love', whence *filius*, as in 'parental love'. But as Bridanus says in his *Questions arising out of Aristotle's Economics*, a father's love exceeds a son's in practical expression, while a son's exceeds a father's in simple esteem. And we see this ourselves, how a father will love his son and want him to be richer than himself, but not more honoured, and the son would like to see his father highly honoured, rather than richer. And in so far as we have so much love to give, we must see to it that our children are educated and are reared in the social graces, as they owe us their obedience and we owe them their upkeep and education.

There are four categories of children: the natural and (f. 92') legitimate who are born in regular matrimony; the natural, born to unattached men and women who may yet marry; the simply legitimate, that is, adopted children, and finally the illegitimate, that is, bastards, born as the result of adultery or incest or some other union prohibited under the law, and these are excluded from all hereditary rights.

When conceiving a child, be sure not to lie with a woman during her menstruation, because leprous children will result, nor after lunch, while food is being digested in your stomach, because you will have sickly children who will generally not live long. After they are born I favour their being breast-fed by their mothers, because children inherit much through that milk. None the less, if the mother cannot suckle, as can be the case, you must find a robust and comely wet nurse, well-mannered, healthy and with a pleasing presence, and above all things not a drinker; as long as your children are drinking her milk, she must abstain from wine, because her blood will be tainted.

And remember that women can conceive up to the age of fifty, while men can procreate even at eighty. And Solinus tells us that Masinissa, king of Numidia, fathered a son, Mathuma, at the age of seventy-six; Cato the Elder, at eighty, conceived the grandfather of Cato of Utica with Solon's daughter, one of his freedmen. And it can happen that a pregnant woman can conceive and deliver another, as we read of the half-brothers Hercules and Iphicles, each of whom was born according to the moment of his conception; or the maid of Proconnesus,[7] who had two children from adulterous liaisons, each resembling its father. And if women would not put (f. 93) the embryo at risk they must abstain from sneezing after coitus.

Indications of pregnancy will start to appear ten days after conception, with headaches, restlessness, clouding of the vision, reactions to foods, loss of appetite, and if it is a boy the mother will acquire a better colour and the infant will start to show signs of life after thirty days, if it is a girl, after ninety-six, and the mother in this case will be pallid. And if the expectant mother eats too many salted things her issue will lose their finger nails.

---

[7] That is an isle of the Sea of Marmara: see Plinius, *Nat. hist.* VII 48.

And the children once born, must be hardened to the cold, as Aristotle says of the Macedonians that they used to douse their little children in the river to get them used to the cold and to make their constitutions more robust. And similarly we read of Pliny the Elder, that, as he writes in a letter to his nephew the Younger Pliny, he used to strip off and bathe in cold water and then stretch out in the sun to toughen his constitution. And he himself explained how men born in hotter climates are smaller and darker, as the outer heat dissolves their inner heat and hampers their growth, whereas in colder parts men are taller and whiter because their natural warmth, on account of the exterior cold, is closed up inside them and stimulates growth and multiplies the vital spirits. And in this manner they must learn to endure hardships, to sleep or not to sleep, eat or not eat, put up with heat and cold, coming and going, and so on, every sort of change, so that they will become impervious to sudden alterations which then, should the time come, will not adversely affect their health.

Once the child has been taken from its wet-nurse, he should be entrusted to a good tutor who will teach him good manners, (f. 93') Latin and Rhetoric. He must be taught some skill to earn his crust with, so that if he should lose the patrimony fortune has given him, he will not end up in poverty: in fact a merchant without money is useless in his profession, like a workman or goldsmith without his tools.

Then, as soon as they are grown, they should be placed with a good and knowledgeable merchant so as to learn their trade, because although many want to become masters without a master, this is not possible. Even so, there are more than a few among us who have ended up in trade without a mentor, and these are fools, who do not know how to pick up a pen or seal a letter; because, I tell you, the art of trade is not like painting pictures, which many can pick up without a master, even if one would still be useful to teach you how to mix the colours: my advice is to learn everything from your master, which is why Boethius says in his *Discliplina Scolastica*[8]: "There can be no master who has not learned to be a pupil", and it is indeed a miracle when one is able to discover everything for himself. And those who neither learn for themselves, nor from others, can be placed among the dumb creatures. Thus Aristotle, in the

---

[8] Again, *De disciplina scholarium (see note 8, p. 58).*

first book of his *Ethics*: "Undoubtedly the best is he who having discovered everything for himself, has achieved great things on his own, being his own instructor. But he is also worthy in his turn who, without finding out for himself, trusts another to set him on the right way. On the other hand, one who neither sees for himself, nor trusts in another to put him on the right way, is good for nothing whatsoever".

And see to it that they look up to you and show respect when talking to or of you, because "The old jug will preserve the flavour it knew in youth". And your sons should absorb this good and respectful habit so that even in their own decrepitude they continue to honour (f. 94) their father's name. In the Kingdom of Sicily they do the opposite, and often the sons grow up with such a lack of reverence that they descend to the folly of quarrelling with their fathers and fighting against them. And among other things, they usually from childhood call their fathers by name, like brothers, and do not follow the good practice of places such as Venice, Genoa or Florence, where they say '*messere*' or 'Sir', because this word is so respectful that there they grow up retaining a permanent reverential image of their father. Better still is the Catalan usage, where they say 'My Lord' and never pronounce their father's name, either in his presence, nor abroad. And next, be sure not to let your son handle money until he understands what money is, what it is worth and the effort required in gaining it.

Which is why in our city we have a fable concerning a fine fellow who travelled and traded widely in the Levant, and had warehouses full of pepper; but his wife was open-handed and generous by nature and gave away the pepper to any of her friends and neighbours who asked for it, so that what the husband accumulated she dissipated. One day her husband, having been unable to break her generous habit, took her with him in a galley to Alexandria, and the good woman was given a tiny space to herself near the stern, and sometimes a sailor might even tread on her stomach by mistake, as can happen, and as is the way in galleys she suffered such privations that her return home seemed a thousand years off. And when she finally returned, her neighbours asked her about the pepper trade and she answered "You have no idea how it is purchased: with blood!" Likewise, a son who appreciates the difficulty of turning a profit (f. 94') will rein in his youthful prodigality.

And remember that if his first voyage ends for some reason in loss, this may be better than if he had gained: he will understand the difficulties and work all the harder, while should the opposite occur, that is, he becomes convinced that he will always gain as much as the first time, he will become foolhardy and arrogant, and suffer many losses. What difficulties lie in wait for you, I am sure of it! When you are wiser you will say "I know nothing". All those who believe they know little or nothing are able men; those who presume to know everything know nothing. Which is why the Florentine said: "Whoever knows little knows much, whoever knows too much knows little, whoever knows everything knows nothing, but he who knows how to give advice knows most".

Chapter VIII On Servants

Servants are of many types: some become servants at birth, that is, are the children of an existing servant. Some become slaves by international convention, such as those captured in a just war. Some are servants under the civil law, such as those who, having reached the age of twenty, opt to be sold and participate in agreeing their price. And these three categories are covered by the statute *De iure personarum.*

There also servants who become so by under the law, such as the freedman who is guilty of ingratitude; or similarly under canon law, such as the abductor of a woman who becomes her slave, or one who on a mission to the heathen is taken prisoner and becomes the slave of his captor. There are also bondservants known as *ascripticii* or *originarii* who are tied to a particular landholding (f. 95) which they may not leave and are obliged to cultivate. These are bought and sold with the land, and are sometimes called 'sharecroppers' and are similar to our Ragusan vassals.

But to concentrate on the servants a merchant should have, these should be largely of the last category, trained to work on the land, and he should treat them humanely, but, living among them, make his superiority evident, and reward one more than another according to their merits and demerits. The other kind he will have, both male and female, are house-servants, either bought or hired, and he should see to it that they are clean, neat, loyal and trustworthy, because both money and expensive goods are handled in a merchant's house. He should not employ men of the lowest class; and because one needs to be able to trust a merchant's apprentice, try to take on lads whose parents you know, and if you can get a recommendation, so much the better.

And given that the tasks in a merchant's house are various, he should also have some young men of good family and the sons of persons of good rank, and these are ideal for office work and business matters. He will also need domestic servants, including a steward who will oversee and deal with all things to do with eating, a boy to look after the horses. And the head of the family must see that all know their place and not become over familiar with them, be ready to laugh and participate in the party, but not to go too far: you must show yourself to be temperate in all things, and not be arrogant or partial.

And when you take on a servant, look closely at their appearance, which should be amiable, biddable and graceful, not foreign-looking, and not given to some reprehensible activity; and he should not be one-eyed (f. 95') nor lame nor similar, as we said in the first book of one who should reflect credit on your business.

And you should try to educate them as if they were your own children, and if you fail to do this, you commit a sin: as Seneca says, "When one, being able to, does not stop another from committing a wrong, he has seconded him in committing it". And the Church calls such men "shameless dogs", *di.* LXXXIII, *Nemo*, C. *Error*, C. *Nihil.* Nor should there be forgiveness in these cases, because pardoning one you encourage others to transgress, like an epidemic: "A too easy forgiveness is an incentive to crime", XXIII, *q.* IIII *Est iniusta*, and following.

But nor should you be cruel or severe, *di.* XLV, *Licet* et C. XXX, and as is also written in XXII[9] *q.* V, *Prodest*: "Only thus, by punishing and forgiving, do you do right, so that men's lives are set on the right track". And do not let them over-indulge in eating, drinking or in dress, have them work hard, and do not spare the rod when they go wrong. And certainly in this respect I am a great admirer of the Catalans, who keep their servants well fed and dressed, but work them like dogs and when they are disobedient do not hesitate to take a stick to them.

---

[9] Instead of XXIII.

Chapter IX On Landholdings

Here follows a note on landholdings which are the goal of a merchant and function as his tools and equipment, because the merchant can hardly exist who lacks capital and a sound assets. But these too, as we have said, must be within reason: he should have some property outside the city, a vine to drink from and a house to live in will suffice, as too extensive vineyards distract a merchant from his proper business, and many properties require too much overseeing.

Therefore (f. 96) as the Pugliese rightly says: "Land enough to see all of it, vines enough to drink from, roofs sufficient to live under". And once you have acquired these things you should administer them in the manner I believe I have already shown you.

Chapter X On the Merchant's Last Years

Generally speaking the art of trade requires a keen intellect, high spirits and a bold outlook, things which in men over fifty years old tend to cool and atrophy, as day-to-day experience teaches us: as soon as a man reaches that age, his natural fervour abates, his blood calms down, his intelligence dims and his memory becomes less quick, so that he risks committing many errors in his business. And this is especially true of those who are naturally libidinous and continually wasting their energies.

It is not that one is not just as acute in civil and political matters, and certainly one's judgement is sound at that age, but trading requires something more; and therefore this is the moment when a man should rest from his labours for the above-mentioned reasons, and also in order to be able to dedicate himself to more important things, which we will come to. And after so many hours put in on projects, white nights, trafficking, book-keeping, drawing up contracts, travelling by sea and by land, quarrelling, sweating, flattering, trusting, finally, after so much worry and immense labour of mind and body, it is good that he rest. He wanted money: he has it; good name: he has it; possessions: he has them; he has married off his sons and daughters, he has made his pile, fathered and reared children, he has seen them learn his trade, he is fifty or sixty years old: what more does he want? "I want to carry on without interruption and not let myself go, so that (f. 96') no-one can call me a layabout" etc.

I tell you that you are condemned on many counts: first, under our own Catholic law; secondly, under the civil law; thirdly, under natural and physical law; fourth, under the laws of nature herself; fifth, under the moral and political law. And you who call yourself a gentleman, are condemned even by gentility and should be banned from the activities and company of gentlemen, you put yourself beyond the law, not just of men but of the mute beasts, in that your presumption is limitless.

What demands of man or society insist that you must perforce go to Rome by way of Campania, or that having been to Rome you must come back by Campania? And keep on going round and round, like a wheel that turns , or the bottomless tub in Tartarus to be filled forever by the daughters of Danaus, as the poets have it? Would you have inflicted so much on yourself as a penance? I truly believe that such that such a thing might have been awarded as a foretaste of hell or a first dose of damnation.

Unhappy man, that you understand nothing! Oh, human intelligence, where are you? Gentle soul, gifted with so many excellent abilities, with memory, intellect and willpower, have you got into such a twist as to have lost the ability to grasp the goal of our beatitude? Are you so far out of yourself that you have lost the ability to remember? How you have lost your motive willpower, so as to be so forgetful, when you should be wanting the most reasonable things! Have you not seen that for every thousand that are born into this world, hardly two arrive at the age of fifty, and you with already one foot in the grave, have you forgotten that? And since good sense has deserted you, you must recapture it reading these words, and lucky if you do.

When you are reaching the end and can (f. 97) rest, dispose of your possessions, given that you must die. Make arrangements for your house, for your daughters, if you have any, while putting your sons in the right track, and giving them a portion of your money, keeping the rest for your remaining needs, as you see them.

Do not leave everything in your sons' hands; choose one of your farm-holdings and retire in one far from the city, where you can live off your income with your wife and servants according to your needs.

Have a chaplain on hand to celebrate the mass, dedicate yourself to your prayers and commend yourself to God. Go through your old account books, and see to it that you have a clear conscience, righting any wrongs done, and read the Holy Scriptures regularly. Do not return to the city nor think of it and the world's novelties. Think continually of our eternal life and matters of Paradise, and never let yourself be idle, praying, writing, dictating, reading, engaging in manual activities; be active always, and your life will be prolonged in tranquillity, peace of body and mind; speak sparingly with men of the world, and live thus until Almighty God close your earthly eyes and lead you to eternal life.

Oh, blessed life, beyond all praise, angelic, holy life, philosophical life, as has been longed for and eulogised not only by our Catholic faith, but by every country and religion as a universal ideal! Virtue without transgression, life free of doubt, lived according to our essential needs, the salvation of us Christians, which the ancients called the solitary life and we the heremitic life, in so far as it ought to be lived in a hermitage or a wilderness. Such a life entails the inestimable privilege of complete liberty, (f. 97') allows complete freedom of mind and is always available; nor does anything in our present existence compare with it. No one gives you orders nor lords it over you, you are your own sole commander and answer only to the heavens.

One who lives thus cannot be an arbiter or a judge, a most dangerous race of men, nor an impious liquidator, nor a crooked lawyer, nor a false witness, neither accuser nor accused, nor an unhappy millionaire beset with worries, nor does he fear to be poisoned, nor is he a slave to Venus or Bacchus, he does not need to be crafty or cunning, he does not get inflamed or embittered by envy.

He does not speak ill of others nor stick his nose in others' business, does not colour at the prosperity of others, nor live trusting in random benevolence, nor proudly count himself among the frivolous, nor hail men insincerely, nor be always inventing words for the next lie.

He does not sit up late and eat poorly, worrying over middlemen and ships' cargoes, he does not steal nor is robbed himself, he does not spend the day weeping over his will, regretting its beneficiaries and thinking of those who will be surprised by it and those he might not wish to inherit, and last and not least he lives without lust or lasciviousness, which cannot be said of many in the city.

This is the life the blessed live, like that of the saints, which alone allows us to serve God and philosophy: happy the man that reaches this point! Be content with having enough to eat and to wear and nourish your soul on virtue; do your best in this life to hone your intelligence, enter into a dialogue with men who have written on the good things of the universe.

Oh happy life, oh joyful night-watches, oh softest of sleeps, oh (f. 98) most delightful ease, oh happy exercise of body and mind, with nothing lacking to live blessedly well! Live it to its utmost, praying, reading, living in the country, and you will live, work and study far from all the contrariness of our lives here. And prolong your old age into longevity, as nothing ages a man so much as the daily worries and fears of the merchant, and the nervous waiting on uncertain outcomes, which tire our lives out so much, fast-flowing though they seem to us.

Blessed then is the life which has shrugged off the burden that weighs so heavy on mortal men and leads them, dying by stages, to death. Thus the rustic Gens Curia, thus the ancient Coruncanii, thus the Fabritii of venerable memory, when the wars were commuted to truces, left their laurels in the lap of Jupiter Capitolinus, and so that their virtues might not perish through inactivity, these once triumphant heroes went to live in the country with their ploughs.

There we are, my dear Francesco, we have talked, briefly enough, of the life and death of the true merchant, under which title many shelter and call themselves merchants. And if I have on occasion failed to satisfy your whole mind, be patient and blame the adversity of the times, which give me little rest from my labours. And all this has been written in an unsettled spirit, in that it has been my lot to be away from my joyful homeland, and in a place where I have to put up with inconveniences and discomfort (f. 98'), and separated in particular from my library, which deprives me of many things.

Where, on the other hand, I have satisfied you, I am glad; where not, blame these exiled times. And also the fact that from being secluded here from the plague, which is now in Naples, in the Castle of Serpico, my Lord the King Don Ferdinand has now entrusted me with an embassy to your parts, and I did not want to bring with me an unfinished work. Nor would I ever have finished it for the pressure of work, for all that I have always been most anxious to satisfy your prayers and entreaties, which as they were ever ready to seek my guidance, I beg you may they be similarly prompt in indulging the results, thanks to which you can achieve a blessed end and the glory of everlasting life, for ever and ever, Amen.

Here ends the book entitled *The Art of Trade* written by Benedetto dei Cotrugli for Francesco di Stefano, *Deo gratias*. At Serpico, while an epidemic was devastating the City of Naples. In the year of Our Lord 1458, on the 25th day of August, in health. Amen.

Part III

Essays

Benedetto Cotrugli, Merchant Writer

Tiziano Zanato

Thanks to its fortunate geographical position, Ragusa (today's Dubrovnik) enjoyed a considerable degree of political autonomy from the later middle ages onwards, even during the period from 1205 to 1358 when it was a Venetian protectorate. The Venetian presence can still be felt, not least in the language, tingeing the local dialect, of Neo-Latin provenance, with a noticeable Venetian patina, overlaid by mainland Veneto influences, with an admixture of Tuscan borrowings, particularly numerous in the fourteenth and fifteenth centuries with the expansion of commercial contact with Florence and Prato. Commerce was in fact proving the key to the prosperity of the Dalmatian city, a port well placed to afford access to the East for goods (chiefly cloths and woollen goods) originating for example in Barcelona and worked in Florence. As a consequence

T. Zanato (✉)
Department of Humanities, Università Ca' Foscari Venezia, Venice, Italy
e-mail: zanato@unive.it

C. Carraro, G. Favero (eds.), *Benedetto Cotrugli – The Book of the Art of Trade*, DOI 10.1007/978-3-319-39969-0_8

a wealthy merchant class had emerged, to which the Cotrugli family belonged, among whose members we find the author of *L'arte de la mercatura* (*The Art of Trade*).

It was very likely not intended that Benedetto follow in the footsteps of his father and brother, or at any rate not immediately, his energies being initially directed towards academic study. After completing the earlier part of his education, including Latin, in his home country, he had set off for Italy, apparently to enrol at Europe's oldest and most distinguished university, Bologna, and study civil and canon law, taking a degree, as the saying was, *in utroque iure*. We can read what Cotrugli himself has to say on the subject in *L'arte de la mercatura*:

> since destiny and ill-luck contrived it that right in the midst of the most pleasurable of philosophical studies, I was seized from studying and made to become a merchant, a trade I was obliged to follow, abandoning the sweet delights of study, to which I had been utterly dedicated.[1]

This "seizure" from studying is a potent metaphor employed by Benedetto to underline the real violence of his experience, particularly considering that he must have been well on the way to his degree, to judge from the deep and detailed knowledge of legal texts evident in *Libro de l'arte de la mercatura* and his subsequent essay *De Navigatione*. None the less, he did in fact abandon his studies and was "rimpiantato nela mercatura", not in the sense of returning to ply that trade, given that he had not done so before (he was, as he says, "utterly dedicated" to study), but in the sense of being 'forcibly placed' therein, as underlined by the following clarification ("I was obliged to follow"). We need not waste time speculating on the precise circumstances that constrained Cotrugli to return home and take up trading, but since we find him shortly afterwards in Naples (in 1434), where his father had held the position of Master of the Mint, we can follow Piero Falchetta, *De navigatione*, 20 in assuming that he was taking over the latter's affairs, given that his father died shortly afterwards in Ragusa.

[1] Pr., f. 2. ["li fati e la fortuna permiseno che in sul più bello del nostro philosophare io fui raputo da lo studio e rimpiantato ne la mercatura. La quale per necesità mi convéne seguire, et abandonare l'amenità e la armonia dolcie de lo studio, a lo quale ero totalmente dedito"].

Naples was to be only the first of many cities Benedetto visited or lived in for varying periods of time. Among others were Barcelona, where he was certainly resident between 1444 and 1446; Florence, where he is known to have been at least during the summer of 1439; Venice, where we find him in 1440, ready to embark for Aigues-Mortes in a galley captained by "lo magnifico misser Arsenio Duodo" and owned by "misser Maffio Contarini et misser Piero Zen".[2] Cotrugli must have travelled extensively by land and sea between the principle commercial centres of Italy, France and Spain, to have acquired his evident experience both of navigation and, more assiduously, trade, the two fields about which, in late middle age and now far from the markets, he settled down to write his treatises, *L'arte de la mercatura* and *De Navigatione*.

After spending a good eighteen years of his life in this peripatetic fashion, Benedetto decided, quite abruptly it seems to our eyes, to move to Naples and take up residence there; he would stay in fact for a further eighteen years, from 1451 to 1469, when he died. He was able to settle in Naples thanks to the patronage of Alfonso the First (and Fifth of Aragon) 'the Magnanimous'. Initially he continued with his own business affairs, largely financial (debt recovery) by this stage, but worked also in the service of the King, who sent him on a number of diplomatic missions, as well as appointing him a judge and legal consultant (his juvenile studies proving useful in the end), and Superintendent of the Mint into the bargain.

In Naples Cotrugli was able to breathe a very different intellectual air to any he had known in Ragusa. Alfonso from his first arrival in the kingdom (1442) had gathered men of culture about him and entrusted them with important political responsibilities, not only Neapolitan humanists, but men from every part of the realm and from elsewhere in Italy too, Tuscany in particular. Chief among them was Antonio Beccadelli, known as 'il Panormita' from the Latin (*Panormus*) for his native city Palermo. From a legal background, he had done the rounds of the cities and courts of Italy, before becoming first an adviser, then secretary to King Alfonso, who looked to him for a Neapolitan cultural renaissance, centred on the Academy, initially given the name *Porticus Antoniana,* after its founder.

[2] *De navigatione* II iii, p. 117.

At the regular sittings of this institution, frequently in the presence of the sovereign, the classics were read and discussed, particularly the historian Livy, but also philosophers, poets, orators, rhetoricians. Very likely Cotrugli participated in these events, which were rigorously conducted in Latin, the *lingua franca* of the humanists, but also a medium favoured by Beccadelli, who composed several works, in verse and prose, in that language, renouncing the vernacular, denied nobility by its presence in the mouths of the vulgar horde.

A similar insistence on Latin was characteristic of another leading humanist, Giovanni Gioviano Pontano, who in fact succeeded Beccadelli at the helm of the Academy and in his political functions. He too was an outsider, hailing from Cerreto in Umbria. He arrived in Naples in 1448 and soon made a name for himself, thanks to his ability to write well on any subject, including treatises and moral dialogues, the area to which the works of Cotrugli, who would certainly have known him, belonged.

Other 'foreigners' at the court of Alfonso, and subsequently of his successor (from 1458) Ferdinando, were Flavio Biondo, a historian, geographer and linguist from Forlì, who stayed in the capital in 1451–52, and Enea Silvio Piccolomini, the future Pope Pius II, poet, historian and composer of epistles, from Corsignano (Tuscany), in Naples in 1456. More important from our point of view was the presence of Bartolomeo Facio and Giannozzo Manetti. The former, from La Spezia in Liguria, arrived in the city as Genoese ambassador in 1444 and stayed there until his death in 1457. Facio was appointed royal historian and it is for a historical work that he is best known, his *De Rebus Gestis ab Alphonso Primo Neapolitanorum Rege* ('The Deeds of Alfonso I King of Naples'), which went to consolidate the 'legend' of The Magnanimous, to which Cotrugli himself was not immune. He was also responsible for a moralising Latin dialogue, *De Humanae Vitae Felicitate* ('The Felicity of Human Life', 1444), with which Benedettto was probably familiar, as also a similar treatise, *De Dignitate et Excellentia Hominis* ('The Dignity and Excellence of Man'), penned in 1452 by Manetti, in Naples, where he was resident from 1445 to 1459, the year of his death. Giannozzo was a Florentine, a native therefore of the cultural capital of Italy, a city with which Cotrugli had had dealings throughout his time as a merchant.

In reality Benedetto's Florentine contacts had not been of a purely commercial nature: as Luca Boschetto has pointed out (*Tra Firenze e Napoli*, 705–6), his relations over many years with the Neroni, a prominent merchant family, but also men very much in the swim of the new humanism, were "such as to open up to him, if he had so wished, the right channels to establish a wide contact with the humanistic culture of the city". A culture that had already produced, among so much else, the two dialogues in the vernacular perhaps generically closest to the *Arte de la mercatura*, that is, Leon Battista Alberti's *Libri de Familia* and Matteo Palmieri's *Vita Civile*, both in four books (as would be Cotrugli's treatise). The first, from the pen of the great artist, architect, essayist, poet and more, deals with the topics of educating one's children, of marriage, of appropriate activities for the young, of the household (from an economic perspective), and of friendship, while the more or less contemporary (1430s) *Vita Civile*, opens with a hymn of praise for the vernacular and moves on to discuss children's education, the four cardinal virtues, individually examined, and finally profit and loss, or economics. Its author, Matteo Palmieri, a Florentine from a non-aristocratic family, had followed the path of politics and diplomacy, as well as letters. Upon entering Florentine humanistic circles, he had become notable for his championing of vernacular literature, and in fact wrote *Vita Civile* in his mother tongue, setting himself apart from almost the entire intellectual class.

In a city like Naples, even the 'foreigner' Benedetto Cotrugli was welcomed openly and generously by Alfonso and the intellectuals he had gathered about him as his court. The Magnanimous king in fact mistrusted the Neapolitan barons and preferred to choose his administrators from outside, as our author explains:

> And we were able to observe, thanks to my long acquaintance with his court, how that divine and glorious prince, Alfonso King of Aragon, such was his great generosity, never allowed himself to be outdone in courtesy. And therefore, out of his greatness of soul, he was wont to raise up men of low condition and make them officials and functionaries of his kingdom, so that his liberality was reflected by them, since none of these beneficiaries could claim to have earned their position through their own merits, but only through the great generosity of their sovereign. And, from his

> commitment to this virtue, he preferred to reward those who were worthy of it, rather than those who seemed to him born and shaped for preferment.[3]

Cotrugli, too, while not becoming a 'gran maistro', that is a court notable, profited from Alfonso's generosity and was received with honour into his circle of intellectuals and dignitaries. He entered this academy with a confidence deriving from his juvenile legal studies and his Florentine and other cultural contacts, participating in events arranged by the intelligentsia and thriving on the stimulating air of these encounters, the ex-merchant becoming himself a humanist, as testified by the preparation and publication of no less than three treatises.

The first of these has not come down to us. What we know of it comes from the author's own words in *Arte de la mercatura*:

> Although we have already written an autonomous work on the theme *De Uxore Ducenda*, dedicated—as you will know—to Messer Volce de Baballio, in which we have discoursed at some length, in the Latin tongue, of all the matters in which a wife should obey, of her duties, of the education of her children, and of all the instructions that ought to be followed by each member of the household, we will none the less, in so far as this chapter requires us to touch on the same material, make a few further observations.[4]

We gather from this preamble that before composing his *Arte de la mercatura* (1458) Cotrugli had tested the waters with a "singular", that is autonomous, stand-alone, work in Latin entitled *De Uxore Ducenda*,

[3] *Arte de la mercatura* III xiv, f. 73 ["Et vedemo nel glorioso principe, divo Alfonso re d'Aragona, per longa pratica che ò avuto in sua corte, che, per la grande liberalità, mai vidi che di cortesia si lasasse vincere, et però per grandeça d'animo usava rilevare homini da poco et facievalli gran maistri, che risplendesse la sua liberalità, che nissuno di sui criati poteva dire havere *ex merito* quello che aveva, si non per grande liberalità del signore. Et vinto proprio di quella virtù, piutosto facieva gracie a quelli che nol meritavano che a quelli che li pareva fusseno acti et nati a meritare"].

[4] IV vi, f. 84' ["Non obstante che *de uxore ducenda* ne habiamo facto un'opera singulare altre volte, come sai, a misser Volce de Baballio, dove s'è decto diffusamente in sermon latino d'ogni observancia de mugliere et de lo officio loro, et de alevar figlioli, et di tuti ordini deveno essere obervati *in unocoque* de la famiglia, ma perché qui la materia ci inducie lo capitullo, pure alcune cose diremo generali"].

dealing with the taking of a wife. We have no reason to doubt the existence of this lost text, given that the author himself goes so far as to specify a dedicatee, his fellow countryman the nobleman ("misser") Volce de Baballio, in Croat Vuk Vlahov Bobaljević (1420–'72), a business partner of Cotrugli's (see: Spremić, *Dubrovnik*, 278) but also a man of letters and a writer of verses in Latin under the name Volcius Blasii de Bobalio (Metzeltin, *La Dalmazia*, 325), which may explain why this work in the Roman language was dedicated to him. Furthermore we have the precise, if terse, summary given above in which Cotrugli states that he has dealt "at some length" with everything that concerns a wife, her duties, children's education, instructions for every servant (each member of the household). Now, in the *Arte de la mercatura*, he revisits the subject in broad terms, not only in this sixth chapter of the fourth book, which is one of the longest in the entire treatise, but also in the chapters following, as follows:

ch. vi De la muliere (on a wife)
ch. vii De li figlioli (on children)
ch. viii De servi et famigly (on servants)

We are dealing then with a summary of a pre-existing Latin text, but now in the vernacular, and thus accessible to those who had not studied *gramatica*, that is, the Latin language. This aspect, the retrieval of a work originally in the language of the educated, and legible therefore by only a limited circle of intellectuals, and its re-presentation in a more 'popular' vernacular version, is consistent with a tendency of the mature humanism of the fifteenth century to no longer consider the vernacular a paltry medium and Latin as the only worthy vehicle of culture. In this sense *De Uxore Ducenda* may be seen as the price that Cotrugli had needed to pay to render himself acceptable to the Academicians as a fellow intellectual. At the same time the work had served as a badge of recognition for the new Benedetto Cotrugli, seeking a position for himself in the Neapolitan cultural ambiance rather different from his earlier roles, embarking now on a literary route, and instructional besides. His chosen field was one of the more crowded ones of the age: the Venetian Francesco Barbaro had written a *De Re Uxoria* around 1416, dealing with the same topics as

Cotrugli, and Alberti and Palmieri had, as we have seen, had their say on the subject in the vernacular. Naturally, in a Naples where the intellectuals only read and wrote in Latin (occasionally in Greek), Benedetto had chosen, or felt himself obliged, to adopt the same medium, to establish himself on the same level as the many other men of letters made welcome at Alfonso's court.

Cotrugli's other two works, the *Libro de l'arte de la mercatura* and the *De Navigatione*, have on the other hand both come down to us, with differing and interesting manuscript and printing histories. In the case of *L'arte de la mercatura* it would be best to start at the end, by having a look at the *explicit* which closes Manuscript n. 15 in the National Library of Malta in Valletta.

> Here ends the book entitled *The Art of Trade* written by Benedetto dei Cotrugli for Francesco di Stefano, *Deo gratias*. At Serpico, while an epidemic was devastating the City of Naples. In the year of Our Lord 1458, on the 25th day of August, in health.[5]

Such specific information could only come from the author himself. He is telling us then that:

1. *L'arte de la mercatura* is dedicated to Francesco di Stefano (or Francesco Stefani), whom Janeković-Römer, *Libro*, identifies as Benedetto's brother-in-law, the husband of his wife's sister, a relation and fellow Ragusan therefore, and a merchant himself.
2. The work was completed at Serpico Castle, now Sorbo Serpico, near Avellino, of which only the ruins now remain but at the time belonged to the Aragonese crown (having been confiscated from a rebellious noble, one Carlo Capece Galeota: Tucci, *Il libro dell'arte di mercatura*, 31).
3. His sojourn at Serpico was circumstantial, being due to a plague epidemic that had hit Naples causing King Ferdinand (who had just succeeded Alfonso) and his court, including Benedetto, to flee the capital.

[5] F. 98' ["Finisse l'opera che 'Mercatura' è dita per Benedicto de Cotrulli ad Francisco de Stephano, *Deo gratias*. Apud Castrum Serpici dum epidimia vexaret urbem Neapolitanam. Anno Domini MCCCCLVIII, die XXV° augusti, feliciter"].

4. The treatise was completed on August 25, 1458.
5. This information is repeated and slightly amplified on the last page of *L'arte de la mercatura*, where Cotrugli, his labours done, addresses his dedicatee in the following words:

> There we are, my dear Francesco, we have talked, briefly enough, of the life and death of the true merchant, under which title many shelter and call themselves merchants. And if I have on occasion failed to satisfy your whole mind, be patient and blame the adversity of the times, which give me little rest from my labours. And all this has been written in an unsettled spirit, in that it has been my lot to be away from my joyful homeland, and in a place where I have to put up with inconveniences and discomfort (f. 98'), and separated in particular from my library, which deprives me of many things. Where, on the other hand, I have satisfied you, I am glad; where not, blame these exiled times. And also the fact that from being secluded here from the plague, which is now in Naples, in the Castle of Serpico, my Lord the King Don Ferdinand has now entrusted me with an embassy to your parts, and I did not want to bring with me an unfinished work. Nor would I ever have finished it for the pressure of work, for all that I have always been most anxious to satisfy your prayers and entreaties, which as they were ever ready to seek my guidance, I beg you may they be similarly prompt in indulging the results, thanks to which you can achieve a blessed end and the glory of everlasting life, for ever and ever, Amen.[6]

Here we have confirmation of the dedicatee's name, Francesco (Stefani), the place where the treatise was completed ("the Castle of Serpico") and the reason for his not being in Naples (the plague). New is the informa-

---

[6] Ff. 98–98' ["Ecco, Francesco mio caro, decto ve habiamo con multa brevità il vivere e 'l morire del mercante vero, sotto lo quale nome multi falsamente albergano et chiàmanose mercanti. Et se alcuna volta son mancato a la satisfacion de l'animo tuo, habi pacientia et la incomodità del tempo incusa, lo qual non mi lassa riposare de le mie fatiche. Et con inquiete de l'animo vi ò scripto tuto, perché m'è destinato de star fuor de la mia patria iocosa, dove si pate disagi et incomodi, specialmente de la mia libraria, la qual mi fa multo povero de varie cose. Se pur a l'animo tuo satisfacio, piàcieme; se non, lo tempo e l'exilio acusarai. Et se non che, confinato da la peste, la qual al presente è in Napoli, in Castello de Serpico, lo Signor mio Re don Ferrando mi have imposta questa legatione da le bande vostre, e non ò voluto venire con opera inperfecta. Ancora non l'arei fornuta per la varietà di faciende, per ben che sempre fui desiderosissimo de satisfare a le tue preghiere et peticioni, le qualli come furno prompte ad volere consiglio, così ti prego siano sollicite a li effecti, mediante li quali possi conseguire il fin beato e la gloria di vita eterna, *in secula seculorum, Amen*"].

tion regarding any imperfections in the treatise (a conventional excuse, but reinforced here by the author's estrangement from his personal library, left behind in Ragusa), but of much greater interest is the reason for Benedetto's having had to hurry to finish his book, his forthcoming embassy to Ragusa, or that general area ("your parts") at the behest of King Ferdinand, probably to seek military support for the arduous task of securing his succession to Alfonso's throne. In essence Benedetto had to return to his homeland and had promised himself not to do so with empty hands and his chosen gift to his relations (or his brother-in-law at least) would be this intellectual rather than material offering. We have no evidence to confirm that Benedetto set off immediately for Dalmatia, but from what he writes at the close of his treatise we may assume that he left in the same year, 1458, carrying a fine copy of *L'arte de la mercatura* to present to Francesco Stefani. This manuscript, though lost to us, must have arrived in Ragusa, as it has been philologically demonstrated that it was used, a century or so later, by the merchant Giovanni Giuseppi, who had it copied and took it with him to Venice to be printed from, an operation sponsored by Francesco Patrizi, who edited the text that was published in 1573 by the 'alla Elefanta' press.

The codex now in Malta, mentioned above, must derive, directly or indirectly, from the original copy of the treatise, which had not left Naples, as the copyist himself tells us at the end of the *explicit* already cited: "Copied by the hand of Marino de Raphaeli of Ragusa, in 1475". Marino Raffaelli, merchant and fellow countryman of Cotrugli, was in Naples for that year, as we learn from an appendix to the manuscript,[7] and it is his intervention that we have to thank for the fact that, seventeen years after its completion and six years from the death of its author, the *Libro de l'Arte de la Mercatura* could be preserved in its first state, the original still being consultable in Naples at that time.

Almost from the outset then *L'arte de la mercatura* met with the approval of the merchant community, only later, and indirectly, coming to be valued as a literary text. Nor would we have expected any other

[7] "Laus deo M°iiij^c^lxxu adj xuiij° decembris in neapoli" (f. 101'). ["Praise be to God, 1475, December 15, at Naples"].

reception for the *Arte*, given that this was the very public Cotrugli had in mind when writing his work:

> it was beholden on me to write in the language that was most commonly used and comprehensible to those merchants at whom the work was aimed. [...] And being desirous that our book be useful not only to merchants in our present century, but also to those coming after, into whose hands it may happily fall, we have decided to proceed with our treatise according a particular scheme.[8]

Benedetto is addressing therefore not only, or not so much, contemporary merchants as those to come, as he had declared in the opening lines of his introduction, underlining how he intended to trust to "the eternal memory of the written word, so as to spread their knowledge among future generations".[9] He is writing for future merchants, but also for his contemporaries, especially "the young and adolescents" "who genuinely aspire to attaining an honourable return" of the profession.[10] It is clear however, as Ugo Tucci has observed (*Il libro dell'arte di mercatura*, 47), that "his ideal reader was an established merchant" keen to acquire "a basic profile of his proper place in society; essentially what it means to live as a merchant, and what precepts apply, in short to locate and inhabit his own myth", which will be identified with that of the erstwhile merchant, now writer, Benedetto Cotrugli. And he is clearly looking to his work to bring him fame, as he has invested a great deal of expectation in the treatise he is embarking on, well aware that his chosen subject is a completely new one that "has never perhaps been written before from the creation of the world down to our own times".[11] It is a project that has been in his mind for many years, from when he was still in Ragusa, and

---

[8] Pr., ff. 3–3' ["mi parve ch'el fusse necessario lo scrivere in quella lingua che fusse più comune et più inteligibille a mercanti, a l'utilità de qualli era hordinata l'opera nostra. [...] Et desiderando che questa nostra opera sia utille non solo a quisti nostri de lo presente seculo, ma eciamdio a' posteri, a le man de quali per aventura ella perverrà, habiam deliberato di prociedere in questo nostro tractato con hordine singulare"].

[9] Pr., f. 1 ["a la eterna memoria di scripture per seminare doctrina a li posteri"].

[10] Pr., f. 2' ["li gioveni et li adolescentuli" "li quali ànno voluntà di conseguire lo fructo laudevelle"].

[11] I ii, ff. 6–6' ["da la creation del mundo in fino a la nostra età per aventura da nisuno scriptore per ancora è suto facto"].

only now has he finally resolved to tackle it, thanks to the prompting of his brother-in-law Francesco:

> For this reason I have many times and again promised myself to take up my pen and offer some instruction and lay down some salutary axioms concerning this profession, eliminating the errors and abuses that have reduced it to a joke, a profanity surrounded by lies, faithlessness, perjury and licentiousness, neither venerated nor cultivated, lacking modesty and commitment, completely without any sense of our duty towards humanity, and marred by acts of great incivility. And having omitted for a long time to set these things down, due to various pressing claims and responsibilities, and particularly from having lived away from my lovely homeland, which is so dear to me, as you will read, it was you that came to my aid, dearest Francesco, my prompter and petitioner, and it is to satisfy your entreaties that I am resolved to write what I think of the art of trade, not least because I do not doubt that in writing to you I will do a service to many, and especially those that desire and are prepared to trade in things with honour and without offence to God or their neighbour.[12]

Here we have made explicit both the subject ("the art of trade") of the treatise and its scope, consisting in useful suggestions for those who want to make money ("trade in things") while maintaining their honour and without committing offences against God or their fellow men. To achieve this end, however, it will first be necessary to carry out a cleansing operation on the current state of the profession, since, as Benedetto writes:

> I found the state of general education inadequate, ill-organised, arbitrary and useless, to the extent that my compassion was aroused and it pained me that this useful and necessary activity had fallen into the hands of such

[12] Pr., ff. 2–2' ["Il perché multe volte mi disposi a scrivere et dare doctrina et porgiere regula salubre di decta arte, levando li errori e le abusioni, [sendo] reducta in fazetie, turpiloquio, falsità, infidelità, spergiurio, inverecundia; senza veneratione, senza culto, senza modestia, senza gravità, senza alcuno officio *penitus* de humanitate, con ogni enorme et impolito giesto. Et avendo pretermiso lungo tempo lo scriverne, per varie e diverse e urgente necesità et ocupatione, et *maxime* per lo advenare fuor de la mia patria iocosa, la quale m'è sì cara come si legie, occoresti tu, Francisco mio carissimo, solicitatore et pregator mio, a li pregi de lo quale intendendo a satisfar, mi sono mosso a scrivere quelo sento de la arte de mercatura, et eo *maxime* che non dubito che con lo scrivere ad vui proficto ad molti, et *presertim* ad quelli che ànno volontà e desiderio d'aquistare roba con honore et senza ofendere Dio et lo proximo"].

> undisciplined and uncouth people, who carry on without moderation or orderliness, ignoring and perverting the law, and that this profession should be considered of so little importance and be so neglected by the wise, and so mangled and given over to those who know nothing, a forum for empty chatter where anything goes.[13]

These last two passages we can take together: we receive from them an extremely dark and negative idea of the contemporary merchant, uneducated, incompetent, irresponsible, a criminal, ignorant, foul-mouthed, false, shameless, untrustworthy, a perjurer, ruthless and irreligious. Obviously, it is a hyperbolic catalogue, thrown at the reader to startle him, stun him almost, and so render him receptive to the solutions to all these evils which the author has prepared for him in his treatise where he intends to "offer some instruction and lay down some salutary axioms concerning this profession".[14] In truth, Benedetto is unsure whether trade is an exact "science", or an art, that is, an activity with defined rules, or an "unclassifiable discipline", as "its necessarily multiform diversity" and "the variety each day brings to it" might lead one to suppose; these last are "governed none the less by specific rules, both general and particular, which must be understood".[15]

To arrive at these, Cotrugli will base himself on "what we know from our daily exercise of the art, and what we have discovered by the application of our intelligence",[16] and he is speaking of course of his own long experience and intellectual capability.

After having laid down the foundations of his work in this way, Benedetto had to deal with a very important issue: whether to write in Latin according to the humanistic model, as he did in his previous *De*

[13] Pr., f. 2 ["trovai lo culto inepto, disordenato, soluto e frustro, in tanto che mi condusse ad conpassione et dolsemi che questa arte tanto necesaria et tanto bisognosa et utille sia divenuta in mano de li indocti et indisciplinati homini, et governata senza modo, senza ordene, con abusione et senza legie, et da li savii posposta et pretermisa et data in delaceratione et preda a li inscipienti et fabulla a li eranti"].

[14] Pr., f. 2 ["dare doctrina et porgiere regula salubre di decta arte"].

[15] Pr., f. 2' ["La quale mercatura, per ben che si chiami arte, over disciplina irregulare, per la sua multiforme mutabilità che àve e dè havere in sé, per le varietà occorente per giornata in essa, niente di meno ella have alcune singulari regole in sé in genere et in specie"].

[16] Pr., f. 1' ["quello che per cotidiano exercitio mediante l'ingegno intrinseco sapemo e sentimo"].

uxore ducenda, or in vernacular Italian, which was considered a less noble language for this kind of treatise. He deploys two different levels of argument, one of a purely theoretical and axiomatic nature, sustaining the superior dignity of Latin (elegant, the language of the ancients, refined to perfection, etc.), the other practical, contingent, linked to the necessity of being understood by the public at whom the treatise was aimed, those merchants "ignorant of letters" (i.e. Latin). Cotrugli was well aware that he was writing in a cultural context, mid fifteenth century Naples, inhospitable to the vernacular, but he was equally conscious that his work is not intended for a humanist readership, was not written for the restricted circle of Academy intellectuals; it aims a bit lower than that, at the middle class, or even upper middle class, largely excluded from cultural discourse. It was a choice going against the grain of Neapolitan culture, but not Florentine, given that the same issues had been faced twenty years earlier by Leon Battista Alberti, and resolved in the vernacular's favour, as we can see for example in the preface to the third book of *De Familia*, composed in the mid 1430s. Here, having stated that by "writing in such a way as all can understand me" he can "be useful to the greatest number", he continues:

> I will readily admit that the ancient Latin language is a very rich and elegant one, but I do not see why our modern Tuscan should be so hated that we should condemn any thing in the language however well written. It seems to me that I can say exactly what I wish to in this tongue, and be understood, while these gentlemen so ready to condemn know only how to be silent in Latin and in Tuscan know only how to insult those who speak.[17]

Like Alberti, whose works he knew and in whose *Libri de Familia* he had found inspiration when compiling *L'arte de la mercatura*, Cotrugli had made a choice entirely consistent with his target, apologising, briefly and purely as a matter of form, to the *literati*. That linguistic choice makes

[17] Alberti, *Famiglia*, 190 ["Ben confesso quella antiqua latina lingua essere copiosa molto e ornatissima, ma non però veggo in che sia la nostra oggi toscana tanto d'averla in odio, che in essa qualunque benché ottima cosa scritta ci dispiaccia. A me par assai di presso dire quel ch'io voglio, e in modo ch'io sono pur inteso, ove questi biasimatori in quella antica sanno se non tacere, e in questa moderna sanno se non vituperare chi non tace"].

L'Arte the first treatise written in the vernacular in Naples, and not just in the fifteenth century, which is a not inconsiderable claim to fame in no way diminished by Benedetto Cotrugli's Ragusan origins, not least as had in fact become a citizen of the Kingdom.

The linguistic element of the treatise that most immediately strikes us is the vocabulary, where we find an absolute explosion of Latinity, sometimes very crude adaptations, being used for the first time in the Italian language or very early imports, and among these a profusion of technical commercial terms, never previously recorded in Italian. It will be worth pausing to examine some of these, of considerable interest both to the linguist and to the economic historian, beginning with the expression that has earned Cotrugli a certain (limited) renown in the field of accounting technique, *dupple partite* (double entries).

> In your Records in the Scrap Book you must write all contracts and obligations taken on and your exchange transactions, and everything you do as soon as you have engaged to do it, before actual transactions derive therefrom that need entering in the Day Book: there are in fact many things you agree to, that do not become entries in your account books, but which none the less it is necessary to remember and have noted down in your records. And remember that any one making use of the exchanges must record in his double entries when he disburses the cash: that is, one line for the calculation of the equivalent value in the currency of the city you are trading in, and another, with appropriate symbols, accounting for monies corresponding to the currency in which you are accustomed to keep your Day Book, according to the usage of your city. You do this in order to be always be in control of situations you are involved in. And in these lines you will record the profit and loss.[18]

This is, at least from the linguistic point of view, the earliest occurrence of the syntagm 'double entries', which would become widespread

[18] I xiii, ff. 34'–35 ["Ne le ricordançe deve scrivere tucti li contracti, promissioni et cambii, et ogni cosa che fai sùbito che l'ài firmato, nançi che ne nascano partite al giornale, perrò che sono multe cose che se ne fa contracto sença farne partite a lo libro et tamen sono sença dubio necessarie a ricordarsene et averle notate a ricordançe. Et nota che chi costuma fare de cambi deve mettere *dupple partite*, io dico ne lo caciare de le monete fuori: cioè una linea per abacho de la moneta pertinente ad quello de quella patria dove trafichi, et l'altra linea con figure, catiando fuori ad monete che à' costume a tenere lo tuo libro secundo lo costume de la tua patria, per poser sempre afrontare con cui ài da fare: et ne le qual linee apare l'utile e lo danno"].

only much later, written here in Latinate script and in the plural. But it is not *L'arte de la mercatura*'s only claim to lexical primacy: it is replete with technical commercial terms, used by Cotrugli for the first time, such as for example:

accomanda: "Devono con li decti denari afanarse la persona et non fare [...] accomande in altri" (I x, f. 25'—"they will have to commit themselves personally and not enter into partnerships"), in the sense of 'commercial partnerships'.

excomputare reddito: "devesi lo redito exconputare de lo debito principale" (II iv, f. 49'—"any such gain should be discounted from the original debt"). The expression means 'subtract the income' and is made up of a noun still relatively rare in old Italian (it appears in Venetian documents from the early fourteenth century) and a verb entirely new to the language.

intraprenditore: "è necessario ch'e mercanti non aspectino lo stentare del vendere le cose ad una ad una, ma è de bisogno le vendano in grosso; et in grosso non si trova intraprenditori e compratori ad contanti, et però è necessario, si non vol perdere lo guadagno e lo capitale, che si conduca a vender al termene" (I vii, f. 17'—"merchants cannot waste the further time required to sell their goods retail, but must dispose of them wholesale; and since in wholesale transactions it is rare to find buyers or entrepreneurs ready to pay in cash, the merchant, if he does not want to lose his profit and his investment, must opt for selling on credit"): the meaning is very close to the modern 'imprenditore' (businessman/entrepreneur);

quadernista: "lo mercante non solamente, come s'è decto, deve essere bon scriptore, abechista, quadernista, etc." (III iii, ff. 64–64'—"the merchant, as we have already said, should not only be a good writer, mathematician, keeper of accounts etc."); that is 'the man who keeps the books of accounts': a newcomer to the vocabulary.

ripetere: "l'ài pigliato ad usura et vòi ripetere lo interesso che tu ài patuto" (II iv, f. 51'—"you have borrowed from a usurer and wish to seek a judicial award of the interest you have agreed"), in the previously unknown sense of 'request the repayment of a given sum'.

L'arte de la mercatura is divided into four books, respecting the canonical format for practical philosophy treatises. In contrast to the comparable works, cited above, by Alberti (*Libri de familia*) and Palmieri (*Vita civile*),

Cotrugli abandons the schema of a dialogue between various protagonists, keeping to his own voice, although notionally in conversation with his friend Francesco Stefani, in practice some way distant from Naples. Everything therefore passes through the personality of Benedetto himself, a writer speaking of his own role as a merchant, and a merchant describing his own actions with his skills as a writer. This is not for all that an autobiographical work, despite its many first person references, for Cotrugli's aim is to provide a proper regulatory framework for a merchant's activities, and raise the profile of an occupation widely held to be a secondary one in comparison to other human endeavours, among which it ought rather to occupy a foremost if not the undisputed prime position. Such a pre-eminence for commerce is unique to Cotrugli: neither Alberti nor Palmieri took the same view, the latter indeed placing agriculture first in his hierarchy of the professions. Going further, Cotrugli exalts trade *in itself*, not as a step along the way to higher things, politics for example. The merchant's role is sufficient unto itself and has no need of 'transmutation' into something else to achieve nobility. Viewed from another angle, we might say that the treatise is lacking in the specifically political/civic dimension to be found in other authors, Palmieri in particular.

The four parts of *L'Arte de la Mercatura* are quite distinctly structured, Cotrugli being at pains to emphasise, at the end of his preface, the necessity of proceeding "con hordine singulare" [according a particular scheme], as follows:

> and in the first we will deal with the origins, types and essence of trading; in the second, the manner in which the merchant should make his religious observances; in the third the attitudes proper to the merchant relative to the moral virtues and politics; in the fourth and last of the individual merchant and how he should administer his house, his family and his budget.[19]

[19] Pr., f. 3ʾ ["ne lo primo tractaremo de la invencione, forma et quidità d'essa mercatura; nel secundo, de lo modo dè observare lo mercante circa la relligione e lo culto divino; ne lo terço, de li costumi de lo mercante circa le virtù moralli et politiche; ne lo quarto et ultimo, de lo mercante e lo suo governo circa la casa e la famiglia e lo vivere iconomico"].

We see immediately how the matter of the book is split between the first book, which is dedicated to the actual subject in hand, trade, and the other three, which focus on the figure of the merchant himself, that is, to an active practitioner. This is no more than the traditional division between *obiectum* and *subiectum*, confirming that Cotrugli wants to proceed "per auctorità de philosophi" [by the authority of the philosophers], as he puts it in the first line of the first chapter of his first book; a chapter which, as he will have occasion to point out in the following three books, functions as an extra preface (after the general introduction which we have looked at) to each of the four sections. And it is with a properly scientific approach in mind that Cotrugli begins his second chapter in the following manner:

> To keep things in their proper order, we will describe what trading is, because, as Cicero says, if we want to understand things properly, we must begin by defining them.[20]

We have then an entirely standard opening, sanctioned besides by Cicero, but before proceeding with his definition of trade, Cotrugli makes a preliminary distinction between *mercatantia* ('goods' or 'merchandise') and *mercatura*, which

> is an art, or rather a discipline, practised between qualified persons, governed by the law and concerned with all things marketable, for the maintenance of the human race, but also in the hope of financial gain.[21]

There follows a close dissection of each part of this definition, going into what the *disciplina* consists in, who are the persons legitimately qualified to trade, and who not, why the occupation is useful for the maintenance of mankind and why financial gain is also one of the proper aims of the merchant. In setting down and explicating these details Benedetto buttresses his argument with citations from authoritative sources, which

[20] I ii, f. 6' ["Per observare l'ordine naturale, diremo che cosa è mercatura perché, come vol Cicerone, volendo intender le cose bene devéno principare da la definitione"].

[21] I ii, f. 6' ["è arte overo disciplina intra le persone legiptime, iustamente ordinata in cose mercantili, per conservatione de la humana generatione, con sperança niente di meno de guadagno"].

in these opening chapters, and largely throughout the work, are prevalently juridical. Here Cotrugli's youthful university immersion *in utroque iure* is much in evidence, provoking a whole string of substantial quotes, including from the Bible, a major source. Naturally for the humanist that Cotrugli would have certainly considered himself to be, the range of possible authorities could be wider still, the great Latin authors in particular, while our author does not, on the other hand, appear familiar with the Greeks, at least not in the original. On the other hand he does cite a number of vernacular authors, possibly less obvious than the Latin writers, but not wholly surprising, given the language employed in the treatise. The authorities in question are the so-called 'Three Crowns' of Italian *trecento* literature, Dante, Petrarch and Boccaccio. And Dante is also present in person, cited as an example of how "when a cultivated man stands out from the crowd, he is criticised and despised, or even killed, or crushed and persecuted by the common horde" [dove intra lo vulgo si trova homo literato, egli è o biasimato, o despregiato, o morto, overo discaciato et persequitato da lo vulgo] as happened to Socrates and in this case to Dante, who "hounded from his homeland, died in Ravenna" [discaciato da la sua patria, morì in Ravenna].[22]

The first book of *L'arte de la mercatura* is the most technical of the treatise, and it is not by chance that we find there the syntagma *dupple partite* discussed above. Of particular importance, above all for what we might call their 'secular' stance vis-à-vis issues connected with usury, are chapters seven ('Selling on credit') and eleven ('On Exchanges'), where Cotrugli "audaciously" fulminates against certain theologians:

> And I am certainly astonished that exchange, being so useful, easy and entirely necessary to the conduct of human affairs is condemned by so many theologians, ancient and modern, as impermissible, embracing as it does uncertain gain, the circulation of goods, simple exchange, lending, the paying of interest, particularly hard work, realism, the risk of having credits pending on many occasions and being in a situation of potential profit or loss.[23]

[22] III iii, f. 66.

[23] I xi, f. 30' ["Et per certo, esendo tanto utile, commodo et *omnino* necessario a lo guverno de la humana generatione, multo me stupisco di molti moderni et antiqui theologi li quali damnano

But having rehearsed all the possible (theological) objections to the legitimacy of exchange, Benedetto sweeps away any doubts on the point, holding that he, as a merchant, knows more about the matter than anyone of the cloth:

> I have little doubt that the matter has not been understood by those who have returned this negative verdict. I am a merchant myself and understand this art of exchange, but I was practising it for two years before grasping it fully, and my intelligence is above the mean and I was determined and desirous of grasping it. So that churchmen should not marvel that I so audaciously declare that it is more or less impossible for a man of the cloth to understand this art from simply having heard about it, and consequently he cannot make a judgement, 'like a blind man with colours'.[24]

Boschetto (*Tra Firenze e Napoli*, 710–11) has rightly pointed out that such a critical stance may also owe something to a certain atmosphere of secularity that informed the Aragonese court at Naples, mixed here with a justifiable pride on our merchant-author's part in his command of such complex material and his consequent ability to speak as a true expert on the art.

Such outbursts of criticism directed at the religious authorities are not confined to this part of the book only, but are counterbalanced immediately and at length in the following second volume, dedicated to the "religione che convene a lo merchante" [the religion incumbent on the merchant]. Here Cotrugli lays out his devout and wholly orthodox personal position, founded not only on his Christian *pietas*, but also on his technical juridical knowledge, since, as he begins by saying, "to no man more than themselves [merchants] is it necessary to know canons".[25]

---

questo cambio come illicito, sendoci in lui incerto lucro, corso reale, comutatione vera, acomodaçione, vitaçione d'interesso, industria sola, realità, periculo dal credere tante volte et di posser perdere et guadagnare"].

[24] I xi, ff. 30'–31 ["Io non dubito che lo caso non fo inteso da coloro che deteno questo iudicio. Io sono mercante et intendo l'arte, et dui anni ò fato lo exercicio avanti che l'habia posuto intender, et ò avuto non mediocre ingiegno, et ò voluto et desiderato de intenderlo, sì che non se meravigli-eno li religiosi si tanto audacemente dico che l'è *quodanmodo* impossibile ad uno religioso intenderlo per informatione et *per consequens* non può iudicare «tamquam cecus de coloribus»"].

[25] II, pr., f. 42' ["a nulla generacione di homini è più necessario il sapere di canoni quanto" ai mercanti].

It comes as no surprise to find the book particularly replete with *in utroque iure* adjuncts, particularly thick on the ground in his fourth chapter "On matters of conscience: what is; and what is not permissible", which becomes an extended treatment in the manner of the medieval canonists, such as the Dominican Bartolomeo da San Concordio, in a work actually entitled *Summa de casibus conscientiae.*

In the third book we turn to "what the moral virtues are that a merchant ought to have",[26] these embracing not only the four cardinal virtues (prudence, justice, temperance, courage) but also more personal gifts. Among these last, a linguistic education looms large, particularly a knowledge of Latin (*gramaticha*), a propos of which Cotrugli condemns those "ignorant folk" (as he calls them) who refuse to allow the possibility of a merchant being an educated man, and proficient in Latin, which would in fact prove useful to him for a number of reasons, including practical ones:

> But I maintain that the merchant, as we have already said, should not only be a good writer, mathematician, keeper of accounts etc., but should be above all well-educated, and a good rhetorician, as this will be extremely useful to him: Latin besides renders a man capable of properly understanding a contract, and merchants make contracts every day; it allows him also to understand the detail of laws, or privileges and everything pertaining to a contract; it helps him to understand the languages of many races, because it is common to many ethnical groups, and of different people like the Hungarians, Germans, French and many others. Latin will also help him to understand properly many aspects of the Christian religion, such as the mass, and the prayers and those things he may like to read for his personal devotions. It will also allow him to hold his own among nobles and men of importance, make him extraordinary (Latin *egregius*—'apart from the herd', 'superior to the crowd').
>
> To be a rhetorician is useful not only because it makes a man proficient in Latin, but also fluent in the vernacular, which also a distinction in a merchant. Latin also teaches him to write letters elegantly, to address nobles and persons of importance in the proper manner; thus, when necessary,

[26] III, Pr., f. 60'.

merchants know how to write formal missives and open them in the approved manner.[27]

We have here nothing less than a humanist hymn to the utility and merit of the Latin language, which will open the merchant many doors, from the ability to read contracts and laws to the possibility of communication with foreign peoples through an intermediary language, as well as enabling him to understand the mass, prayers and religious texts, notoriously all still in Latin; and particularly familiarity with the ancient language of Rome will make him "comparesciente", that is, let him shine, in being able to speak it to kings and gentlemen and powerful men of every stripe, and raise him above the vulgar horde, those who can speak only the vernacular.

So persuaded is Cotrugli by his own assertions that he even thinks it useful, necessary even, that women be introduced to Latin and rhetoric:

> And many have criticised me because I have had my daughters learn Latin and recite many lines of Virgil from memory. I do this not only to make them perfect Latinists and rhetoricians, but to make them sensible, wise and with good, sound and healthy memories.[28]

Which is a surprisingly forward-looking stance, not least because Cotrugli himself, in the fourth book of his treatise, presents women, particularly

[27] III iii, ff. 64–64' ["Et io dico che lo mercante non solamente, come s'è decto, deve essere bon scriptore, abechista, quadernista, etc., ma eciamdio lo mercante deve essere literato prima et almeno bono retoricho, però che questo gli è necessaryssimo, ché la gramaticha fa l'huomo inteligente ad cognoscere bene uno contracto et lo mercante ogni dì fa li contracti. Lo fa eciamdio intendere uno comandamento, uno privilegio et *quod maximum est* pratico a lo contraere. Lo fa eciamdio intendere multe nacioni, però che è idioma commune con molte nationi, et diverse gienti, come Ungari, Todeschi, Francesi et multi altri. Lo fa eciamdio intendere multo de la christiana religione, come sono le messe et le oracioni et quelle cose che, per sua divocione, si delectasse di legiere. Lo fa eciamdio la grammatica comparesciente intra signori et magnifici homini, et lo fa essere egregio, che vòl dire "*extra gregem*", "superiore al vulgo". L'essere rhetorico è necessario perché non solamente l'arte de la rhetorica fa l'homo eloquente in lingua latina, ma e' lo fa eciamdio diserto in vulgari, la qual parte è multo ornamento de la persona de lo mercante. Falo eciamdio sapere ornatamente scrivere in litere et fare superscripcioni a signori et a gran maistri, et quando è di bisogno sanno epistolare dove bisognia et exordire"].

[28] IV vi, f. 87 ["Et però multi me ànno ripresso perché io faccio imparare le mee figliole gramaticha et recietare multi versi de Virgilio a mente. Fàciolo non solamente per farle perfecte gramatiche et retorice, ma per farle prudente, savie e di bona, salda et sana memoria"].

in their role as wives, in a thoroughly traditional framework and from a strictly masculine point of view, as we can see from the following extracts:

> women have different natures: for some kind words are best, and these will be noble creatures brought up with delicacy and grace by their fathers at home. Harshness would be pointless with them, because their very nature is disdainful of harsh words or blows [...].
>
> There are others who need to be cowed with a frown, and these are by their natures shrinking and timid: there tends to be little substance to them and they are unintelligent and learn with difficulty. And such women must be educated with a degree of cunning, you must give them freedom and encourage their initiative [...].
>
> Some are proud and fractious and in their father's houses they have been brought up in a squalid and disorderly fashion and roughly, rubbing shoulders with the servants, from whom they pick up any number of bad habits. These, as soon as they have arrived at their husband's house, believe themselves transferred from a prison to a castle, and with their overbearing and arrogant ways they think themselves great ladies [...].
>
> Others are women of little intelligence, and superficial; they would like to do better, but in their fickleness they forget and cannot remember things, and these have been brought up since infancy without any education. It is essential for the memory that it be put to work in learning, as with use memory will strengthen and become more useful [...].
>
> And others are slow-witted and half-asleep, dull of intellect, fat in body, somnolent and unkempt, all flesh and no spirit. These have lived in their fathers' houses in complete freedom, without having to think of practical things, in foolish company, where they thought of nothing but stuffing their faces, and remember too that there are places where the women habitually eat soup with malvasia in the morning and then continue to sit down to such meals throughout the day.[29]

---

[29] IV vi, ff. 86–87' ["Diverse sono le nature di donne: alcune vogliono bone parole, et queste songo creature gentille et alevate in casa di loro patre dilicatamente et veçosamente, et non vogliono aspreça, perché la natura loro piglia disdegno de l'aspreça de parole o batiture [...].

Alcune sono che vogliono aterrirse di vulto turbato, et queste sono di natura sua timide et inaudacie et *ut plurimum* son da poco et bestialli, et duramente imparano. Et queste talli se volno con multo ingiegno adoctrinare et darli libertà et spingere l'audacia [...].

Alcune songo superbe et bestiali, et queste songo alevate in casa di lor padre, et tenute vile et mal in ordine, et *potissime* in conversacion di schiave, da le quali imparano ogni mal costume. Le qual, come vengono in casa di suo mariti, lor par essere venute di prigione in signoria, e lo far di superbia bestialle lor par essere madone [...].

Returning to Latin, Cotrugli emphasizes how, thanks to that language, the merchant has access to philosophy, astrology, theology and jurisprudence, leading him to conclude: "And so *ad infinitum*, we will find that everything a man might know may be helpful to a merchant".[30] As we see from these lofty claims, Cotrugli is constructing an idealised merchant, in whom are united the highest practical skills and the greatest intellectual and spiritual virtues. The point of view has shifted somewhat, from that of the merchant to that of a man *tout court*, and his manual on the art of trade is becoming a treatise *de excellentia hominis*.

As far as *excellentia mercatoris* is concerned, Benedetto seems to have in mind a specific, flesh and blood person, identifiable as "that glorious prince of merchants, Cosimo di Medici", still at that time (1458) an active protagonist of the civil, economic and political life of Florence, which he had ruled for half a century. And concerning Cosimo, he relates the following anecdote:

> having been asked by a foreigner, who seemed a respectable and trustworthy person, for 300 ducats, which this man claimed to have deposited in his bank, but which there was no trace of in the accounts, and was in fact a complete invention, did not Cosimo take him by the hand and see that he was given the money, not wishing his reputation for honesty to be damaged or sullied in a any way. He thereby demonstrated that the honesty and trustworthiness of the merchant must be established and maintained more keenly than riches.[31]

Alcune son done di poco ciervello, ligiere, voriano fare, ma ligieremente si dimenticano et smemorano, et queste sonno alevate da puericia sença doctrina, che *maximum memorie est* frequentarla et imparare, perché frequentando si fa più salubre et più efficace la memoria [...].

Alcune sono hebete d'ingegno et adormentate, grosse d'intelecto, grasse di corpo et dormigliose et stracurate, et sono tucte carne sença spirito. Queste son quelle che sono vivute in casa di lor padre in libertà, schitate di faciende, con conpagne bestiali, dove s'è ateso al pachiare, et *maxime* che son algune terre dove usano multo le done mangiare la matina suppa con la malvasia et poi *infra diem* fanno le colacioni"].

[30] III iii, f. 67 ["Et cusì *in infinitum* transcorrendo, trovariamo tuto quello che dè sapere uno homo convenirse debitamente a lo mercante"].

[31] III vi, ff. 68–68' ["sendo iniquamente interpellato da uno forestiero, lo qual pareva homo di auctorità et di fede, di ducati CCC, li quali dicieva havere diposati nel suo banco, la qual cosa non solamente non era scripta ne li soi libri, ma anche era falsissima, et Cosmo, volendo in nula parte non ledere nen maculare la fama della sua vera integrità, pigliandolo per la mano li fecie dare la decta pecunia. Mostrò quanto più deve essere servata et culta la integrità et la fede de lo mercante che lo denaro"].

This is, so far as I know, one of the first reported pieces that will go to make up the mosaic of legend accumulating around the grandfather of Lorenzo the Magnificent, which will win in the course of time a wide literary currency.

The third book also deals with a theme ever popular among composers of treatises, but especially so in the humanist or Renaissance era, concerning the relationship between Fortune and the energy and abilities of the individual. In the fourth chapter, speaking of 'the merchant's confidence', that is, his faith in himself, Cotrugli maintains that "in all circumstances, and especially in times of misfortune, the merchant should be confident and bold, and the more that fate buffets him the more he should face it with strength and resolution".[32] *Face* ("invadere") having here the sense of 'take it on', Benedetto being of the opinion that the battle needs to be taken to Fortune before she turns her guns on us, a point of view that cannot but bring to mind what Niccolò Machiavelli would write fifty years later in the *The Prince*, employing the identical words and recommending the same attitude towards fate: "I am sure of one thing, that it is better to be impetuous that cautious", better to take the initiative than hang back, "because Fortune is a woman and if you want to get the better of her you must rough her up a bit".[33]

The fourth book focuses "on the manner in which a merchant should conduct himself with regard to the economics and administration of his household and family", because "he should not be intent on merely accumulating money but must look to the running of his family and acquire houses and possessions, because he can never know what fate might have in store for him".[34] This constitutes a fundamental part of his treatise, where Cotrugli clearly feels himself profoundly engaged, at the emotional level even, as can be seen from the sudden switch of pronoun,

[32] III iv, f. 67' ["in ogni evento, et masime in adversa fortuna, lo mercante dè essere confidente et audace, et quanto più la fortuna lo percòte, più robusto et animoso la deve invadere"].

[33] *Il Principe*, XXV 26.

[34] Book IV, pr., ff. 78–78' ["in che modo lo mercante si dè havere circa la vita yconomica e governo de la casa et de la famiglia", because "non bisogna che solamente sia intento ad acumulare pecunia, ma deve resguardare al governo di sua famiglia et havere possessioni et case, perché non sa li casi de la fortuna che potrebono avenire"].

from the third to the second person and the accompanying recourse to direct address, often accompanied by the affectionate possessive *my*:

> Therefore the merchant, while he is steadily making money, must set aside some part of his profit and invest it in solid things, because, my dear merchant, every rational man must do all the things he does with some end in view; but if your only aim is continually piling up riches on riches, so that if you lived for a thousand years you would accomplish nothing else, I should think you an animal, a beast without a brain, and no man.[35]

In this final volume Cotrugli turns to the merchant's personal property and in what way it should be turned to the benefit of his family, and of himself as *pater familias*, moving on to expatiate, as we have already seen, on his wife, children and servants, material already covered in *De Uxore Ducenda*, and at least as thoroughly by the Florentine essayists, Alberti at their head. The final chapter is dedicated to the "last years of the merchant", that is, what we would now call his retirement: this should come at the age of fifty, or at most sixty, and be such that the merchant, withdrawing into "a private and virtuous life", will think to sorting out any outstanding business, and concentrate on the health of his soul.

It is an end to be looked forward to, recommended by philosophers and the Christian faith, as Dante had described in the fourth essay of the *Convivio*, "after so many hours put in on projects, white nights, trafficking, book-keeping, drawing up contracts, travelling by sea and by land, quarrelling, sweating, flattering, trusting, finally, after so much worry and immense labour of mind and body".[36] Needless to underline the stylistic effectiveness of this piling up of noun and verb, which leaves the reader, like the aged merchant, out of breath.

---

[35] Book IV, pr., f. 78' ["Però lo mercante, lo qual guadagna al continuo, deve trahere alcuna parte da lo suo guadagno et investire in cose stabile, perché, mercante mio, ogni homo racionale tute le cose che fa le dè fare ad qualche fine, ma se lo fine tuo non è si non sempre acumulare denari sopra denari, et se mille anni vivessi, voresti acumulare *in infinitum*, sença altro fine, io te stimo per animale et per bestia irracionale et non per homo"].

[36] IV x, f. 96 ["dopoi di tanti orlogii, disegni, vigilie, trafichi, scricticare, contracti, navegare per mare et per terra, altercha re, sudare, lusingare, contare, et infine, dopoi tante solecitudini et fatiche immense di mente et di corpo"].

Such stylistic felicity seems however to be more the exception than the rule in the *Libro de l'arte de la mercatura* as a whole. While making allowances for its hasty composition, frequently lamented by Cotrugli, and possibly too for the vicissitudes of the work's transmission, with inevitable errors accumulating from copy to copy, it remains the case that the text, particularly from a syntactical point of view, is muddled, convoluted and difficult. It is a hard enough work for even the specialist to take on, and certainly holds few charms for the general reader, who has to battle with the breadth and novelty of its lexicon: though this last, as we have said, is one of the book's most important and interesting aspects from a linguistic and cultural viewpoint.

In the third chapter of the third book, where Cotrugli turns to talk of the "sciencia de lo mercante", that is, the learning that he also needs to possess concerning practical matters, he specifies that he should understand:

> Cosmography, for example, which is important for knowing how the world is made up and the names of the nations, regions, provinces and individual cities, but also to understand trading conditions and usages, tolls, the nature of all the merchandise and various things that are transported and exported from every part, because in ignorance of such things the merchant cannot know what is required for each season and place. And he must besides know distances, places, ports, landings, and especially sea charts to understand charters and insurance.[37]

Speaking of the necessity of studying cosmography, or geography, our author seems to be anticipating a new field of enquiry for himself as an essayist, which dovetails nicely with what he was working on at that moment. The idea will take shape some years later in the form of *De Navigatione*, where, in the preface to the fourth volume, he will again emphasise the importance of geography and sea charts:

[37] F. 66' ["la cosmographia, la quale è di bisogno non solamente sapere lo sito de l'orbe e lo nome de le patrie, regioni et provincie et terre particulari, ma è di bisogno eciamdio sapere le condicioni et li usi mercantili, et gabele di quele, et condicioni d'ogni robe et mercanthie che si meteno et tragono d'ogni parte, però che, nol sapendo, non intende quello che ad ogni parte et in sue stagioni si convene. Et più li bisogna sapere le distancie, li siti, porti, spiagie, et multo bene la carta de lo navigare per sapere noligiare et asicurare"].

> After many had wandered the seas in a disorderly manner without measurements, comes Claudius Ptolemy of Alexandria, who wrote his *Geography* in Greek, which is called *Cosmography* in Latin, as *cosmos* in Greek translates as world in Latin. This Ptolemy was a great astrologer and geometer, and divided up systematically the extent and proportions of the sea, the sky and the earth, and measured all these with a celestial compass [astrolabe] and constructed an *orbis pictus* from which we derive our sea charts, which enable us to navigate without error.[38]

Cotrugli's third and final treatise then is fashioned from a rib of *L'arte de la mercatura*, being *L'Arte del Navigare* (as Benedetto calls his work from the very first line of the first book) an expertise profoundly rooted in the former material, though not altogether contained by it. This is the case at least in the personal experience and perceptions of the author, who refers in the preface (written in Latin) to "The numerous and various voyages of my life and its continual sea crossings"[39]: an activity not undertaken for pleasure, but to supervise commercial cargo and merchandise on the principal trade routes. On one of these voyages he found himself "In the violent hands of certain sailors",[40] brutish, evil and lawless men and realised that he had put his life at their mercy "so rashly and without forethought",[41] which brought home to him how low the art of navigation had sunk, with the consequent duty on his part "to put into written form the theory of navigation" and "to publish individually the rules and regulations pertaining to it".[42]

As we see from the opening lines of this preface, Cotrugli's motives in composing his new treatise are actually very similar to those for *L'arte de*

[38] I quote, here and subsequently, from Falchetta's transcription of the Schoenberg 473 codex (Falchetta, *De navigatione*, 182) ["Da poi multi erranti per mare sensa ordine et sensa mesura, trovo Claudio Ptolomeo alexandrino, in greco *Geographia*, in latino *Cosmographia*, perché *cosmos* in greco vol dire in latino mundo, lo qual Ptolomeo fo [...] gran astrologo et geometra, et ordinò et divise le mesure et le proportioni delo mare, celo et terra, et mesurò tucto per lo compasso celeste et descripse lo mappamundo donde nui havemo la carta delo navigare, la quale ce insegna lo andare per mare et non ce lassa errare"].

[39] P. 67 ["tot tantas variasque aetatis nostrae navigationes assiduosque tranandi maris transitus"].

[40] P. 67 ["in violentas quorundam navigantium manus"].

[41] P. 67 ["tam temerarie inconsultoque"].

[42] Pp. 67–68 ["Committendam litteris eiusdem navigationis disciplinam" and "unam quamque disciplinam ac leges edi"].

la mercatura, a situation of general degeneracy in the profession, which he intends to remedy through a written essay, viewed by him as a proper vehicle for civilising and instructing. One would assume therefore that *De Navigatione* was directed at men of the sea, but Benedetto does not explicitly specify his intended public, while offering a notably elitist profile of his implied readers, who are those "who are used to immersing themselves in such studies".[43] These words would appear to restrict the target audience of *De Navigatione* to a few intellectuals interested in maritime affairs, or the odd Latin-educated seafarer, but the real reason for the narrow profile is to be found in the explicit dedicatees of the treatise, the Venetian Doge and patriciate, "To whom every aspect of maritime concern and the very dominion of the seas belongs".[44] More specifically:

> I thought it opportune therefore to dedicate this work above all to yourselves, not because you are ignorant of maritime matters, but because you are men equally expert in enterprises on land and sea, and gifted with the science of navigation, so that you are in a position to recognise exactly when a man has performed well and honestly and judge him fairly.[45]

To conceive a treatise providing a regulatory framework for particularly ignorant sailors, and end up by dedicating it to the Doge and patriciate of Venice, entails something of a contradiction, from which the author tries to extricate himself by clutching at straws somewhat: the Venetians can employ it, he suggests, as a sort of maritime code and use it as a basis for evaluating seamen. Of course this is a trumped up solution, which we might explain by hypothesising that the dedication was added (as is often the case) after the work was finished, in which scenario Cotrugli has already planned and written his treatise before thinking of dedicating it to the Venetians (as we will make clear below). The temporal disparity between the dedication and main text of *De Navigatione* seems also to be clearly reflected in his use of two different languages, Latin for

[43] P. 68 ["Qui eiusmodi studiorum oblectari solent"].

[44] P. 67 ["Quibus maritimarum rebus cura omnis et dominium est"].

[45] P. 68 ["Vobis itaque id operis dedicandum in primis censeo, non tanquam rerum maritimarum ignaris, sed ad viros qui rerum terra marique bene gestarum instituti sunt, navigationisque scientia praediti, utque alii bene honesteque gesserunt probe cognoscere et eque iudicare possitis"].

the former and the vernacular for the latter. In addressing the highest Venetian authorities Cotrugli had perforce to employ the official language of diplomacy, as required by protocol and due deference, but having done so he closes his preface with the following lines:

> Wherefore, O illustrious and glorious senate of princes, I beg you to receive favourably this essay on things maritime, written however in the vernacular, so that with the blessing afforded by the dignity and glory of your name, they may also learn from it who know only their common mother tongue, who are besides in the majority.[46]

It is clear from this that the treatise was planned and written in the vernacular, being aimed at speakers of nothing else, who can only be those seamen involved in one way or another with navigation. Cotrugli thus repeats the choices made in the *Arte de la mercatura*, where he had declared that he "wished to write in the language commonest among and most intelligible to merchants", adding the gloss "for whose benefit our work was conceived", which we may assume holds also for *De Navigatione*, substituting sailors for merchants.

We might enquire what was Benedetto's motive, or motives, in dedicating his work to the Doge and Venetian patriciate, given that he was still living in the kingdom of Naples. Before attempting an answer it is worth pinpointing the exact period of its composition, for which, as Falchetta, *De navigatione*, 27 has noted, two date clues are available to us:

1. In chapter 25 of the first book, after a reference to current political events concerning "the Kingdom of Sicily [i.e. Naples], which besides being his legitimate inheritance from the divine Alfonso, King of Aragon, in present times has been subdued by our glorious King Ferdinand against a general uprising of the barons" he goes on to specify that "the present day" is the year 1464[47];

[46] P. 68 ["Quare, ducum inclite gloriosissimeque Senatus, hanc maritimam institutionem vobis caram accipite oro, vulgari tamen idiomate conscriptam ut ob dignitatem ac gloriam nominis vestri illi etiam discant quibus est solum materna lingua communis, quorum potior est numerus"].

[47] P. 95 ["Regno di Sicilia, lo quale ultra la heredità de divo Alfonso re de Ragona, al presente ha conquistato lo glorioso S. re Ferdinando contra la universale rebellione deli baroni"—"lo presente iorno"].

2. In the third book, chapter 13, in a caption attached to a lunar table, in the course of demonstrating its uses, he declares: "For example, in March 1465, the moon will turn on the fifteenth day, at the seventeenth hour, at point 637".[48] As this involves a forecast it is probable that it refers to an imminent date, and that therefore the writing of this part of the book would have taken place not long before March 1465.

It can be established then that the bulk of *De Navigatione* was composed between 1464 and 1465, although this latter date ought properly be extended forward a little, because it refers to the third book and does not allow for the fourth, which we have only in incomplete form. The missing finale is a firm datum, as can be seen from the brevity of the fourth book (it only contains about a third of the pages present in the other volumes) and the fact that a navigational chart, intended to cover in detail the entire Mediterranean coastline, starts from Gibraltar and via Africa reaches Venice, where it stops. On the basis of this textual evidence the question is whether Cotrugli had for some reason to abandon the work, or whether one or two final fascicles are missing. I would be inclined to favour the second hypothesis, given that the text of *De Navigatione* comes equipped with a dedicatory preface, very likely written last of all (as we have seen), after the completion of the rest of the work.

To return to the question we posed earlier concerning the Venetian dedication, round about 1465, if not later, when, as we have just heard, King Ferdinand had resolved victoriously the troubles attending his succession, and a relatively prolonged era of peace was in prospect, the adoptive Neapolitan Benedetto Cotrugli, reaching the end of a work on navigation that he might legitimately, and advantageously, have dedicated to the sovereign then reigning over the Gulf of Naples, decided instead to pay homage to the Venetian Doge, at that time Cristoforo Moro, and patriciate, emphasising on more than one occasion in his preface, the power and reach of the Serenissima, to the extent that it "rules over the seas no less than the Romans ruled over the land".[49] Such hyperbole is

[48] P. 169 ["Ut puta nel 1465, marzo, volta la luna die XV, XVII hora, punti 637"].

[49] II v, p. 120.

customary of course when addressing the powerful, and common enough among writers seeking political protection. Coming from the pen of Cotrugli, it might perhaps indicate a possible plan of moving to Venice, which we know was never realised, but which Benedetto may have been toying with for a while.

The four books of *De Navigatione* focus on, respectively, "the sea", "ships, their rigging and sails", "the winds"[50] and finally on "navigational charts".[51] As one would expect, the most technical sections are the second and the fourth, whereas the first and third derive largely from literary sources, often with long quotes in, or translated from, Latin, with a considerable amount of what one can only call 'cutting and pasting'. Naturally 'scientific' authors are to the fore, from Ptolemy (as we have mentioned) to Pliny, Solinus, Albertus Magnus; Aristotle is there of course, though as physicist rather than moralist, and even such as St. Augustine and St. Ambrose get a look in, more for their technical than for their ethical or religious writings. The Bible continues to be among the books most quoted, mainly the parts regarding the creation of the world, and jurists too, so dear to the heart of the author of *L'arte de la mercatura*, make an appearance, though less pervasively. It comes as no surprise to find, among the *auctoritates* most mined by Benedetto, the poet Virgil, with all three of his canonical works, then, one after another, Ovid and Seneca, the latter as much for his *Naturales Quaestiones*, a 'technical' text, as for his plays. Following on through, we come, as in his earlier treatise, to the vernacular poets, specifically to Dante, whom Contrugli cites on 'geographical' grounds, for all that the extract is a savage piece of invective against Pisa (*Inferno* XXXIII 82–84):

> In this sea we find the little islands of Capraia and Gorgona, of which Dante said: "let the Capraia and Gorgona move, and hedge up the Arno at its mouth, that it may drown in thee every living soul".[52]

---

[50] As listed in a themed summary rehearsed in the preface to Book III, p. 134.

[51] IV i, p. 184.

[52] I xvii, p. 93: but he is clearly quoting from memory, as can be seen from the approximate rendering of the last line (which should read "sì ch'elli annieghi in te ogne persona"). ["Nel dicto mare è Capraria et Gorgona, de la quale Dante dixe: «Movase la Caprara et la Gorgona et facian sepe a l'Arno in su la foce, sì che in te annegi ogne persona»"].

The roster of contemporaries cited continues through a passage from the previously mentioned Antonio Beccadelli, 'il Panormita,' "the inhabitants of Amalfi invented the magnetic compass",[53] a claim which later became, even down to our own times, something of a commercial for Amalfi. We should not overlook the fact that here he is bringing in the greatest poet of the Neapolitan court at the time, still active when Benedetto was sitting down to compose *De Navigatione*, and certainly greatly admired by him. But there is another author, also a guest of King Alfonso's court, who had died little more than a year earlier (1463), Flavio Biondo, whose geographical treatise *Italia Illustrata*, written between 1448 and '58, and thereafter continually updated in manuscript, enjoyed a wide currency, so that Cotrugli was able to refer to it on no less than three occasions.

Like *L'arte de la mercatura,* only on a wider scale, *De Navigatione* has frequent recourse to the authority of popular wisdom contained in proverbs. The examples being too numerous to list, we report only the following sample:

> Generally a prosperous hinterland comes as a result of a prospering port, as the saying goes: "Port, porkers, orchards and the dead make a man rich". And again: "On land served by the sea, what's not there in the evening you will find in the morning".[54]

> A helmsman should be strong and imperturbable; as the well-known proverb has it: "Who travels with calm, arrives without harm".[55]

> When the South Wind, or Scirocco, makes for turbulent weather and the sea is unsettled by these winds, that produce rain and thunderstorms, and it sometimes happens that the middle of the sky clears while the edges remain cloudy, it means that the bad weather will persist; and above all when the wind drops for a while, then the sailors say "the weather turns upside down (?) and the foul weather rests and the dead calm makes us shit

---

[53] III iv, p. 142.

[54] I xlviii, p. 103 ["Communemente le bone terre se fano da boni porti, et però se usa dire: «Porto, porco, orto et homo morto fa riccho l'homo». Però anche se dice: «Terra de marina, quel che non c'è la sera se trova la matina»"].

[55] II vii, p. 124 ["Lo nauchieri deve essere saldo et reposato, che como dice lo comune proverbio: «chi va adascio fa bona iornata»"].

ourselves"—sometimes, reporting the exact speech of the sailors, I have to be indecorous.[56]

As well as such proverbs, Cotrugli sometimes reports snatches of maritime jargon, for example noting the commands shouted out by the helmsman, with the sailors' replies:

> when the helmsman whistles, the sailors must reply "oho", after which the helmsman can communicate many things in a single word, as when he says "strisci mantichi in man!", which means "some of you man the yards, the rest look to the pumps", to which the sailors respond "fatee".[57]

And here we enter into the vast, rich, almost overwhelming lexicon of marine terms, so specialised as to represent on occasions a sort of a systematic sub-vocabulary of the Italian language and its dialects. We only have to open the third chapter of the second book and take a look at the various parts of a ship, which furnish at least a hundred specialist terms, many of which make their only known appearance in these pages. There is nothing to compare with it in *L'arte de la mercatura*, for all the latter's rich harvest of specialised words, including nautical ones. In this great plethora of technical terms, the base language is Venetian, but often equivalences are cited from other sea-powers, such as the Genoese or the Catalans, these being the three navies of reference for our author:

> And just as in ancient times maritime expertise was the province of the Athenians, the Carthaginians, the Phoenicians, the Egyptians, the Etruscans, latterly it died out in such places and the baton was passed to the Venetians, the Genoese and the Catalans, the Genoese with their great

[56] III v, pp. 144–45 ["Quando l'Ostro overo Scilocho fanno turbulento tempo et lo mare è agitato da decti venti, et fa fortuna con pioggia, et alcuna volta schiarisce lo mezo delo cielo, remanente le extreme parti delo celo nubilose, significa che lo tempo è da durare; et maxime quando reposa *aliquantulum* lo vento, li marinari dicono «lo cielo fa chiricha, et lo tempo reposa, et bonaza fa chachaza»—ad me bisogna alecuna volta usando proprii vocabuli marinarischi deshonestarmi"].

[57] II vii, p. 123 ["quando fischia deveno li marinari respondere «oho», et allora lo nauchieri dice in una parola multe cose, como quando dice: «strisci manthichi in man!», vol dire: «l'uni vadano a li strisci, e gli altri piglino li mantichi in mano», e li marinari rispondeno «fatee»"].

ships, the Venetians with their large mercantile galleys, the Catalans with their speedy piratical craft.[58]

It would be superfluous to underline Cotrugli's personal experience of each of these fleets, from which indeed he had drawn a sufficiently broad knowledge to hazard some quite sharp comparisons, like the following, hardly flattering to the Venetians (and presumably written at a time when Benedetto had yet to have the idea of dedicating his treatise to the doge and patriciate):

> The ship's master should stay continually with his ship, and not just temporarily. The Genoese stick to this rule, and are critical of the arrangements of the Venetians, who rarely have permanent ship's masters, but hired men, foreigners as often as not. And while the Venetians are very thorough and scrupulous when arming and equipping their galleys, in peace and in war, when they send them out to sea they are quite disorganised, with temporary masters and sailors and officers from anywhere. I have nothing but praise for the Genoese system in this, whose ship's masters are gentlemen and commoners from Genoa itself, while the officers and men are also from the city or thereabouts, so that the master has every interest in safeguarding his ship and its cargo, and when one is in need they are all united in heart and soul, and one will defend the other valiantly, so that they stand or fall together.[59]

What shines through *De Navigatione*, as indeed *L'arte de la mercatura*, is Benedetto Cotrugli's own human experience, to the extent that he could

---

[58] II i, p. 107 ["Et como antiquamente la disciplina navale era in li Athenisi, Carthaginisi, Phenicei, Egyptii, Etholi, poi è spenta da questi et è remasa ad Venetiani, Genoisi et Catalani; Genoisi in navi grosse, Venetiani in galeaze grosse da mercantie, Catalani in galee sottili da curso"].

[59] II vi, p. 122 ["(lo patrone) deve essere participe dela nave, non postizo, et in questo Genuisi me pareno observanti, et loro accusano lo stile et l'ordine Venetiano, che raro vel *nunquam* hanno patroni se non postizi, et lo più de le volte foresteri. Et como ne lo armare dele galee tanto in guerra quanto in mercantia Venetiani sono ordinatissimi et regulatissimi, così nelo mandare le loro navi sono inordinati, havendo patroni postizi et marinari et officiali de mille vescovati. Laudo multo in questo la consuetudine de Genoesi, che li patroni de le loro navi o sonno gentili homini, o populani Genoisi, et li marinari et officiali Genoisi da entro o de fora, in modo che lo patrone ha grandissima cura dela nave et de la roba, et quando è ad uno bisogno, sono tucti de uno animo et un sangue et *per consequens* virilemente defende l'uno l'altro, et de esserno oppressi o vincitori tucti quanti sono in uno gradu"].

well apply to himself the definition of *magnanimo* 'all-encompassing' given in the preface, in the sense of one who has seen "many different lands and many different customs among men"[60]: almost calling up the imprint of Dante's Ulysses, committed "a divenir del mondo esperto/e de li vizi umani e del valore" [A full experience of the world to gain—of human vice and worth] (*Inferno* XXVI 98–99). Benedetto had gained his experience in many different places and observed the customs of different and far-flung peoples, and learned to listen to and take to heart even the humblest voices, snatches of which he sometimes reproduces unmodified with the verve of a born storyteller, at home in the narrative mode, as in the following passage, which appears as a self-contained little fable, complete with moral:

> I had not quite grasped this principle until a peasant from Cerignola in Apulia kindly put me right. I had just arrived in Cerignola, where it had rained all day, but seeing a rainbow appear towards evening, I said, thinking to be on the button, "A rainbow at evening: we'll get the good weather tomorrow". But the peasant replied laughing: "No, sir, it will be the opposite! We'll have a lot more rain". I asked him why and he told me that if a rainbow was to mean fine weather, it must appear in the west in the evening, or in the east in the morning, while this rainbow was shining over the east at evening, and that meant rainy weather. And in fact I observed that it rained all night and the following day. Since then I have trusted the peasant, that an auspicious rainbow must stand in the west at close of day.[61]

The two treatises we have been looking at, *L'Arte de la mercatura* and *De Navigatione*, are the mature fruits of a vernacular humanism which we might define as Tuscan-Neapolitan, in that it first developed in Tuscany, in Florence particularly, and transplanted to Naples, largely thanks to

---

[60] Pr., p. 67 ["Multas [...] terras et diversos hominum mores"].

[61] III v, p. 145 ["questa regula e' non me pare al tucto intesa, ma uno rustico ala Cirignola in Puglia me la deschiarò gintilemente. Arrivando io ala Cirignola essendo piovuto quello giorno al continuo sensa repusare, vedendo io lo arco che già era verso la sera, credendome indovinare dixi: «Arco de sera haveremo bon tempo». Respuse lo villano ridendo: «Signore, lo contrario; nui haveremo grandissima acqua». Io lo domandai perché, e mi dixe che arcu de sera se intende quando appare de Ponente, et de mane quando appare de Levante, et questo arco pare da Levante, però è tempo da acqua. Siché io vidi che tucta nocte piobe, et lo giorno sequente. Però attenti ala sententia delo rustico, che l'arco sia de sera et da parte occidentale"].

Benedetto Cotrugli. And he, combining the learning acquired from his university studies, curtailed though those were, with the practical experience, initially forced on him but increasingly relished, of commerce and the navigational know-how deriving from it, found a path all his own towards unifying these two elements, primarily with a view to dignifying the so-called 'mechanical' practical arts through the application to them of a humanistic, largely classical, culture. This intellectual elevation was directed at the less educated, in the sense at least of those not knowing Latin, for whatever reason: hence the choice, by no means a foregone conclusion, nor arrived at without misgivings, given the time and the place, of the vernacular. By employing this linguistic medium, Benedetto could achieve a double result: bring a degree of 'noble' culture to those who had had no means of familiarising themselves with it, a descending process therefore, from above to below, and at the same time leaven the rather arid intellectual world of the elite with a new range of knowledge, no longer considered 'base' or inferior, enriching the dry garden of the *literati* with a vital new stream drawn from the crafts and the professions, the process this time working in the opposite direction. It was through this dialectic that the famous expression 'double entry' (*dupple partite*) entered the language, and therefore the culture, of the time, came, as it were, to 'exist', not only as a mercantile procedure, but as a linguistic concept, finally as a concept tout court. Certainly the particular linguistic mesh of the two treatises ended up by including a considerable amount of Latin intermixed with the mother tongue, both through continual citings and at the lexical level through a superabundance of Latinist neologisms. This factor, confirmed by the limited circulation of the manuscripts, in the end actually tended to limit the audience for his works to an elite public, the major merchant families and naval officers, both capable of a degree of bilingualism, and of course to humanists. It will not be until the middle of the sixteenth century, with the emergence of print editions of *L'Arte de la Mercatura*, that the treatise would begin to reach a wider public, and belatedly give its author his due, Ragusan by birth, Venetian and Bolognese by education, Catalan, French and Florentine through the practice of trade, finally Aragonese-Neapolitan by cultural choice—truly a *homo europaeus*.

The Printed Editions of Benedetto Cotrugli's Treaty

Mario Infelise

Ugo Tucci wrote on the printed tradition of Benedetto Cotrugli's work in 1990.[1] No other element able to shed completely new light on editorial events has emerged since then. It is still, however, possible to look again at just how much Tucci took into consideration and try to see if other suggestions can emerge.

Therefore, the book was published for the first time in Venice in 1573 in octavo format with the title *Della mercatura et del mercante perfetto. Libri quattro di M. Benedetto Cotrugli raugeo. Scritti già più di anni CX & hora dati in luce. Utilissimi ad ogni mercante.* It did not carry the name of the printing house or the bookseller, but only its device "In Vinegia, all'Elefanta, 1573". The title page also featured the image of a she-elephant nursing her calf along with the Latin motto *non sine spe* (not without hope). The publishing symbol is very rare. It appears on

[1] Tucci (1990, 3–17).

M. Infelise (✉)
Department of Humanities, Università Ca' Foscari Venezia, Venice, Italy
e-mail: infelise@unive.it

C. Carraro, G. Favero (eds.), *Benedetto Cotrugli – The Book of the Art of Trade*, DOI 10.1007/978-3-319-39969-0_9

only three editions, all from 1573, and allows for a documentation of an original editorial firm brought to life by a neo-platonic philosopher by the name of Francesco Patrizi and his nephew Giovanni Franco, the owner of a bookshop named "All'insegna dell'Elefanta" and situated in Venice in Calle delle Acque, off of the Mercerie, which was the main location for the concentration of bookshops in the city.[2]

The fact that Patrizi had very intense intellectual activities and, among other things, had been put on trial by the Holy Office for his anti-Aristotelian *Nova de universis philosophia* must not be misleading. Patrizi had a long and great life where his commitment to study and philosophical research was on par with other occupations as well as his travels from one part of the Mediterranean to the other. He himself recounted of his adventures in an autobiographical letter written in 1586.[3] He was descended from a Christian Bosnian family who took refuge in Cherso in the Quarnaro Gulf in order to escape the Turkish advance. He was born there on April 25, 1529 and from there was sent at a very young age to an uncle in Venice, to abacus school with the intention of making him a merchant. In the meantime, young Francesco, having discovered an inclination for law, began his studies in grammar alongside a priest who did proofreading for the great publishing house of Giunti. Following this, his father sent him to study in Bavaria in Ingolstadt, where he was then directed to studies in Padua in 1547. It was in the Paduan ambiance that he learned the rudiments of Greek and philology. In the 60's, he was in Cyprus, where he dealt with improving the conditions of property of the Contarini dal Zaffo Venetian family where they had enormous holdings (Nicolau-Konnari 2013). On the eastern Mediterranean island, he also busied himself with reclamations and collaborated with the bishop of Cyprus Filippo Mocenigo in governing some villages. In the meantime however, he became interested in Greek manuscripts (Grivaud 2013). From Cyprus, he continued on to Barcelona, as "philosopher" to the viceroy of Catalonia, the Prince of Francavilla, Diego Hurtado de Mendoza y de la Cerda. It was on this occasion, that not being able to collect the

[2] On the device of the elephant, Ascarelli and Menato (1989, 425–426). On the publishers' devices Zappella (1986, I, 158; II, fig. 481).

[3] The letter, dated Ferrara 12 January 1587, was sent to the Florentine legal expert Baccio Valori. It was published in Patrizi (1975, 45–51). On Patrizi see Vasoli (1989).

wage promised to him by the viceroy, he began to deal in book trafficking, selling "many crates of books that he had brought with him" and realizing that "one could profit greatly" (Patrizi 1975, 49). Among others, he granted various Greek codices collected in Cyprus to Philip II of Spain for the library of El Escorial.

It was at the end of his Spanish endeavours that Patrizi returned to Venice, in any case with the idea of specializing in publishing, at a moment in which access to the book trade was still a liberal profession, enrolment into the guild of printers and booksellers not yet having become obligatory. It happened therefore, that several different people could operate, true publishers, in the modern sense of the word, who were not professional printers or booksellers, such as what happened with Franceso Patrizi. In 1571, he entered into an agreement with Leonora Caglia, Apulian, "ancilla" of Girolamo Ruscelli, one of the most noted writers of Venice in the 1500's, and who inherited from Ruscelli himself the texts and illustrations of *Le imprese illustri,* one of his last works dedicated to the king of Spain Philip II.[4] The book was published in 1572 by Comin da Trino of Monferrato completely revised and corrected by Patrizi, with a print run of 1125 copies. During these months, he had also published the first volume of *Discussionum Peripateticarum* for Domenico de Franciscis and some manuscripts of Pope Pius II on behalf of Francesco Piccolomini.

The following year Patrizi had to think about giving prominence to his role as publisher, deleting from the cover page, the name of the printer on whom the publishing operations relied and replaced it with the device of the she-elephant, which was associated with the bookshop of his nephew Franco. However, his commitment in that field had not been lucky and remained limited for only a few months, presumably in the second half of 1573, bringing forth only three editions, however not for a lack of ambition.

Dated the 14th of October, 1573 was the dedication to Cardinal Alessandro Farnese from the mathematical treatise of the Vicentine Silvio Belli—regarded by Andrea Palladio as "the greatest building surveyor in the Veneto of his times"—*Della proportione, et proportionalità communi passioni del quanto. Libri tre utili et necessari alla vera et facile intelligentia*

[4] On editorial events about Patrizi see Marciani (1970a, 1970b).

della Arithmetica, della Geometria, et di tutte le Scienzie et arti. It dealt with a brief mathematical text of 40 pages in quarto format published in a beautiful italic typeface. In its presentation, the author predicted the imminent issuing of other mathematical texts which would otherwise have never seen the light of day.[5] In these same months, battle schemes engraved in copper *Gl'ordini della militia romana* based on the writings of Polibio were collected. These engravings predicted the imminent issuing of a further work by Francesco Patrizi on the Latin writer with more images, which, instead, were published in Ferrara 10 years later (Patrizi 1583).

The third volume with the symbol of the she-elephant was the treatise by Benedetto Cotrugli, which he dedicated to the celebrated merchant Giacomo Ragazzoni and was dated the 15th of November 1573. The Dalmatian merchant's book was published in octavo format, but in any case in editorial form, using an elegant italic type.[6]

In the dedication, the only available information on the events of the edition was found. The manuscript was recovered by the Ragusan Giovanni Giuseppi, who would have entrusted its use in a rather casual way ("fu gran ventura ch'ei si abbattesse in me") to Patrizi who, upon recognizing the importance of the piece especially for its practical teachings, would have set out reviewing it. Tucci's evaluation of this work was decidedly negative: "the activity of revision that he employed, certainly with the best of intentions, was disastrous". It is worth considering however, that it was not so much in the intentions of Patrizi to prepare a philological edition in the written version, as to—more simply, render the text more legible than how he received it which surely presented several comprehension problems. It is also worth bearing in mind that it was during this time he was qualified as a honoured merchant of Venice ("honorando negoziante di Venetia"), which leads one to think that the intention was that of releasing a useful document for learning commercial techniques, at a time when, especially in Venice, there was a good demand for tools of this kind.[7] However, it is also true that the revision of the ecclesiastical

[5] On Silvio Belli, see Barbieri (1965).

[6] It is also noted an example with a dedication to the Ragusan merchant Francesco Radagli, kept in the Baltazar Bogišić library in Cavtat (Ragusa Vecchia) (Tucci 1990, 4).

[7] Between 1470 and 1600 at least 136 books concerning generically commercial tecniques were published in Venice. The other major publishing centers were far behind: Antwerp with 84, Frankfort 76, London 59, Lyon 53 (Hook et al. 1991).

censorship had occurred, as was common in those times, modifying here and there the original text. Tucci noted that references to priests, friars and theologists were expunged.

Still, business did not go very well and the symbol of the she-elephant ceased publications soon after, even if Francesco Patrizi did not altogether end his editorial activities. It is, however, certain that the titles he edited had low circulation. The treatise was re-printed with no significant changes only one time in 1602 in Brescia—a hub for editorial activities in those years (Spini 1988)—in a shared edition (with two different title pages) by Comino Presegni and by Giambattista Bozzola (Cotrugli 1602a, b). It also had a translation into French in 1582 with the title *Traité de la marchandise, et du parfait marchand* in Lyon at the heirs of François Didier, à l'enseigne du Fénix, which in any case, had low circulation.[8] The translator was Jean Boyron, a literary from Annonay, in the vicinity of Lyon, and author of other translations from Latin into French.

Italian Editions:

1573

Della mercatura et del mercante perfetto. Libri quattro di M. Benedetto Cotrugli raugeo. Scritti già più di anni CX. & hora dati in luce

In Vinegia, all'Elefanta, 1573, [8], 106, [2] c.; 8°

Fingerprint: 4141 e,,e rela anco (3) 1573 (R)

1620

Della mercatura et del mercante perfetto. Di Benedetto Cotrugli Raugeo. Libri quattro. Doue si tratta il modo di lecitamente negotiare ... Opera ad ogni mercante, e deuoto christiano vtilissima Nuouamente datta in luce

In Brescia, alla libraria del Bozzola, 1602, [6], 213, [i.e. 203], [1] p.; 8°

Fingerprint: nore tei, a-er coEr (3) 1602 (R)

Della mercatura et del mercante perfetto. Di Benedetto Cotrugli Raugeo. Libri quattro. Doue si tratta il modo di lecitamente negotiare ... Opera ad ogni mercante, e deuoto christiano vtilissima Nuouamente datta in luce

[8] A replica of the French translation was edited by Luc Marco and Robert Noumen for the publisher L'Harmattan (Cotrugli 2008).

In Brescia, appresso Comino Presegni, 1602, [6], 213, [1] p.; 8°
Fingerprint: nore tei, a-er coPe (3) 1602 (R)

French translation
1582
Traicté de la marchandise et du parfaict marchant disposé en quatre livres. Traduict de l'italien de Benoit Cotrugli raugean, par Iean Boyron…,
Lyon, par les héritiers de François Didier (27 Oct. 1582), 179 [-13] f.; in-16°
Bibliothèque Municipale de Lyon.

A Note on the Text

Vera Ribaudo

The English translation of Benedetto Cotrugli's *The Book of the Art of Trade*, by John Phillimore, is based on my critical text, of which I provided also a version in modern Italian with a few explanatory notes. The critical text in fifteenth century vernacular, published for Edizioni Ca' Foscari—Digital Publishing, is available at the following link: http://edizionicafoscari.unive.it/it/edizioni/libri/978-88-6969-088-4/

The introduction to the Italian edition contains explanations on the formal criteria adopted in curating the text as well as on the criteria according to which the critical apparatus was constructed. Let us now have a look at the tradition of the text.

Benedetto Cotrugli's *The Art of Trade* has come down to us in the following versions: R (ms. of Malta, copied in 1475), S (Strozzi's ms., copied

V. Ribaudo (✉)
Department of Humanities, Università Ca' Foscari Venezia, Venice, Italy
e-mail: veriba@unive.it

C. Carraro, G. Favero (eds.), *Benedetto Cotrugli – The Book of the Art of Trade*, DOI 10.1007/978-3-319-39969-0_10

in 1485), M (Marucelliano, datable to 1480s), P (*editio princeps* of the treatise, published in 1573).

Cotrugli's treatise was published in 1990 in an edition edited by Ugo Tucci, who had only versions S, M and P to work from. Tucci established the relationship between S and M, excluding the derivation of one from the other. He further hypothesised that P belonged to a different lineage, tracing to an autograph copy by a different route. S's evident superiority to the other copies available persuaded him to use the Strozzi version as the basis of his edition. His critical apparatus listed the variants (other than simply orthographic) in M and the points at which he had adopted its readings over manifestly erroneous passages in S. P's reworkings of the original excluded it from consideration, except where its readings were of evident interest or where it made specific the '*et cetera*' of S or M.

Janekovic Romer's (2009) edition is essentially a diplomatic edition, and not moreover always an accurate one, of R. Variant S and M readings are regularly noted, but without adequate explanation.

The relationship between the four extant versions has been closely examined by Tiziano Zanato (1993), to which I refer the reader for a detailed analysis of the various readings. There are no existing direct copies, as is evident from the chronology: R, being the oldest manuscript (1475) cannot derive from S, copied ten years later (1485), nor from M, attributable to more or less the same period as the Strozzi version; still less can P, the first printed edition, from 1573, have been a referent of R, S or M. The second consideration emerges from a collation of the editions: the *lectiones singulares* in R, S & M do not allow the possibility that one version can have been the model for another. Without extant copies, the common errors of S and M testify rather to the existence of a common ancestor (*f*). R and P's derivation from the same progenitor (*n*) is proved by a number of errors quite distinct from the *f* branch, for all that the textual emendments of P, paralleled by R, stand in the way of any close comparison between S & M and R & P. The existence of an archetype (*alpha*) is proved by a series of errors common to S, M and P and corrected in R, or in R, S & M, and corrected in P, who tends to intervene on the basis of his superior classical culture: the possibility of a double original drafting can thus be excluded.[1]

[1] For errors in the prototype see Zanato (1993, 36–41).

The two branches differ notably in their approach to the text: where *f* is inclined to trim or jib at neologisms and over-colloquial or notably pungent usages, P wears rather both the hat of the grammarian, smoothing over textual difficulties, at the risk of trivialising on occasion, and that of the rhetorician 'improving' the original wording, to render it more consonant with the expectations of a later sixteenth century reader. In contrast, R seems to stick closely to the readings of his model text and emerges therefore as a more reliable transmitter of the legacy. Zanato's stemmatic hypothesis proves its validity in our editorial practice: taking R as our base text, we have adopted S and M's readings when they correct evident errors of R & P, or when *f*, or S or M singly, in agreement with P, displace on the basis of lineage R's authority as being a *lectio singularis*.

Conversely, the corrections applied on the basis of Patrizi's personal classical learning, correcting errors due to memory lapses on Cotrugli's part, who found himself without his reference books at Castel Serpico, or otherwise present in the archetype, have not been carried over into our text. Conjectural interpolations have been kept to a minimum, for the most part adjustments aimed at restoring the text in cases where an obvious lacuna is repeated in all versions. These are clearly signalled in the notes.

However, it is worth noting that a substantial number of variants found in R and not in P S M might be due to a different configuration of the manuscript, with R alone representing an entire branch accounting, therefore, for 50 % of the whole tradition. The critical apparatus records the various modifications applied to R's text over the full lineage of all the versions.

The table below provides a brief description of the witnesses:

R ms. n. 15, Valletta, National Library of Malta

Paper ms, pp. 122, original numbering upper righthand corners. The ms was copied in 1475 by Marino Raffaelli from Ragusa, as recorded in the *explicit*, on p. LXXXVIII*v*: 'Finisse l'opera che mercatura è dita per Benedicto/ de Cotrulli ad Francisco de Stephano, *Deo/gratias*. Apud Castrum Sercipici dum epidimia/vexaret urbem Neapolitanam. Anno Domini/MCCCCLVIII, die xxv° augusti, feliciter. Ammen. Ammen./Copiato per mano de Marino de Raphaeli de Ragusa in 1475'. Pp. CI*r*-CXXI*r* contain a series of mercantile notes. On p. CXXII*v* a few lines of a religious nature in another fifteenth century hand.[2]

S Magliabechiano XIX 97, from Strozzi's library, 4° n. 613, Florence, Biblioteca Nazionale Centrale.

Paper ms., later half vellum binding, perhaps nineteenth century. On spine: 'Ben. Di Cotrullo. Trattato di mercatura'. Recent ink Roman numbering on first two pp. On recto of p. I a *pater noster* and a prayer to the Virgin inked in a sixteenth century hand. Copy made by Giovanni di Matteo di Giovanni Strozzi, completed on March 17th, 1485.[3]

M Marucelliano C 16, Florence, Biblioteca Marucelliana.

Paper ms., miscellany, comprising 4 gatherings of 12 pp., pencil numbered in a modern hand. The pages of L'*Arte de la Mercatura* are numbered 56–103, book III chapter 18 defective, lacking part of last gathering: on the final page of the fourth gathering the copyist breaks off at the words 'lenticchia o orzo'. The ms is datable to the 1480s.[4]

P *editio princeps* of the treatise, Venice, 1573, edited by Francesco Patrizi.

DELLA MERCATURA/ET DEL MERCANTE PERFETTO/LIBRI QUATTRO/Di M. Benedetto Cotrugli Ragueo./Scritti già più di anni CX./& hora dati in luce./Vtilissimi ad ogni Mercante./CON PRIVILEGIO//IN VINEGIA, all'ELEFANTA./MDLXXIII

For printing circumstances, see Mario Infelise's essay in this volume.

[2] Kristeller (1989, II, 328); Zanato (1993, 20–21).

[3] Kristeller (1963, I, 126); Tucci (1990, 9, 26); Zanato (1993, 19).

[4] Tucci (1990, 18); Zanato (1993, 19; n. 7).

References

Alberti, Leon Battista. 1994. *I libri della famiglia*, edited by Ruggero Romano and Alberto Tenenti. Turin: Einaudi.

Alfieri, Vittorio. 1891. *La partita doppia applicata alle scritture delle antiche aziende veneziane*. Turin: G.B. Paravia.

Appendini, Francesco Maria. 1803. *Notizie istorico-critiche sulle antichità, storia e letteratura de' Ragusei divise in due tomi e dedicate all'eccelso Senato della Repubblica di Ragusa*, vol. 2, 98–100. Ragusa: A. Martecchini.

Arlinghaus, Franz-Joseph. 2004. "Bookkeping, double entry bookkeping." In *Medieval Italy: An encyclopedia*, edited by Christopher Kleihenz, v. 1, 147–150. New York: Routledge Chapman & Hall.

Ascarelli, Fernanda, and Menato, Marco. 1989. *La tipografia del '500 in Italia*. Firenze: Olschki.

Bačeković, Alika. 2006. "Benedikt Kotruljević, Knjiga o umiječu trgovanja." *Prilozi za istraživanje hrvatske filozofske baštine* 32(63–64):293–298.

Bacotich, Arnolfo. 1930. "Benedetto Cotrugli da Ragusa, primo scrittore di scienze mercantili (1458)." *Archivio storico per la Dalmazia* 9:182–190.

Baletić, Zvomir. 1996. "Benedikt Kotrulievjć – glasnik merkantilnog drustva." In *Dubrovcanin Benedikt Kotruljevic. Hrvasti i svjetski ekonomist XV stoljeca*, edited by Vladimir Stipetić and Mladen Hebek, 173–192. Zagreb: HAZU. Dubrovnik: Hrvatski racunovoda (Monumenta Historica Ragusina).

C. Carraro, G. Favero (eds.), *Benedetto Cotrugli – The Book of the Art of Trade*, DOI 10.1007/978-3-319-39969-0

Barbieri, Franco. 1965. "Silvio Belli." In *Dizionario Biografico degli Italiani*, vol. 7, 680–682. Rome: Istituto dell'Enciclopedia Italiana.

Bariola, Plinio. 1897. *Storia della ragioneria italiana*. Milan: the author.

Bertelli, Sandro. 2002. "La mercantesca." In *I manoscritti della letteratura italiana delle origini, Firenze, Biblioteca Nazionale Centrale*, 70–73. Florence: Edizioni del Galluzzo.

Boschetto, Luca. 2005. "Tra Firenze e Napoli. Nuove testimonianze sul mercante-umanista Benedetto Cotrugli e sul suo Libro dell'arte di Mercatura." *Archivio storico italiano* 163(4): 688–715.

Branca, Vittore. 1990. *Boccaccio medievale e nuovi studi sul* Decameron. Florence: Sansoni.

Bratić, Bojana. 1995. "Uno scrittore mercante raguseo del XV secolo: Benedetto Cotrugli e il suo trattato 'Della mercatura et del mercante perfetto'." *Italica Belgradensia* 4:121–141.

Buzadzić, Miroslav. 1996. "Utjecaj djela Benedikta Kotruljevica na suvremene racunovodstvene postupke." In *Dubrovcanin Benedikt Kotruljevic. Hrvasti i svjetski ekonomist XV stoljeca*, edited by Vladimir Stipetić and Mladen Hebek, 325–341. Zagreb: HAZU. Dubrovnik: Hrvatski racunovoda (Monumenta Historica Ragusina).

Buzadzic, Miroslav, Habek, Mladen, and Stipetić, Vladimir, 1998. "Benedikt Kotruljević (Benedetto Cotrugli) of Dubrovnik on double-entry bookkeeping in the year 1458 – before L. Pacioli." Abstract presented at the 21st Annual Congress of the European Accounting Association, Antwerp, April 6–8, 1998. ftp.cs.bham.ac.uk

Coronella, Stefano. 2015. "Benedetto Cotrugli. Il primo illustratore della partita doppia." *Contabilità e cultura aziendale* 15:145–148.

Corradi, Alfonso. 1972. *Annali delle epidemie occorse in Italia dalle prime memorie fino al 1850: aggiunte e correzioni fino all'anno 1700*, 4 vols, Bologna: Forni.

Corti, Gino. 1952. "Consigli sulla mercatura di un anonimo trecentista." *Archivio storico italiano* 110:114–119.

Cotrugli, Benedetto. 1573. *Della mercatura et del mercante perfetto. Libri quattro di M. Benedetto Cotrugli raugeo. Scritti già più di anni CX. & hora dati in luce.* Venice: all'Elefanta.

Cotrugli, Benedetto. 1602a. *Della mercatura et del mercante perfetto... Opera ad ogni mercante, e deuoto christiano vtilissima. Nuouamente datta in luce.* Brescia: appresso Comino Presegni.

Cotrugli, Benedetto. 1602b. *Della mercatura et del mercante perfetto... Opera ad ogni mercante, e deuoto christiano vtilissima. Nuouamente datta in luce*. Brescia: alla libraria del Bozzola.

Cotrugli, Benedetto. 1990. *Il libro dell'arte di mercatura*, a cura di Ugo Tucci. Venice: Arsenale.

Cotrugli, Benoit. 1582. *Traicté de la marchandise et du parfaict marchant disposé en quatre livres. Traduict de l'italien de Benoit Cotrugli raugean, par Iean Boyron....* Lyon: par les héritiers de François Didier.

Cotrugli, Benoit. 2008. *Traicté de la marchandise et du parfaict marchant disposé en quatre livres. Traduict de l'italien de Benoit Cotrugli raugean, par Iean Boyron. À Lyon, par les héritiers de François Didier (27 oct. 1582*, replica edited by Luc Marco and Robert Noumen. Paris: l'Harmattan.

de Polo Saibanti, Claudio. 1985. "'Arte del navigare'. Manoscritto inedito datato 1464–65." In *Imago et mensura mundi. Atti del IX Congresso Internazionale di Storia della Cartografia*, 3, 71–79. Rome: Istituto dell'Enciclopedia Italiana.

Del Treppo, Mario. 1973. "The Crown of Aragon and the Mediterranean." *Journal of European Economic History* 2(1):161–186.

Doni, Federica. 2007. *La teoria personalistica del conto: Aspetti evolutivi ed approfondimenti critici*. Milan: Giuffré.

Falchetta, Piero, ed. 2009. "Il trattato De navigatione di Benedetto Cotrugli (1464–1465). Edizione commentata del ms. Schoenberg 473 con il testo del ms. 557 di Yale," *Studi Veneziani* 57:16–334.

Falchetta, Piero. 2012. "Benedetto Cotrugli et son traité *De navigatione* (1464–65)." *Historical Review/La Revue Historique* 12:53–62.

Farlatus, Danielis, and Coletus, Jacobus. 1800. *Illyrici Sacri tomus sextus*. Venice: Jacobus Coletus.

Fejić, Nenad. 1983. "Dubrovcanin Benko Kotruljevic pred sudom kraljice Marije Aragonske u Barceloni." *Istorijski casopis* 29–30:77–83.

Franc, Viktor. 1996. "Povijest izdavanja djela Dubrovcanina Benedikta Kotruljevica u Hrvata." In *Dubrovcanin Benedikt Kotruljevic. Hrvasti i svjetski ekonomist XV stoljeca*, edited by Vladimir Stipetić and Mladen Hebek, 53–69. Zagreb: HAZU. Dubrovnik: Hrvatski racunovoda (Monumenta Historica Ragusina).

Grivaud, Gilles. 2013. "Une liste de manuscrits grecs trouvés à Chypre par Francesco Patrizi." In *Cyprus and the Renaissance (1450–1650)*, edited by Benjamin Arbel, Evelien Chayes, and Harald Hendrix, 125–156. Brepols: Turnhout.

Gruujić, Nadi. 2006. "Benedikt Kotruljevic o vili." In *Kultura ladanja. Zbornik dana Cvita Fiskovica*, edited by Nadi Gruujić, 41–47. Zagreb: Institut za povijest umjetnosti u Zagrebu.

Habek, Mladen. 1994. "Kotruljevicevo djelo u svjetskoj racunovodstvenoj misli." *Racunovodstvo, revizija i financije* 4:XI–XIV.

Habek, Mladen. 1996. "Kriticka analiza o vodenju poslovnih knjiga u rukopisma B. Kotruljevica." In *Dubrovcanin Benedikt Kotruljevic. Hrvasti i svjetski ekonomist XV stoljeca*, edited by Vladimir Stipetić and Mladen Hebek, 277–290. Zagreb: HAZU. Dubrovnik: Hrvatski racunovoda (Monumenta Historica Ragusina).

Hernandez Esteve, Esteban. 1992. "Benedetto Cotrugli, precursor de Pacioli en la exposicion de la partita doble." *Cuadernos de Estudios Empresariales* 2:87–99.

Hook, Jochen, Jeannin, Pierre and Kaiser, Wolfgang. 1991. *Ars mercatoria : Eine Analytische Bibliographie*, vol. 1, *1470–1600*. Paderborn: Schoningh.

Janeković Römer, Zdenka. 1996. "Obitelj u Dubrovniku u kasnomu srednjem vijeku i njezin teoretski odraz u djelu Benedikta Kotruljevica." In *Dubrovcanin Benedikt Kotruljevic. Hrvasti i svjetski ekonomist XV stoljeca*, edited by Vladimir Stipetić and Mladen Hebek, 123–134. Zagreb: HAZU. Dubrovnik: Hrvatski racunovoda (Monumenta Historica Ragusina).

Janeković-Römer, Zdenka. 2009. "Benedikt Kotrulj u potrazi za savršenim trgovcem." In *Benedikt Kotrulj, Libro del arte dela mercatura*, edited by Zdenka Janeković-Römer, 13–111. Zagreb: HAZU, Zavod za povijesne znanosti u Dubrovniku. Dubrovnik: Hrvatski racunovoda (Monumenta Historica Ragusina).

Jouanique, Pierre. 1994. "Benedetto Cotrugli reencontrado." *Tecnica Contabile* 46:205–216.

Kheil, Carl Peter. 1906a. *Benedetto Cotrugli Raugeo. Ein beitrag zur Geschichte der Buchhaltung*. Vienna: Manzsche Buchhandlung.

Kheil, Carl Peter. 1906b. "Benedetto Cotrugli Raugeo. Contributo alla storia della Ragioneria." *Rivista Italiana di Ragioneria* 6(6):233–250.

Kheil, Karl Peter. 1906c. *Benedetto Cotrugli Ragugeo (Dubrovcan), prispevek k dejinam ucetnictvi*. Prague: Bursik a Kohout.

Kotrulj, Benedikt. 2009. *Libro del arte dela mercatura*. Edited by Zdenka Janeković-Römer. Zagreb: HAZU, Zavod za povijesne znanosti u Dubrovniku. Dubrovnik: Hrvatski racunovoda (Monumenta Historica Ragusina).

Kotruljević, Benedikt. 2003. *De navigatione*, edited by Damir Salopek. In *Hrvatska knjizevna bastina*, edited by Dunja Falisevac, Josip Lisac, and Darko Novaković, vol. 2, 15–129. Zagreb: Ex libris.

Kotruljević, Benedikt. 2005b. *Knjiga o umijecu trgovanja*, prev. Zarko Muliacic. Zagreb: Binoza Press.

Kotruljević, Benedikt. 1985. *O trgovini i savrsenu trgovcu*, edited by Rikard Radicevic, Zarko Muliacić, and Vladimir Stipetić. Zagreb: Djela znanosti Hrvatske 1.

Kotruljević, Benedikt. 1989. *O trgovini i o savrsenu trgovcu*, edited by Zarko Muliačić. Dubrovnik: U. Dubrovnik.

Kotruljević, Benedikt. 2005a. *De navigatione. O plovidbi*, edited and translated by Damir Salopek. Zagreb: Ex Libris.

Kotruljić, Benedikt. 1963. "O trgovini i o savrsenu trgovcu." In Zebić, Milorad., *Zivot i rad Dubrovcanina Benka Kotruljica i njegov spis o trgovini i o savrsenom trgovcu*, 111–203. Titograd: Udruzenje knjigovoda Crne gore.

Kovacević-Kojic, Desanka. 1988. "Dvojno knjigovodstvo u Dubrovniku i Benko Kotruljevic." *Godisnjak Drustva istoricara BiH* 39:57–64.

Kovacević-Kojić, Desanka. 2008. "Business records of merchants in Dubrovnik in 15th Century." *Racunovodstvo, revizija i financije* 8:155–165.

Kristeller, Paul O. 1963. *Iter Italicum: Accedunt Alia Itinera: a Finding List of Uncatalogued or Incompletely Catalogued Humanistic Manuscripts of the Renaissance in Italian and other Libraries*. London: The Warburg Institute. Leiden: Brill.

Kristeller, Paul O. 1989. *Iter Italicum: Accedunt Alia Itinera: A finding list of uncatalogued or incompletely catalogued humanistic manuscripts of the Renaissance in Italian and other libraries*. London: The Warburg Institute. Leiden: Brill.

Ljubić, Sime. 1856. *Dizionario biografico degli uomini illustri della Dalmazia*. Vienna: Rod.Lechner libraio dell'I.R. Università. Zara: Battara e Abelich libraj.

Luzzati, Michele. 1984. "Cotrugli (Contrugli, Cotrulli, Kotrulja, Kotruljevic, Kotrulj, Kotrljic), Benedetto (Benko)." In *Dizionario Biografico degli Italiani*, vol. 30, 446–450. Rome: Istituto dell'Enciclopedia Italiana.

Marciani, Corrado. 1970. "Ancora su Francesco Patrizio e Giovanni Franco." *Bibliofilia* 72:309–310.

Marciani, Corrado. 1970. "Un filosofo del Rinascimento editore-libraio: Francesco Patrizio e l'incisore Giovanni Franco di Cherso." *La Bibliofilia* 72:177–198.

Mari, Libero Mario. 1993. "La vita e l'opera di Benedetto Cotrugli: Della mercatura e del mercante perfetto." *Quaderni di Scienza e tecniche Aziendali* 10:41–90.

Mari, Libero Mario. 1998. "Il Libro dell'Arte della 'Mercatura' e il 'Mercante Perfetto' di Benetto Cotrugli da Ragusa." In *Atti del IV Convegno Nazionale della Società Italiana di Storia della Ragioneria*, 341–358. Rome: Rirea.

Metzeltin, Michele. 1992. "La Dalmazia e l'Istria." In *L'italiano nelle regioni: Lingua nazionale e identità regionali*, edited by Francesco Bruni, 316–335. Turin: Utet.

Miller, Walter, trans. 1913. Cicero. *De officiis*. Cambridge, Ma.: Harvard University Press.

Momcinovic, Helena. 1997. "Trgovacka arbitraza u djelu Benedikta Bene Kotruljevica 'O trgovini i o savrsenom trgovcu' iz 1458 godine." *Pravo i porezi* 6:173–176.

Muliačić, Žarko. 1997. "Petric nakladnik Kotruljeviceva remek-djela." *Dubrovnik* 1–3:4–585.

Muliačić, Žarko. 1958. "Kotruljević – nas jezik i poslovice. Znacajni jubilej nase kulture: Petstota godisnjica djela dubrovackog ucenjaka bena Kotruljevica." *Zadarska revija* 4:329–355.

Muliačić, Žarko. 1958. "Znacajni jubilej nase nauke: Beno Kotruljevic: Autor prvog teoretskog djela o ekonomici preduzeca i dvojnog knjigovodstva." *Slobodna Dalmacija* December 13:3.

Muliačić, Žarko. 1995a. "Slicnosti i razlike Petrisova izdanja Kotruljeviceva traktata (Mleci, 1573, P) i najistarijeg dosad poznatog prijepisa (Napulj, 1475, R) izgubljenog autografa (1458)." *Prilozi za istrazivanje hrvatske filozofske bastine* 22(41/42):57–65.

Muliačić, Žarko. 1995b. "Frane Petri Kao izdavac traktata o trgovini Dubrovcanina Bene Kotruljevica (1573)." *Filozofska istrazivanja* 15:157–168.

Muliačić, Žarko. 1996. "U potrazi za izvornim Kotruljevicem." In *Dubrovcanin Benedikt Kotruljevic. Hrvasti i svjetski ekonomist XV stoljeca*, edited by Vladimir Stipetić and Mladen Hebek, 3–17. Zagreb: HAZU. Dubrovnik: Hrvatski racunovoda (Monumenta Historica Ragusina).

Nicolau-Konnari, Angel. 2013. "Francesco Patrizi's Cypriot connections and Giason and Pietro de Nores." In *Cyprus and the Renaissance (1450–1650)*, edited by Benjamin Arbel, Evelien Chayes, and Harald Hendrix, 157–204. Brepols: Turnhout.

Novaković, Darko. 1996. "Novopronadeni rukopis Benedikta Kotruljevica." In *Dubrovcanin Benedikt Kotruljevic. Hrvasti i svjetski ekonomist XV stoljeca*, edited by Vladimir Stipetić and Mladen Hebek, 19–32. Zagreb: HAZU. Dubrovnik: Hrvatski racunovoda (Monumenta Historica Ragusina).

Patrizi, Francesco. 1583. *La Militia Romana di Polibio, di Tito Livio, e di Dionigi Alicarnaseo*. Ferrara: Domenico Mamarelli.

Patrizi, Francesco. 1975. *Lettere ed opuscoli inediti*, organized by Danilo Aguzzi Bargagli, Florence: Istituto Nazionale di Studi sul Rinascimento.

Postma, Johanna, and Van der Helm, Anne J. 2000. "La riegola del Libro: Bookkeeping instructions from the mid-fifteenth century." In *Accounting and History: A selection of papers presented at the 8th World Congress of Accounting Historians, Madrid, Spain, 19–21 July 2000*, 147–178. Madrid: AECA.

Privitera, Claudio. 2003. *Origine ed evoluzione del pensiero ragioneristico*, Milan: Giuffrè.

Privitera, Claudio. 2010. Benedetto Cotrugli, un antesignano del Pacioli. *Rivista Italiana di Ragioneria e di Economia Aziendale* 110:514–522.

Proklin, Petar. 1996. "Kotruljević je prvi priopcio svijetu otkrice o dvostavnom knjigovodstu." *Racunovodstvo, revizija i financije* 6:146–149.

Proklin, Petar. 1997. "Benedikt Kotruljević: prvi "izumitelj" dvostavnog knjigovodstva." *Racunovodstvo, revizija i financije* 7:506–507.

Ravlić, Pavao. 1999a. "Benedikt Kotruljevic kao preteca Luce Paciolija u prikazu dvostavnog knjigovodstva." *Racunovodstvo, revizija i financije* 9:109–114.

Ravlić, Pavao. 1999b. "Usporedni prikaz dvostavnog knjigovodstva po Kotrljevicu i Pacioliju." *Racunovodstvo, revizija i financije* 9:111–118.

Resetar, Milan. 1927. "Kotruljević Beno." In *Narodna Enciklopedia: srpsko-hrvatsko-slovenacka*, edited by Stanoje Stanojević, vol. 2, ad vocem. Zagreb: Bibliografski Zarod.

Rigobon, Pietro. 1892. *Di un contributo del prof. Vittorio Alfieri alla storia della Ragioneria e di Benedetto Cotrugli, primo espositore della partita doppia*. Milan: Tipografia Golio.

Runjić, Andelko. 1989. "On Beno Kotruljevic and his work." In Benedikt Kotruljević, *O trgovini i o savrsenu trgovcu*, edited by Žarko Muliačić, 510–517. Dubrovnik: U. Dubrovnik.

Sangster, Alan. 2014a. "Preface." In *Libr. XV: Cotrugli and de Raphaeli on Business and Bookkeeping in the Renaissance*, presented by Alan Sangster, 1–2. Stirling: Lomax Press.

Sangster, Alan. 2014b. "Introduction." In *Libr. XV: Cotrugli and de Raphaeli on Business and Bookkeeping in the Renaissance*, presented by Alan Sangster, 3–15. Stirling: Lomax Press.

Schiffler, Ljerka. 1996. "Eticko-humanisticka misao Benedikta Kotruljevica." *Prilozi za istrazivanje hrvatske filozofske bastine* 22(43/44):117–142.

Sladović, Eugen. 1942. "Dubrovcanin Benko Kotruljevic preteca privredne nauke u preduzecu." *Alma mater croatica* 4(2):49–56.

Spini, Ugo, ed. 1988. *Le edizioni bresciane del Seicento: Catalogo cronologico delle opere stampate a Brescia e a Salò*. Milan: Bibliografica.

Spremić, Momcilo. 1970. "Presuda Benku Kotruljevicu." *Zbornik Filozofskog fakulteta u Beogradu* 11(1):365–398.

Spremić, Momcilo. 1986. *Dubrovnik e gli Aragonesi (1442–1495)*. Palermo: Accademia nazionale di scienze lettere ed arti.

Stipetić, Vladimir. 1994a. "Beno Kotruljevic prvi je upoznao svijet s dvostrukim racunovodstvom: iznenadujuci novootkriveni rukopis Bene Kotruljevica." *Racunovodstvo, revizija i financije* 4:I–VIII.

Stipetić, Vladimir. 1994b. "Kotruljevic preuzima primat u povijesti dvostrukog knjigovodstva." *Racunovodstvo, revizija i financije* 4:IX–X.

Stipetić, Vladimir. 1996a. "Svjedocanstvo Filipa de Diversisa o dubrovackom gospodarstvu u vrijeme Kotruljeviceve mladosti (1434–1440 godine)." *Racunovodstvo, revizija i financije* 3:657–658.

Stipetić, Vladimir. 1996b. "Ucenje o kamati pri trgovinskom poslovanju u djelu Benedikta Kotruljevica." *Hrvatska gospodarska revija* 45:1–10.

Stipetić, Vladimir. 2001. "Dubrovcanin Marin Rafaeli o dvostanom knjigovodstvu 1475 godine (otkrice nepoznate knjige i nepoznatog pisca)." *Anali Zavoda za povijesne znanosti HAZU u Dubrovniku* 39:497–502.

Stipetić, Vladimir. 2002. "Marin Rafaeli of Ragusa on double-entry bookkeping in 1475: A recent discovery by Anne J. Van der Helm and Johanna Postma." *Dubrovnik Annals* 6:123–129.

Tafuri, Giovanni Bernardino. 1760. *Istoria degli Scrittori Nati nel Regno di Napoli*, vol. 3, part 5. Naples: Giuseppe Severini.

Tagliente, Giovanni Antonio. 1533[1525]. [*Luminario di aritmetica, libro doppio*] *Considerando io Ioanni Antonio Taiente quanto e necessaria cosa a li nostri magnifici gentilhomeni & adaltri mercatanti el laudabile modo de tenere conto de libro dopio cioe, el zornale, el libro con lalphabetto secondo el consueto de questa inclita citta di Venetia, io qui seguendo con lagiuto del mio carissimo compagno Aluise da la Fontana, vi daremo lo amaestramento che con facilita lo potrete imparare, laqual opera ancor sara di molta utilita vniuersalmente ad ogniuno, come ne lopera vedereti*, Venice: per Giovann'Antonio di Nicolini da Sabio.

Tenenti, Alberto. 1978. "Famiglia borghese e ideologia nel Quattrocento." In Tenenti, Alberto. *Credenze, ideologie e libertinismi tra Medioevo ed Età Moderna*, Bologna: Il Mulino.

Trovato, Stefano. 2009. "Il manoscritto *De navigatione* di Benedetto Cotrugli in Marciana. Cronaca di un acquisto mancato tra 1913 e 1914," *Studi Veneziani* 57:549–558.

Tucci, Ugo. 1990. "Introduzione." In Benedetto Cotrugli, *Il libro dell'arte di mercatura*, edited by Ugo Tucci, 3–128. Venice: Arsenale.

Vasoli, Cesare. 1989. *Francesco Patrizi da Cherso*. Rome: Bulzoni.

Vekarić, Nenad. 1996. "Dubrovacki rod Kotrulj." In *Dubrovcanin Benedikt Kotruljevic. Hrvasti i svjetski ekonomist XV stoljeca*, edited by Vladimir Stipetić and Mladen Hebek, 33–52. Zagreb: HAZU. Dubrovnik: Hrvatski racunovoda (Monumenta Historica Ragusina).

Villani, Gianni. 1996. "L'umanesimo napoletano." In *Il Quattrocento*. Vol. 3 of *Storia delle letteratura italiana*, edited by Enrico Malato, 709–68. Rome: Salerno.

Vujić, Mihail V. 1909. "Prvo naucno delo o trgovini Dubrovcanina Benka Kotruljica." *Glas SKA* 80:1–101.

Weissen, Kurt. 2002. "Dove il Papa va, sempre è caro di danari. The commercial site analysis in Italian merchant handbooks and notebooks from the 14th and 15th centuries." In *Kaufmannsbucher und Handelspratiken vom Spatmittelalter bis zum beginnenden 20 Jahrhundert*, edited by Markus A. Denzel, Jean Claude Hocquet, and Harald Witthöft, 63–74. Stuttgart: Franz Steiner Verlag.

Yamey, Basil S. 1994. "Benedetto Cotrugli on bookkeeping (1458)." *Accounting, Business and Financial History* 4(1):43–50.

Zanato, Tiziano. 1993. "Sul testo della Mercatura di Benedetto Cotrugli (A proposito di una recente edizione)." *Studi veneziani* 26:15–65.

Zappella, Giuseppina. 1986. *Le marche dei tipografi e degli editori italiani del Cinquecento*, Milan: Editrice Bibliografica.

Zebić, Milorad. 1963. *Zivot i rad Dubrovcanina Benka Kotruljica i njegov spis o trgovini i o savrsenom trgovcu*, Titograd: Udruzenje knjigovoda Crne gore.

Index

A

accounts, 52, 54, 57, 65, 81, 82, 103, 118, 123
  account books, 73, 170
Adam, 48, 119, 158
adversity, 129, 133, 136, 171
Aegisthus, 158
Aeschines, 36
Aescolanus, 87
Aesculapius, 87
Agamemnon, 158
alchemy, 80, 105
Alexander of Hales, 142
Alexander the Great, 36, 119, 129, 131, 146
Alexandria, 165
Alfonso, King of Aragon, 132, 147
alms, 91–4, 131
Anthony Godswindler, 49
Antigonus, 119, 131
Apelles, 36
Apollo, 87, 120
Apollonius of Alabanda, 36
apostles, 87, 91, 124
Archimedes, 35
Argentinus, 87
Aristides, 119
Aristotle, 25, 34, 35, 38, 39, 41, 48, 51, 59, 82, 104, 119, 120, 126, 129, 130, 136, 138, 141, 142, 146, 153, 154, 156, 157, 162, 164
Ascanius, 162
Astrology, 61, 121
  celestial influences, 34, 61
  constellations, 34
  inclination, 34
Athens, 36

C. Carraro, G. Favero (eds.), *Benedetto Cotrugli – The Book of the Art of Trade*, DOI 10.1007/978-3-319-39969-0

Atlas, 158
Augustine, St, 48, 53, 76, 80, 82, 89–94, 106, 107, 109, 128, 137, 160
Augustus, 146
Averroes, 70
Avicenna, 70, 123
Avignon, 57, 67
Axiotea, 155
B
Bacchus, 170
banks, 68, 143
Barcelona, 53, 64, 67, 74, 103
barter, 29, 33, 42–4
Bellona, 87
benefit, 24, 26, 42, 47, 74, 82, 95, 108, 160
Bible
  New Testament, 158
  Old Testament
    Deuteronomi, 159
    Ecclesiasticus, 90
    Exodus, 88
    Genesis, 79, 82, 146, 158, 160
    Proverbs, 126
bill of exchange, 63, 65, 66, 73, 103, 126
  promissory note, 115
Boccaccio, Giovanni, 148
body, 24, 33, 37–9, 78, 80, 87, 89, 90, 115, 118, 123, 134, 137, 146, 152, 155, 159, 160, 162, 168, 170, 171
  beauty, 23, 65, 119, 151, 152, 159
  death, 38, 92, 94, 113, 114, 134, 135, 159, 171
  grace, 115, 138, 153
  old age, 171
  physical constitution, 121, 132
  physiognomy, 48, 121, 129, 167
Boethius, 58, 59, 80, 116, 129, 136, 137, 164
bon (artisan), 77
Bosnians, 29, 122
Bridanus, 162
brokers, 32, 42, 51, 101
  commissions, 63, 103, 104
  middlemen, 59, 103, 104, 170
Bruges, 66
Bubona, 87
business, 41, 49, 57, 59–63, 65, 69–71, 82, 89, 103, 122, 124, 139, 143, 144, 151, 167, 168, 170
buying, 38, 44, 45, 47, 48, 51, 65, 68, 76, 99, 101, 106, 135, 136, 139
  buyer, 46, 50, 60, 100, 102, 104, 105

C
Calabria, 41
Callisthenes, 146
Campania, 169
Cannae, 147
capital, 46, 55–8, 71, 72, 99, 168
Carmenta, 70
Castle of Serpico, 172
Catalonia, 60, 64, 152
  Catalans, 53, 59, 165, 167
Cato of Utica, 163
Cato the Elder, 163

children, 32, 35, 59, 78, 85, 109, 114, 125, 127, 133, 134, 142, 145, 150, 151, 156–60, 162–4, 166, 167, 169
Christ, 86–9, 95, 106, 124, 126, 158
Chryseis, 158
Cicero, 25, 31, 35, 36, 40, 85, 112, 113, 115–18, 125, 131, 138, 152
Cineas, 70
Circe, 158
Cloelia, 156
clothes, 33, 61, 113, 146, 147, 149, 150, 152
Clytemnestra, 158
Code of Justinian, 32, 40, 69, 78–80, 106, 107, 124, 137, 166
coitus, 135, 156, 163
  seed, 36, 158
common good, 94, 101, 102
Conti, Angelo de, 135
contract, 31, 32, 43, 45, 47, 50, 56, 61, 68, 73, 74, 82, 95, 96, 98, 99, 101, 104, 105, 107, 118, 128, 159, 168
  acivimento ('acquisition'), 101
  stochi ('daggers'), 101
  strangoli ('throttlings'), 101
Coriolanus, 156
Cornelia (mother of the Gracchi), 37
Coruncanii, 171
Cotrugli, Benedetto, 23, 83, 109, 139, 172
counterfeit, 32, 76, 77
country, 46, 49, 65, 66, 101, 118, 127, 138, 141, 143, 144, 170, 171
  homeland, 25, 57, 120, 122, 156, 158, 171
  nation, 58, 113
Crassus, Marcus Licinius, 127
credit, 23, 44–8, 50–3, 60, 61, 65, 71, 72, 89, 93, 100, 115, 124, 143, 167
  creditor(s), 54, 72, 77, 108, 131
culture, 47, 120
  educated man, 23, 25, 36, 118–20, 154, 162
  men of letters, 70
  professors, 51
  reading, 23, 117, 169–71
  students, 51, 66
Cunina, 87
Curia, Gens, 171
custodian, 68, 69
Cynic, 131
Cyrus the Great, 70

D

d'Ascoli, Cecco, 36, 48
Danaus, 169
Dante Alighieri, 120, 134
David, 90, 91
dealings, 45, 46, 55, 60, 76, 82, 116, 144, 148
debt, 47, 50–4, 71, 90, 96, 99, 102, 108, 115, 132
decisions, 56, 106, 116, 133
Deidamia, 150
Demosthenes, 36
deposits, 68, 69, 115, 124
di Marvilla, Simone, 108
di Stefano, Francesco, 23, 25, 171, 172

dignity, 32, 34, 37, 112, 113, 115, 129, 147, 149
diligence, 28, 38, 100, 103, 124
Diogenes, 119
discipline, 25, 29–31, 33, 36, 37, 42, 66, 76, 141, 154, 160
disputes, 40, 70, 74, 128
drapers, 76
  haberdashers, 76
Drepanius, Pacatus, 145

E

Edulica, 87
Egypt, 88
Egyptians, 88
entrepreneurs, 46, 114
entries, 73
  'sums owed,' 72
  'sums owing,' 72
  'surplus,' 72
  double entries, 73
  item, 32, 54, 69, 71–3, 104–7
errors, 24, 51, 55, 79, 80, 86, 112, 116, 136, 168
Esau, 80, 137
Euclid, 35
Eurystheus, 59
Evander, 70
excess, 38, 57, 79, 101, 136, 143, 150, 153
exchange(s), 29, 30, 33, 42–4, 56, 63–8, 73, 81, 103, 104, 114
experience, 23, 29, 36, 41, 49, 51, 56, 63, 121, 123, 136, 139, 168
expertise, 23, 42, 47, 56, 100
Ezra, 88

F

Fabritii, 171
faith, 34, 55, 62, 70, 86, 87, 90, 91, 99, 115, 121, 142, 158, 170
  faithfulness, 157, 159, 162
family, 26, 29, 30, 33, 36, 46, 47, 57, 79, 94, 113, 114, 133, 141–6, 167
Ferdinand, King of Naples, 172
Flanders, 66
Florence, 56, 100, 143, 148, 165
  Florentines, 42, 53, 56, 59, 66, 166
food, 41, 79, 80, 85, 92, 105, 113, 118, 137, 163
  drinking, 38, 80, 87, 135–7, 163, 167
  eating, 38, 80, 87, 136, 137, 156, 167
  hunger, 38, 92, 93
  thirst, 38, 132
  wine, 55, 62, 79, 96, 98, 104, 136, 143, 155, 163
fortune, 23, 24, 37, 62, 77, 122, 123, 129, 132, 142, 152
  misfortune, 24, 49, 58, 62, 74, 75, 116, 122, 133, 152, 154, 157
France, 133
  French, 118
friendship, 81, 95, 96, 139

G

games
  ball games, 78
  cards, 45, 78, 117
  dice, 33, 45, 78, 117

running, 78
throwing the caber or spear, 78
wrestling, 78, 117
Gellius, Aulus, 49, 120
Geneva, 67
Genoa, 165
Genoese, 53, 59, 129, 134
Germany, 133
Germans, 118
God, 24–8, 32, 34, 55, 67, 71, 76, 80, 82, 83, 86–93, 101, 104, 108, 119, 122–4, 126, 127, 133, 134, 137, 142, 147, 149, 151, 152, 157–9, 165, 170–2
creation, 28, 30, 138
gold, 57, 67, 75, 105, 113, 114, 119, 127, 146, 152
good name, 49, 76, 77, 152, 168
goods, 29, 32, 38, 42–6, 48, 50, 51, 54, 61–3, 66, 69, 70, 72, 76, 85, 95, 96, 98, 101, 104, 105, 107, 108, 128, 150, 167
Gospels, 28
Gracchi, 37
Gratiani, Decretum, 32, 45, 87, 89, 90, 94, 95, 97, 104, 106–9, 120, 128, 142, 158–60, 167
Greece, 152
Greeks, 35, 88, 116, 162

H

Hamilcar, 36
Hannah, 90
Hannibal, 36, 147
Hasdrubal, 36
hell, 76, 142, 152, 169
devil, 54, 101, 152
Hercules, 58, 146, 150, 163
Herod, 76
Herodotus, 36
Hesiod, 36, 142
Holy Scriptures, 170
Homer, 36, 158
Honorja, 87
honour, 25, 35, 38, 40, 41, 47, 62, 87, 99, 112, 115, 122, 138, 147, 153, 156–8, 165
Horace, 36
Hortensius, 36
Hostiensis (Henry of Segusio), 68, 89, 90, 101, 105
Hugh of Saint Victor, 89
human race, 27, 29, 31, 33, 55, 70
Hungary, 133
Hungarians, 118

I

ignorant, 26, 39, 85, 86, 92, 103, 119–21, 123
idiot, 78, 118, 150, 152
illness, 40, 78, 79, 121, 135, 150, 160, 162
leprosy, 76, 136
madness, 37, 60, 80, 129, 137, 149, 150
plague, 32, 50, 54, 172
Illyrian, 147
Innocent III, Pope, 101
insurance, 64, 74, 75, 121
assurer, 75
guarantor, 97
intelligence, 24, 28, 34, 39, 55, 59, 66, 133, 155, 168, 169, 171

interest, 62, 66, 96, 97, 99, 102, 103, 115
usury, 95–7, 99, 102, 106, 131
usurers, 41, 52, 96–9, 102, 132
Iphicles, 163
Isaiah, 91
Israel, people of, 27
Italy, 58, 134, 147, 148, 150, 152
Italians, 134, 155

J

Jeremiah, 91
jewels, 113, 114, 147, 152
jeweller, 75, 76
Jews, 88
job, 76
John of Damascus, 89
John Worldfouler, 49
Joseph (Jacob's son), 101
judgements, 40, 128
Julius Caesar, 36, 134, 146
Jupiter, 35, 87, 171
Justin, 36

K

knowledge, 23, 30, 86, 87, 117–21, 139

L

Lactantius, 55, 85
Laërtius, Diogenes, 120
landholdings, 168
farmholdings, 170
language, 26, 118, 134
Latin, 26, 117, 118, 151, 155, 164
vernacular, 26, 118
Lastenia, 155
law, 24, 27, 28, 31, 32, 36, 40, 58, 78, 87–9, 94, 98, 104, 105, 118, 121, 128, 147, 148, 158, 162, 163, 166, 169
canons, 109, 121, 166
lawyers, 40, 128
letter, 63, 73, 118, 125, 126, 164
Levant, 60, 61, 165
liberal arts, 35, 70, 120, 121
grammar, 120
logic, 71, 112, 120, 121
logicians, 121
rhetoric, 36, 118, 120, 138, 164
rhetorician, 118, 155
Licinus, 153
Livy, 36, 147, 156
Llull, Ramon, 89, 90, 97, 99, 101, 106, 159, 162
loan, 68, 69, 95–8, 102, 139
logic
reasoning, 24, 28, 55, 85, 112, 126, 139
loss, 40, 43, 46, 52, 64, 66, 68, 70, 73–5, 79, 97, 98, 101, 104, 105, 107, 116, 128, 156, 163, 166
Lucina, 87
Lucius Scipio, 70
Lycus, 59
Lysimachus, 36

M

Macedonians, 164
Manicheans, 122
marriage, 99, 107, 151, 153, 158–62
  matrimony, 158, 160, 163
Mars, 87
Martial, 152
Mary, Moses' sister, 76
Masinissa, 163
Mathuma, 163
Matthew, 90–2, 106
Maximus, Valerius, 134, 135, 141, 155, 156
mechanical arts, 35, 70, 106, 112
  artisans, 59, 114, 135
  peasants, 32, 41, 52, 135
  porters, 39, 47, 135, 148
  sailors, 47, 55
Medici, Cosimo de,' 123–4
Megara, 59
men-at-arms, 115, 133
  soldiers, 51, 66, 70, 82
merchandise, 31, 32, 41–4, 46, 48–52, 55, 57, 61–3, 65, 71, 72, 76, 81, 100, 113, 121, 126
merchant(s), 24–6, 30–4, 36–43, 45, 46, 48, 51–66, 69–71, 73–83, 85, 86, 88, 89, 92, 95, 100–2, 105, 108, 109, 111, 112, 113–18, 120–39, 141–4, 146, 147, 149, 150, 153, 164, 166–8, 171
  merchant-artisan, 77
merchant's books
  Day Book, 71–3
  ledger, 52, 54, 71–3, 128
  Scrap Book Records, 71, 73
  to keep records, 70
Mercury, 87
Milan, 143
Minerva, 87, 116
moderation, 24, 40, 78, 115, 126, 127, 136, 137, 139, 144, 148, 149, 154, 156, 157
money, 29, 30, 33, 42–8, 51–8, 64–9, 72, 74, 94–100, 102, 104, 108, 114, 123, 124, 127, 128, 132, 139, 142, 150, 156, 164–6, 168, 169
  cash, 42–6, 52, 57, 65, 66, 69, 71–3, 82, 95, 96, 99–101, 142
  ducats, 41, 56–9, 61, 64, 67, 69, 71–4, 99, 100, 123, 126, 128
Moors, 46
Moses, 28, 158
Mudball, Peter, 49

N

Naples, 64, 65, 67, 143, 148, 172
  Neapolitans, 155
nature, 27–31, 33, 35, 40, 41, 47–50, 55, 62, 71, 81, 103, 106, 115, 121, 138, 145, 146, 148, 149, 153, 154, 158, 162, 165, 169
Nepos, Cornelius, 36
Neptune, 87
Noah, 79

nobility, 39, 112, 146, 147, 153
courtier, 103, 121
gentlemen, 31, 40, 52, 59, 66, 76, 103, 113, 114, 133, 135, 147, 148, 169
knights, 31, 66, 146, 149
lords, 114, 115, 118, 119, 130, 135, 139, 147, 170
nobles, 51, 76, 81, 118, 133
noblewomen, 76
princes, 31, 114, 115, 118, 147, 149
North, 61
Numidia, 163

O

obligations, 73, 74, 109, 159–61
Octavian, 58, 152
oratory, 29, 36, 117
eloquence, 37, 112
orator, 36, 82, 121
Ovid, 36, 152

P

Pachivio, 36
Palermo, 67
Paris, 67
partnership, 56, 57, 62, 128
company, 80
Paulus, Aemilius, 112
payment, 42, 47, 48, 50–2, 54, 67, 72, 96, 97, 100, 102, 103
pecunia, 87
Penelope, 158
percentage, 43, 67, 75, 102, 103, 108
Perpignan, 67
Petrarch, Francesco, 139, 152
Phidias, 36
Philip, King of Macedon, 119
philosophy, 24, 28, 35, 117, 119, 121, 171
philosophers, 27, 28, 35, 62, 66, 81, 121, 155
theologians, 45, 66, 119, 121
theoretical speculation, 27, 28
Plato, 35, 146
pledge, 68, 97, 99
Pliny the Elder, 48, 164
Pliny the Younger, 164
poisons, 32, 45
politics, 26, 61
Polybius, 36
Pomona, 87
Porsena, Lars, 156
possessions, 106, 113, 142, 156, 168, 169
buildings, 57, 149
house, 26, 37, 99, 102, 105, 113, 114, 141–6, 149, 151, 154–6, 159, 167–9
furnishings, 113, 149, 150
household, 30, 39, 46, 101, 113, 114, 141, 143–6, 149, 151, 156, 158
office space, 143
villa, 144, 145
washrooms, 144
warehouse, 48, 100, 125
posterity, 26, 28
Potina, 87
poverty, 48, 81, 109, 142, 152, 164
poor, 59, 79, 92–4, 101, 102, 108, 113, 122

practice, 24, 27–30, 32, 34, 37, 40, 42, 47, 53, 60, 63, 66, 67, 73, 75, 82, 83, 99, 113, 143, 147, 148, 162, 165
malpractice, 25, 77
Praxiteles, 36
prayer, 89–92, 108, 118, 170, 172
Priapus, 87
price, 32, 43, 45, 50, 64, 76, 98–101, 103–6, 166
Proconnesus, 163
profession, 24, 30, 32, 33, 36, 38, 39, 49, 52, 56, 60, 63, 64, 86, 101, 114, 116, 126
profit, 31, 33–5, 38, 40, 46, 47, 50, 56–5, 60–2, 66, 68, 70, 73, 74, 82, 97, 101–4, 112, 116, 137, 142, 144, 165
gain, 33, 45, 50, 57, 60, 64, 66, 75, 95–8, 100, 103, 104, 113, 143, 144, 166
premium, 43, 44, 50, 75, 99
projects, 56, 57, 60, 63, 77, 124, 139, 168
promises, 61, 90, 123, 158
Proserpine, 153
Ptolemy, 34, 35, 61, 118
Ptolemy II Philadelphus, 119
public life, 135, 141
Puglia, 147
Pugliese, 168
purchase, 44, 61, 101, 104
Pyrrhus, 70, 150
Pythagoras, 35, 49

Q

Quintilian, 36

R

Ragusans, 57, 59, 166
Ravenna, 120
receipt, 54, 72, 103, 115
recommendation, 93–4, 115, 167
reimbursement, 50, 69, 102–4, 106, 107
religion, 78, 83, 85, 86, 111, 170
Christian religion
Christians, 46, 87, 118, 120, 121, 170
Church, 89, 94, 96, 108, 155, 158, 161, 167
friars, 51, 139
mass, 86–9, 108, 118, 170
priests, 51, 66, 76, 88, 103, 108, 114, 115, 139, 156
rest, 82, 83, 168, 169
restitution, 69, 95, 96, 107–9
retirement, 142, 144, 170
pause, 82, 159
Rialto, 143
rich(es), 24, 32, 41, 47, 52, 55, 56, 59–61, 77, 78, 81, 92, 106, 109, 113, 121, 122, 124, 128, 132, 142, 147, 151
enrichment, 34, 35, 39, 41, 58, 60, 81, 113
prosperity, 57, 113, 129, 133, 136, 170
wealth, 41, 47, 55, 57, 81, 83, 87, 93, 109, 113, 119, 124, 130, 144, 151, 159
risk, 45, 50, 56, 61, 66, 74, 75, 96, 98–100, 102, 103, 122, 125, 139, 161, 163
Rome, 56, 65, 70, 155, 156, 169
Romans, 35, 86, 87, 112, 134, 146, 155

ruin, 39, 40, 46, 48, 57, 58, 75, 80, 81, 114, 139, 143
  bankrupt, 48, 52, 57, 75, 124, 125
  fail, 34, 41, 77, 90, 124, 125, 167
rules, 25, 29, 30, 37, 47, 63, 77, 95, 116, 153
Rumina, 87

S

St. Ambrose, 93
St. Antoninus, 100
St. Basil, 93
St. Chrysostom, John, 89, 91, 124
St. Gregory, 91
St. Isidore, 82, 91, 147
St. James, 90, 124
St. Jerome, 152
St. John (but St Jerome), 32
St. Luke, 89, 91, 142
St. Paul, 32, 57, 76, 79–82, 88, 90, 116, 126, 136, 137, 141, 157, 158, 160, 161
St. Raymond, 79
St. Thomas, 45, 68, 78, 80, 89, 91, 94, 95, 97, 98, 104, 105, 107, 108, 126, 127, 136, 158–61
sale, 31, 32, 43–8, 50, 105
saying, 25, 36, 37, 41, 53, 55, 66, 81, 85, 89, 92, 93, 107, 116, 132, 141, 152
  proverb, 34, 39, 43, 48, 51, 53, 62, 113, 121, 147
sciences, 25, 29, 35, 117, 120
Scipio, 36
Scipio Africanus the Younger, 112
sea charts, 75, 121
Segetia, 87
selling, 38, 43–8, 51, 52, 55, 60, 65, 68, 71, 76, 97, 99, 104, 106, 135, 136, 139
  seller, 44, 45, 104, 105, 148
Seneca, 39, 48, 53, 58–60, 123, 129–31, 133, 149, 151, 158, 167
servants, 32, 55, 58, 79, 88, 94, 119, 127, 133, 134, 143–5, 154, 166, 167, 170
settlement, 52, 139
shipowners, 47, 75
shrewdness, 57, 126
Sicily, 41, 42, 66, 165
  Sicilian, 43
Sigismund of Luxemburg, 147
silk, 46, 57, 147, 149, 152
silver, 57, 87, 93, 105, 114, 119, 127, 146
sins, 27, 68, 76, 78, 81, 92, 95, 97, 101, 102, 105–8, 127, 142, 152, 158–62, 167
  adultery, 86, 160, 162, 163
  avarice, 81, 127
  extravagance, 81
  fornication, 158–60
  fraud, 54, 69, 78, 95, 99–102, 105, 126, 159
  frivolity, 130, 149
  gluttony, 48, 79, 80, 135–7
  greed, 40, 78–80, 101, 127, 136, 137, 142
  idleness, 23, 152
  lasciviousness, 171
  lies, 25, 78, 106
  luxury, 57, 148

negligence, 91, 125
perjury, 25, 45, 78, 106
profanity, 25, 78
robbery, 78
simony, 106
subtlety, 126
theft, 69, 106, 107
vanity, 148
Slavs, 62
smuggling, 80
Socrates, 35, 112, 120, 155
Solinus, 146, 163
Solomon, 48, 119, 152
Solon, 163
Soria, 64
soul, 24, 34, 37, 38, 48, 82, 88–90, 101, 108, 111, 113, 115, 118, 124, 132, 133, 139, 149, 162, 169, 171
Spanish, 64, 155
speed, 40, 143
Stano, 133
state, 25, 29, 94, 113, 146

T

Tacitus, 36
Tarquins, 156
Tartars, 46
Themistocles, 132
Theodosius, 145
Theophrastus, 151
Thucydides, 36
Tiber, 156
Titans, 35
Tobit, 91
trade, 24–7, 31–5, 37, 39, 40, 42, 56, 61, 63, 64, 70, 73, 75–7, 83, 96, 100–3, 106, 107, 111, 113, 116, 121, 126, 139, 142, 164, 165, 168, 169
art of trade, 23, 25, 29–31, 33, 36, 38, 46, 47, 80, 109, 112, 114, 164, 168, 172
mercatantia, 31
mercatura, 31
transactions, 32, 45, 46, 54, 56, 57, 60, 61, 63, 72, 73, 106, 125
Trajan, 146
treatise (this book), 26, 27, 30, 33, 42, 45, 57, 112, 127
Trojans, 116
trust, 55, 78, 86, 115, 124, 156
Turks, 46

U

Ulysses, 158
uneducated man, 31, 32, 52, 120
useful, 24–6, 30, 33, 38, 46, 47, 56, 66, 74, 82, 117, 118, 142, 144, 155, 164

V

Valencia, 65, 67
kingdom of, 41
Valencians, 65
Varro Gaius Terentius, 112
Vendramin (family), 77
Venice, 56, 60, 64, 65, 67, 77, 135, 143, 148, 150, 165
Venetians, 59, 65, 67
Venus, 170

Victoria, 87
Virgil, 36, 62, 122, 145, 155, 162
virtue, 23, 26, 28, 34, 76, 87, 88, 91, 112, 116, 120, 128–30, 132, 136, 151, 152, 159, 171
  application, 125
  benevolence, 130, 170
  civility, 127, 148
  generosity, 130–2
  integrity, 116, 123, 124, 129, 146
  loyalty, 62, 152
  modesty, 25, 78, 130, 134, 148, 152
  piety, 92, 108, 127
  prudence, 75, 103, 116, 117
  sobriety, 129, 148
  solidity, 113, 135, 162
  steadfastness, 129
  temperance, 136, 139, 157
  tranquillity, 132
  uprightness, 134
Volce de Baballio, 151

W

war, 35, 36, 40, 50, 98, 120, 166
West, 61, 143
wife, 79, 85, 107, 127, 134, 135, 142, 145, 151–62, 165, 170
  conjugal obligations, 159
  dowry, 98, 99, 151, 152
  pregnancy, 87, 161–3
William of Ockham, 68, 78, 99, 101, 102, 107, 141, 159, 162
wisdom, 23, 55, 85, 117, 119–21, 152
wise, 23, 24, 34, 48, 58, 80, 86, 115, 119, 120, 122, 126, 137, 148, 151, 152, 154, 155, 157, 161
women, 32, 87, 134, 139, 143, 147–57, 161, 163
wool, 46, 57, 60, 61, 64, 77, 100, 101, 147
writing, 23, 25, 26, 54, 63, 70, 81, 119, 125, 129, 144, 153, 170

Y

young, 23, 25, 32, 35, 48, 53, 117, 134, 139, 151, 152, 155, 167

Z

Zeno, 119
Zeuxis, 36

The manufacturer's authorised representative in the EU is Springer Nature Customer Service Centre GmbH, Europaplatz 3, 69115 Heidelberg, Germany. If you have any concerns regarding our products, please contact ProductSafety@springernature.com

Printed and bound by CPI Group (UK) Ltd, Croydon, CR0 4YY

25/09/2026

02222849-0006